Cybersecurity:

The Ultimate Beginner's Roadmap

ANAND SHINDE

DevOM

Ireland | Poland |Dubai | India | USA

Dedication

"This book is dedicated to everyone navigating the ever-evolving digital landscape, facing its challenges with courage and resilience. It is also a tribute to those tirelessly working to make our online world safer for all. May your journey through the digital realm be secure, informed, and empowered."

With Gratitude,
A Passionate Cybersecurity Advocate.

Anand Shinde

Acknowledgements

"I want to begin by expressing my deepest gratitude to my incredible wife, Shilpa Shinde, and my wonderful daughter, Aarushi Shinde. It's hard to find words that truly capture how much your love, understanding, and unwavering belief in me have meant. Your constant emotional support, patience, and the countless sacrifices you both made throughout this journey have been my strength. Without you, this book would not have been possible. I am beyond fortunate to walk through life with you by my side.

I am incredibly grateful to my spiritual mentor, Shri Rahul Makhi Guruji, who has been guiding me on my spiritual journey. He is responsible for my spiritual, personal, and professional growth. Without his selfless and honest guidance, my progress would never have been possible.

A heartfelt thank you also goes to Rafael Pluta, Karolina Korowacka, Marcel Balazi, and Krzysztof Poznanski. Your encouragement, advice, and belief in my writing have been a source of constant motivation. Your support kept me going, especially when the path ahead seemed unclear. I truly appreciate each of you for being part of this journey.

I am also deeply thankful to Dr Deepak Shikarpur, whose thoughtful guidance and perspective helped me see things from new angles. And to my best friend Saeed Inamdar, your unwavering support and encouragement were vital to keeping me focused and driven. Your faith in my work meant the world to me.

Lastly, I want to express my sincere gratitude to the global cybersecurity community. Your dedication to making the digital world safer inspires me daily. This book is a small way for me to contribute to that effort, and I hope it serves as a token of appreciation for all the work you do to secure our digital future."

Foreword

Dr. John M Nomikos

Director – Research Institute for European and American Studies (RIEAS)

Athens, Greece

In the age of globalization and information technology, the use of the Internet has rapidly increased influence on the functioning of public and private sectors. An important aspect of critical infrastructure and digital security – protection is the understanding of the Manual (book) title "Cybersecurity: The Ultimate Beginner's Roadmap".

The asymmetrical threats of the 21st century require digital protection which is the most significant tool in the battle to protect individual and governmental security. Nowadays, the "invisible enemy" is not conventional but it is a faceless and remote entity.

The Manual thoroughly analyzes fundamental concepts of cybersecurity and provides knowledge to everyone to comprehend the risks and benefits of digital safety. The frequency of cyber-attacks, identity theft cases create a stressful environment on individuals and governments that leads to psychological disasters and chaos.

The "Cybersecurity: The Ultimate Beginner's Roadmap" has a mission to educate and train every citizen in the international community how to avoid the risks of being connected with digital activity. Today's global labor market requires skills, expertise, and knowledge management on how to perform in the digital society. Therefore, the Manual educates you to safeguard yourself and your community in the digital world.

In conclusion, the Manual resembles the "Homer Odyssey lessons" that the Odyssey vividly describes the adventures of Odysseus as he struggles to "adjust his conventional thinking into digital thinking in order to arrive to his home at Ithaca (a Greek island in the Ionian Sea) which is the post digital community. The Manual teaches us that everyone must become a defender of a digital world!

Preface

"Imagine a time when the digital world felt like the Wild West—vast, unpredictable, and full of unseen dangers. Before the rise of cybersecurity, stepping into this uncharted digital territory was like travelling with precious cargo but no map or guide to protect it. We communicated freely, often unaware of the risks lurking in the shadows. Personal details, financial records, and private conversations—all were vulnerable to attackers waiting to exploit any opportunity.

Then came a collective awakening. The surge of cyber-attacks, identity theft, and data breaches forced us to recognize the urgent need for protection—a digital shield we now know as cybersecurity. Just as we locked our homes to ensure safety, we began to understand the importance of securing our online presence. This realization reshaped our relationship with technology, teaching us that safeguarding our digital lives is both a responsibility and a necessity.

This book is your guide to steer through the digital world safely and confidently. It begins with the basics, helping you recognize common cyber threats and providing simple, effective strategies to defend yourself. As you progress, you'll uncover the mechanics of cyber risks like phishing and malware, learning not just how to survive these challenges but how to stay a step ahead. By adopting these practices, you can transform the internet from a place of uncertainty to a space of empowerment and control.

But cybersecurity is more than just a protective measure—it's an opportunity. For those ready to take on the mantle of digital defense, this field offers a dynamic and rewarding career path. From foundational skills to real-world applications, this book explores what it takes to thrive as a cybersecurity professional and turn challenges into opportunities.

By the end of this journey, you will not only understand the fundamentals of cybersecurity but also feel empowered to protect yourself and those around you. Whether you're an individual seeking to safeguard your digital identity, a professional looking to secure sensitive information, or someone aspiring to build a career in cybersecurity, this book will equip you with the tools and knowledge to succeed."

About the Author

"Anand Shinde is a renowned, seasoned Cybersecurity expert, mentor, and author with a wealth of experience in safeguarding digital ecosystems, as a certified professional with credentials from global leaders like Microsoft, Cisco, Amazon, ISACA and the International Society of Automation. Anand has worked on complex cybersecurity projects across India, Poland, Ireland, and the United States. His international career has equipped him with diverse perspectives and practical insights to address intricate cybersecurity challenges effectively.

In addition to his consulting work, Anand is deeply committed to education and mentorship. Since 2015, he has been serving as a student mentor and career counsellor for prestigious institutions, including Novel Group of Institutes and MIT ADT University, guiding aspiring professionals toward successful careers in cybersecurity. His role as a mentor for the International Society of Automation reflects his dedication to fostering talent in the ever-evolving cyber landscape.

Anand has also contributed to the field of cybersecurity and artificial intelligence with an innovative patent application, underscoring his commitment to advancing the industry. His contributions extend to raising cyber awareness through blogs and campaigns that promote best practices for digital strength.

For anyone aspiring to build a career in cybersecurity, Anand invites you to connect through Devom, where he continues to empower individuals and organizations to thrive in the digital age."

Table of Contents

Welcome

"Imagine living in a world where every time you open an email, make an online transaction or browse through social media, a guardian stands by to safeguard you from unnoticeable risks. This guardian is cybersecurity, and in today's technology-driven world, it is more than simply a technical need; it is a critical shield for our personal lives, families, and organizations.

Every day, we rely on technology for vital things like buying groceries online, managing our accounts, and staying in touch with loved ones. While these acts are handy, they put our personal information at risk. Cyber risks are evolving, and the consequences of a hack can be disastrous. The hazards range from identity theft and financial loss to the disclosure of sensitive personal and professional data. This is where cybersecurity comes in to secure our digital assets.

Understanding the fundamentals of cybersecurity and using its tactics can aid in our defense against these attacks. This book will break down the concepts of cybersecurity and explain why it is critical for securely navigating the digital world. We will look at why everyone—from individuals to huge corporations—should incorporate robust cybersecurity practices into their regular online activity. By learning this information and taking a proactive attitude, we can make the digital world safer for ourselves and others around us."

Chapter 1: The Essential Role of Cybersecurity

1.1 Introduction: The Wilson Family's Digital Day

Think of the early days of the internet—a period of wonder and inquiry when the risks of sharing information online were barely addressed. As technology grew, so did the risks, resulting in the development of cybersecurity to defend our increasingly digital lives. This growth has highlighted the vital necessity to protect personal and professional information in our linked society.

Let us take a tour with the Wilson family to understand the relevance of cybersecurity in everyday life. They live in the peaceful community of Greenwood and represent an innovative, technologically aware home. Sarah, a committed 40-year-old high school teacher, and her husband David, a 42-year-old architect who runs a small company from their home, are the joyful parents of Emma, a 15-year-old social media admirer, and Jack, a 12-year-old keen online gamer.

The Wilsons live happily, depending on technology to improve their daily lives. However, their interactions with the digital world come with unintended consequences.

Financial Data: David frequently works from his comfortable home office, organizing client bills and accepting payments online. This essential role is critical to his business, but it is also a possible target for phishing scams. Imagine David receives an email from a trustworthy client requesting him to update payment information on a linked website. Without proper cybersecurity awareness, he might easily be tricked into submitting critical financial information or being sent to a fake payment site, facing considerable financial loss and harming his company's image.

Medical Data: Sarah carefully organizes her family's health information using health apps and online medical portals. She routinely reviews medical records and speaks with healthcare providers. These actions, while helpful, expose their sensitive medical information to possible cyber-attacks. If intercepted due to inadequate security measures, this information might be used by identity thieves. For example, Sarah may connect to a health portal with a weak password, unknowing that it is readily malfunctioning, allowing a cybercriminal to obtain confidential health information and utilize it for fraudulent purposes.

Educational Data: Emma and Jack are both doing well in school and make extensive use of online learning resources. Emma completes her schoolwork and accesses school records, but Jack engages in virtual learning and gaming. However, these platforms are subject to security breaches, which might expose their personal and educational information, such as grades and school IDs. For example, a hacker may take advantage of a weakness in the school's online platform to acquire students' personal information, which could subsequently be sold on the dark web or used to intimidate or harass youngsters.

Employment Data: David's architectural employment involves maintaining and sharing private blueprints and client information online. This rich information is an ideal target for cyber espionage. Consider a situation in which a competitor pays a hacker to access David's networks and steal his creative architectural ideas, allowing him to acquire a competitive advantage in the market. This breach might lead to considerable financial loss and harm David's professional image.

Identity Information: All family members use social media. Sarah discusses her teaching experiences, David shows off his architectural creations, and Emma and Jack hang together with friends. These platforms frequently demand users to share personal information that serves as the foundation for their digital identities. Without suitable privacy settings, people are vulnerable to identity theft. For example, Emma may upload images from her school, indicating its location, while Jack may publish information about his birthday and interests, providing important data for identity thieves to exploit.

Information Online: From online purchasing and forum participation to service subscriptions, the Wilsons leave digital fingerprints everywhere. This includes vital personal information that cyber thieves can obtain if secure browsing habits and privacy awareness are not followed. Consider the family's delight throughout the Christmas season as they browse for gifts online. Without security processes, their credit card information might be compromised, resulting in illicit transactions and financial hardship.

Modern technological advances improve the Wilson family's happy existence. However, these conveniences carry considerable risks. Without effective cybersecurity safeguards, their joyful tale might turn unpleasant, resulting in financial loss, identity theft, or data breaches. This book wants to give their story—and the stories of many other families—a safe and joyful finish.

The Wilsons and other families may safeguard themselves and continue to enjoy their digitally enriched lives safely if they grasp the importance of cybersecurity and learn how to implement its strategies successfully.

1.2 The Basics of Cybersecurity: Understanding the Concept

In the early days of the internet, the necessity to secure our digital interactions may have appeared unimportant. However, as technology evolved and our reliance on it increased, so did the risk of harm. Cybersecurity appeared as an essential strategy for protecting our computers, networks, programs, and data against digital threats. These attacks frequently aim to obtain, change, or destroy sensitive information, extort money, or disrupt corporate operations. With more devices than people today and attackers continually discovering new techniques, maintaining adequate cybersecurity has become more difficult and important than ever.

Let us return to the Wilson family in Greenwood to see how cybersecurity impacts their lives. David, who processes client bills and payments from his home office, is especially vulnerable to phishing attempts. These scams can deceive him into disclosing important financial information, which can subsequently be exploited to empty his accounts or harm his business.

Sarah manages her family's health records using health apps and online medical portals, unintentionally exposing their medical information to possible identity thieves. If intercepted, this sensitive information might result in fraudulent actions and serious privacy violations.

Emma and Jack, who are deeply committed to their studies, frequently use internet platforms to submit homework and check school information. While these platforms are informative, cybercriminals may use them to steal personal and educational information, putting users' privacy in danger.

David's architectural company relies largely on digital technologies to store client data and private information. This data is a treasure for hackers involved in theft and cyber espionage. If compromised, he may lose not just money but also his professional reputation and competitive advantage.

Furthermore, the family's usage of social media and online purchasing generates a digital trail of personal information. If this information is not securely secured, hackers may use it for a variety of unlawful objectives, including identity theft and financial fraud.

The purpose of cybersecurity is to safeguard this data from illegal access and attacks while maintaining privacy, integrity, and availability. As technology becomes more integrated into all aspects of our lives, the number of sensitive data saved online grows, making every one of us a possible target for cyber-attacks.

Why do we need cybersecurity? For people like the Wilsons, a breach can result in the loss of personal and financial information, which can have catastrophic implications such as identity theft and bankruptcy. Organizations face much greater risks, as they must secure not just their operational integrity but also their customers' sensitive data. In a world where digital interactions are the norm, cybersecurity is our primary line of defense against these persistent attacks.

Next, we will examine a key question: "How can individuals and organizations effectively protect themselves against these cyber threats?" If individuals and corporations understand and apply appropriate cybersecurity measures, they can traverse the digital world more confidently and securely.

1.3 Understanding the Necessity of Cybersecurity

Consider the Wilson family to understand the importance of cybersecurity in our daily lives properly. Their stories highlight the essential part that cybersecurity plays in safeguarding us from the numerous threats hiding in the digital environment. As technology advances, so do risks, making it critical to secure both personal and business data.

The Wilson family relies on cybersecurity safeguards to protect sensitive information such as financial data, medical history, educational details, and personal identifying information from unwanted access. Each family member confronts distinct risks.

David conducts his architectural practice from home and relies on the confidentiality of his business information. A data breach might impair his business, causing financial loss and harm to his professional reputation.

Sarah, who manages her family's health using multiple applications and internet portals, is exposed to healthcare data breaches. If this sensitive information is intercepted, it may lead to identity theft and fraudulent activity.

Emma and Jack, who are heavily involved in online educational platforms, run the risk of having their academic records compromised and their online identities stolen.

These vulnerabilities demonstrate how important cybersecurity is in averting serious personal and financial harm. It is important to secure data and ensure the safety and well-being of all family members.

Organizations also rely heavily on strong cybersecurity policies to ensure operational integrity, preserve customer confidence, and protect vital data from cyber espionage and breaches. A data breach can have serious consequences, including considerable financial losses, legal implications, and reputational harm. Companies must secure their data to operate effectively and maintain consumer trust.

The CIA triad of confidentiality, integrity, and availability is fundamental to successful cybersecurity. These concepts are the foundation of security practices:

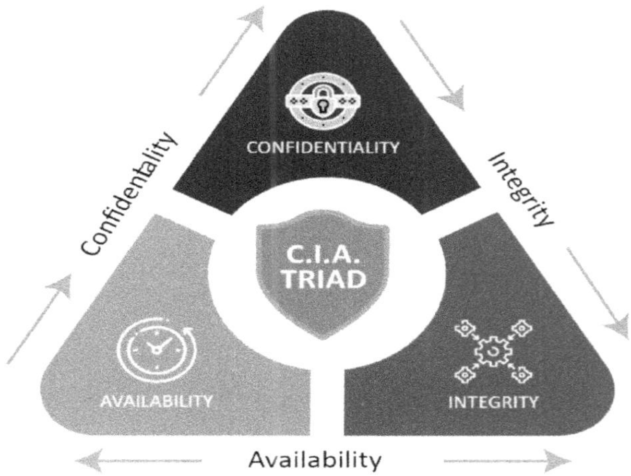

- **Confidentiality:** Limits data access to authorized users. For the Wilsons, this means that their personal and financial information will stay private and protected from unlawful access.
- **Integrity:** This ensures data correctness and completeness while preventing unauthorized changes. It also assures that David's architectural designs are unchanged and exact, preserving his expert labor.
- **Availability:** This ensures that information and resources are always available to authorized users. Sarah benefits from having uninterrupted access to her family's medical records.

Understanding and adopting these principles enables individuals and organizations to interact with the digital world more safely and securely. Adopting robust cybersecurity safeguards allows families like the Wilsons to continue enjoying the benefits of technology without concern while also protecting their privacy, security, and peace of mind.

1.4 Cyber Security for Individuals

For families like the Wilsons, cybersecurity is more than just preserving data; it is essential for defending their everyday lives. As digital technology becomes more and more integrated into our personal and professional lives, the need to protect our data is even more necessary.

Individuals are frequent targets for hackers because they are less likely to utilize strong security measures. Common dangers include phishing scams, ransomware attacks, identity theft, and financial fraud. These threats can cause severe psychological and financial distress, impacting everything from credit ratings to personal relationships.

Protecting oneself in the digital era involves implementing proactive measures to secure personal devices such as computers, cellphones, and tablets, as well as securing home networks. Here are a few important practices:

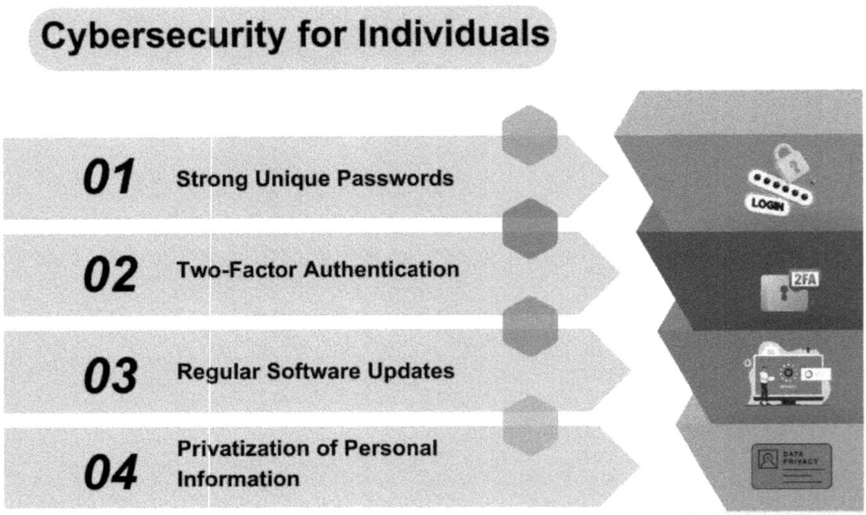

- **Strong, Unique Passwords:** Use strong, unique passwords for each account. For example, David ensures that his business and personal accounts use distinct passwords, reducing the danger of a compromise spreading across several platforms.
- **Two-Factor Authentication:** Use two-factor authentication wherever feasible. This provides an additional layer of protection by requiring a second form of authentication, making it more difficult for fraudsters to get access to accounts.
- **Regular Software Updates:** Keep all software up to date. Manufacturers often offer security upgrades to fix known vulnerabilities. Sarah protects her health applications and internet portals from current risks by upgrading them regularly.
- **Privatization of Personal Information:** Be diligent about sharing personal information online. Emma and Jack learn to think twice before sharing information about their school or birthdays on social media, lowering the risk of identity theft.

Additionally, consumers should familiarize themselves with the security settings on their devices and apps. Understanding these settings can considerably lessen the risk of unwanted data access. For example, by changing their privacy settings on social media, the Wilsons can manage who sees their personal information and shield themselves from danger.

Individuals who use such strategies can establish a robust defense against the majority of cyber-attacks, ensuring that their personal data stays secure in the ever-changing digital environment. For the Wilson family, these steps allow them to continue enjoying their digital life with confidence, knowing they are safe from possible cyber threats

1.5 Cybersecurity for Organizations

Businesses rely on cybersecurity to ensure their operational integrity and continuity. As digital transformation progresses, firms gather vast amounts of data, making them perfect targets for hackers. The consequences of cyber risks extend beyond financial losses to include legal responsibility, reputational damage, and degradation of consumer trust.

Organizations confront a wide range of cyber risks, including data breaches, ransomware attacks, insider threats, and advanced persistent threats. These attacks can interrupt corporate operations, compromise critical data, and cause significant economic and reputational damage. For example, a data breach might reveal personal customer information, resulting in financial losses and a loss of confidence.

To effectively defend their digital landscapes, enterprises must implement a multi-layered security plan. This strategy should include several critical areas:

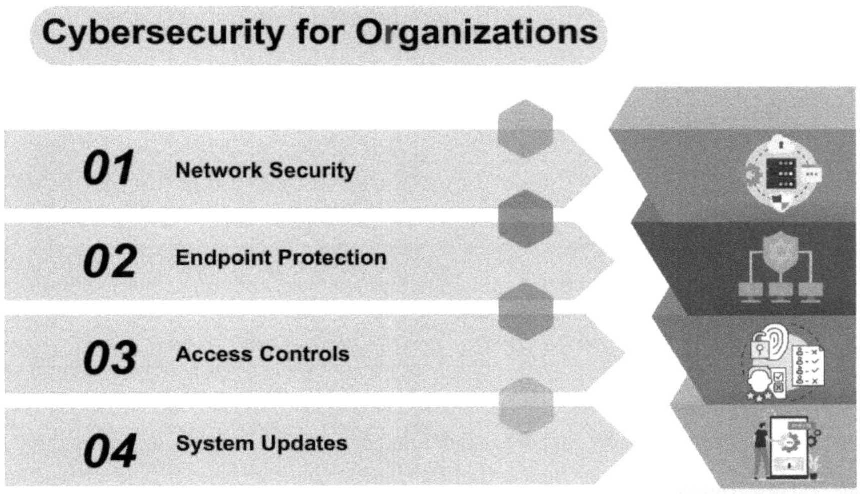

- **Network Security:** Preventing unwanted access and risks to the network infrastructure. This comprises firewalls, intrusion detection systems, and secure network design.
- **Endpoint Protection:** Involves safeguarding network-connected devices, including PCs, cell phones, and tablets. This includes utilizing antivirus software, encryption, and mobile device management solutions.

- **Access Controls:** Implementing strict access restrictions to protect sensitive information. This incorporates role-based access restrictions, multi-factor authentication, and periodic access audits.
- **System Updates:** Systems and software are regularly updated to address any risks. Patches and updates are released on an ongoing schedule to help resolve vulnerabilities that hackers may exploit.

Furthermore, doing regular security assessments and personnel training is critical. Organizations may improve their cyber threat preparation by routinely reviewing security measures and training personnel on recommended practices. For example, training courses on how to recognize phishing emails can greatly minimize the likelihood of falling victim to such attacks.

It is also critical for firms to have robust incident response and disaster recovery strategies. These standards allow for rapid management and mitigation of security incidents, reducing damage and quickly returning to regular operations. Consider a situation in which a ransomware attack encrypts crucial corporate data. An efficient incident response strategy can help control the danger, recover data from backups, and continue company operations with little disruption.

Prioritizing cybersecurity measures protects firms' operational assets while also demonstrating their commitment to protecting their customers' and employees' private information. This commitment to security builds trust and confidence, which is important in preserving a favorable reputation and long-term success.

1.6 Cybersecurity for Governments

Governments are responsible for preserving national security and public safety, as well as maintaining essential infrastructure, making cybersecurity a key challenge. They manage massive amounts of sensitive information, including people's personal data and classified state information, making them great targets for cyber threats such as espionage, sabotage, and terrorism.

The magnitude and diversity of systems that must be protected make safeguarding government networks a massive problem. These systems are necessary for healthcare, transportation, utilities, and other crucial services. A cyberattack on these networks might cause immense disruptions, harming millions of individuals and compromising public trust.

To guard against these attacks, governments must implement comprehensive cybersecurity plans. These techniques should contain the following:

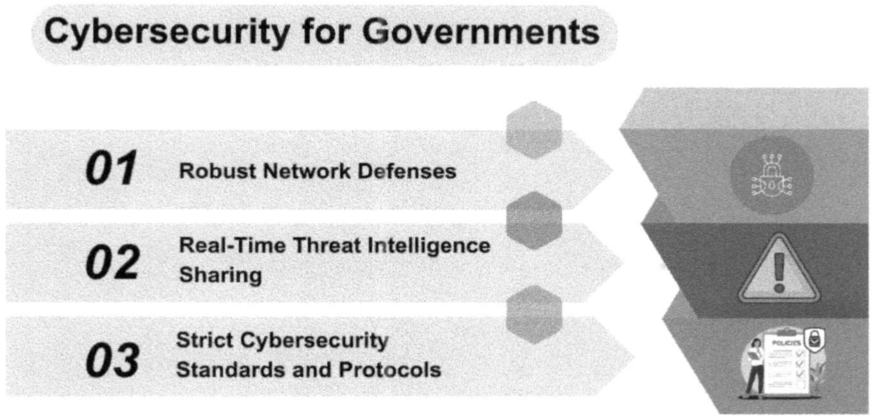

- **Robust Network Defenses:** Implementing robust security measures to safeguard government networks from illegal access and cyber threats. This includes sophisticated firewalls, intrusion detection systems, and secure communication protocols.
- **Real-Time Threat Intelligence Sharing:** Collaborating with agencies, the corporate sector, and international partners to provide real-time information on emerging dangers aids in rapidly recognizing and disarming possible attacks.
- **Strict Cybersecurity Standards and Protocols:** Enforcing strict cybersecurity standards and practices across federal departments. This guarantees a consistent and effective approach to security.

Collaboration with the corporate sector and international organizations is also essential for improving cybersecurity capabilities. Working together, governments and corporations can create more robust security measures and respond more effectively to global cyber threats.

Another critical part is to educate and teach the employees and the broader public about best practices in cybersecurity. Government employees must be informed of the most recent security measures, and individuals must understand how to safeguard their personal information online. For example, public awareness campaigns may educate individuals about the risks of phishing and how to identify questionable emails.

Furthermore, governments must be ready to respond quickly and efficiently to cyber events. A strong incident response strategy guarantees that any potential harm is minimized and that regular activities may be resumed soon. Consider a situation in which a cyber-attack affects a city's electricity system. A well-prepared response team can rapidly isolate the potential threat, restore services, and effectively communicate with the public to preserve calm and trust.

By implementing effective cybersecurity measures, governments can defend their digital infrastructure, maintain the continuity of operations, and assure the protection of their population. This dedication to cybersecurity contributes to the development of a strong and secure nation capable of dealing with the ever-changing cyber threat scenario.

1.7 The Growing Threat Landscape

As technology improves, the complexity and magnitude of cyber-attacks change, bringing new difficulties across all industries. Cyber strategies have evolved to encompass a wide range of sophisticated malware, elaborate phishing operations, ransomware occurrences, and advanced persistent threats (APTs).

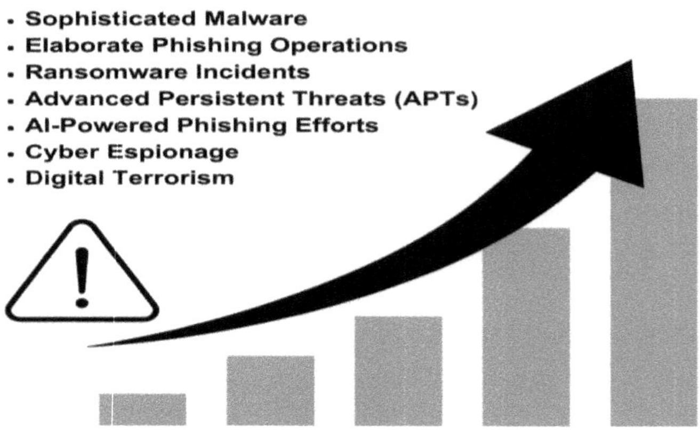

Cybercriminals are integrating cutting-edge technology, such as the Internet of Things (IoT) and artificial intelligence (AI), to create more deliberate and efficient methods of attack. This escalation requires greater attention from people, organizations, and governments.

Growth Aspect: From Personal to Governmental Impact

- **Individuals:** Individuals must protect their personal information from emerging approaches to identity and financial theft. Consider Emma and Jack, who are experiencing increasingly advanced phishing efforts that employ AI to create incredibly convincing false communications. They may protect themselves from these emerging dangers by remaining educated and adopting solid cybersecurity practices.
- **Organizations:** Organizations must enhance their security measures and guarantee continual monitoring to avoid breaches. Consider David's architectural company, which must now deploy more complex security procedures to prevent ransomware and APT attacks. This involves deploying AI-powered security technologies capable of detecting unusual activity and responding to attacks in real-time.
- **Governments:** Governments must secure crucial national infrastructure while also preventing sophisticated cyber espionage and digital terrorism. Consider the huge network of systems that enable public utilities, healthcare, and transportation. Governments must invest in strong cybersecurity policies to keep these important services operational and retain public trust.

Recognizing and responding to evolving cyber threats is vital for developing an effective cybersecurity strategy. Staying updated about the newest advances and adjusting our defenses accordingly allows for more effective protection of our digital spaces from the ever-changing risks posed by cyber activities.

Individuals like the Wilsons can secure their personal information by comprehending the ever-changing danger landscape. Organizations can use advanced security measures to protect their operations, while governments can maintain the safety and security of national infrastructure.

1.8 The Interconnected World: Risks and Challenges

In today's interconnected society, digital technology provides tremendous ease and efficiency. However, these advantages come with substantial risks and challenges that we must overcome in order to preserve our digital lives.

Risks

- **Data Breaches:** These include unauthorized access to sensitive personal and business data. For example, a breach might compromise David's client information, causing financial and reputational harm.
- **Malware Spread:** It refers to the fast propagation of destructive software such as viruses, ransomware, and other malicious applications. Consider Sarah's health applications being infiltrated by malware, putting their medical information in danger.
- **Phishing Attacks:** These include deceptive strategies to obtain sensitive information through fake emails or websites. Emma and Jack might receive appealing emails tricking them into disclosing their login information.
- **Advanced Persistent Threats (APTs):** These are targeted cyber-attacks that steal data or disrupt operations. David's architecture company might encounter an APT aimed at stealing secret blueprints and plans.

- **Identity Theft:** It is the illicit use of personal information for fraudulent purposes. If a cybercriminal acquires access to the Wilsons' personal information, they may experience tremendous financial and mental distress.
- **Infrastructure Attacks:** These can disrupt key services such as energy and communication networks. A cyber-attack on the Greenwood electrical infrastructure might have far-reaching consequences, especially for the Wilsons.

Challenges

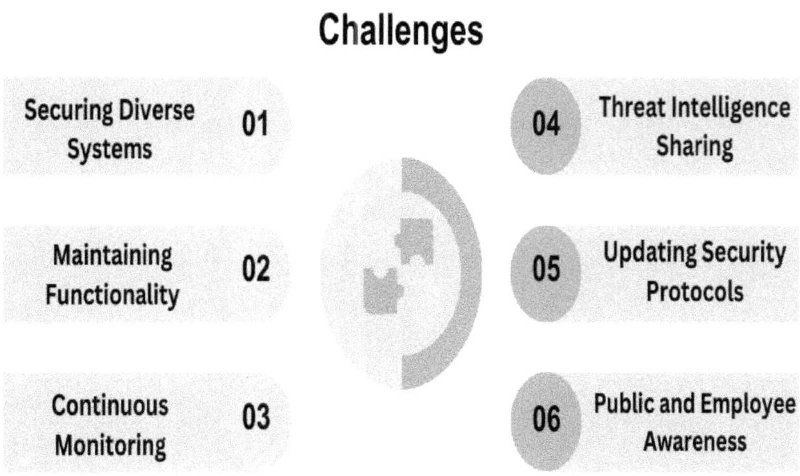

- **Securing Diverse Systems:** The Wilsons utilize various devices and networks, each with distinct vulnerabilities. These devices range from cell phones to home PCs and require distinct security procedures.
- **Maintaining Functionality:** Ensure security measures do not disrupt interconnected systems' efficiency. David needs business solutions that are both safe and functional to facilitate error-free client interactions.
- **Continuous Monitoring:** It is essential for promptly identifying and responding to emerging risks. Regular monitoring enables the Wilsons to keep ahead of prospective cyber-attacks.
- **Threat Intelligence Sharing**: Sharing threat intelligence with other organizations to exchange information on possible and current risks. Sharing insights can help avoid incidents like the ones that targeted Sarah's health information.
- **Updating Security Protocols:** Regularly updating security protocols to address emerging cyber threats. To remain secure, the Wilsons must update their software and security procedures on a regular basis.

- **Public and Employee Awareness:** Educating the public and employees on cybersecurity best practices to reduce human error. Emma and Jack learn about appropriate online conduct, which helps them avoid falling victim to phishing deceptions.

Understanding these risks and challenges allows us to develop more effective ways of protecting our digital surroundings. This maintains the security and confidentiality of our data and systems, allowing us to enjoy the benefits of technology confidently.

1.9 Future Trends and Predictions in Cybersecurity

As we move forward, the cybersecurity landscape will undergo significant changes and new challenges. Technological breakthroughs will continue to affect both the form of cyber threats and the techniques we employ to deal with them. Let us look at some significant trends and forecasts that are expected to affect the future of cybersecurity.

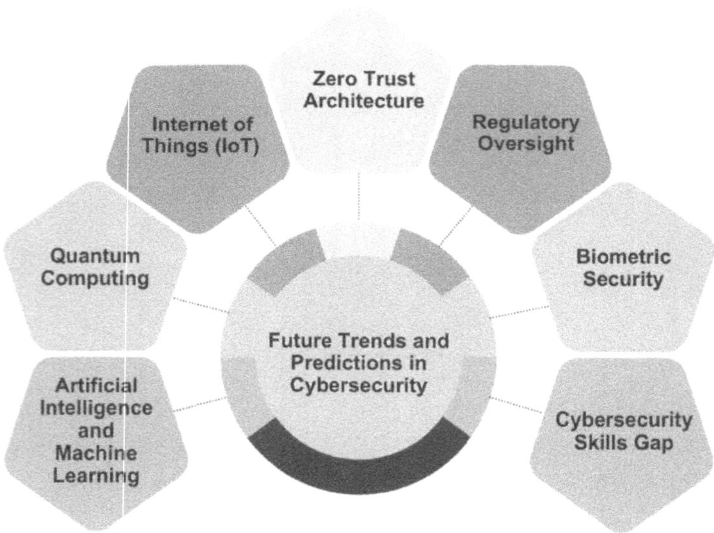

Integration of Artificial Intelligence and Machine Learning

These technologies are crucial for improving cybersecurity defenses. By analyzing massive volumes of data, these technologies can spot abnormalities and forecast future security breaches, allowing for faster and more precise responses. For example, David's architectural business may utilize artificial intelligence to monitor network traffic and detect suspicious activity before it escalates into a significant threat.

Implications of Quantum Computing

While quantum computing has the potential to revolutionize computation, it also poses a danger to existing encryption systems. As quantum technology advances, cybersecurity policies must develop to secure sensitive information. Consider Sarah's health data in danger if encryption technologies are not improved to handle quantum computing capacity.

Security for Internet of Things (IoT) Devices

The growing usage of Internet of Things (IoT) devices in households and enterprises presents unique security issues. These networked devices, ranging from smart home systems to industrial sensors, might provide weak entry points for hackers. For the Wilsons, safeguarding their smart home devices is critical to protecting their privacy and preventing unlawful access.

Adoption of Zero Trust Architecture

Unlike traditional security models, zero-trust involves rigorous verification of all access requests, regardless of origin. This paradigm acknowledges that threats might originate from anywhere, hence improving security against both internal and external dangers. For example, Emma and Jack's school may use zero-trust principles to safeguard their instructional platforms.

Enhanced Regulatory Oversight

Governments and regulatory organizations can adopt stringent cybersecurity regulations. To prevent legal complications and protect their reputations, organizations have to remain updated and comply with these developing standards. David's business, for example, must follow industry-specific cybersecurity standards to secure customer data and avoid fines.

Advancements in Biometric Security

Biometric security technologies, such as fingerprint and face recognition, are gaining popularity as a reliable alternative to traditional passwords. However, these improvements have raised privacy problems that must be addressed. The Wilsons believe that utilizing biometric security can improve the security of their devices, but they must be mindful of privacy concerns.

Addressing the Cybersecurity Skills Gap

The demand for trained cybersecurity experts is increasing. Comprehensive education and training programs are required to provide individuals with the requisite skills. This increases the chances of advancement in cybersecurity, encouraging more people to join the profession.

To summarize, cybersecurity is an important component of our digital life, affecting individuals, businesses, and governments. We can safeguard our digital domains from emerging dangers by studying the existing scene, forecasting future trends, and constantly enhancing our defenses. Moving forward, vigilance and proactivity are required to keep our cybersecurity measures effective and robust.

This chapter emphasized the importance of cybersecurity by discussing fundamental concepts as well as the unique demands of diverse stakeholders. By investigating the evolving threat landscape and forecasting future trends, we position ourselves to negotiate the complex dynamics of the digital world securely and effectively.

Chapter 2: Fundamentals of Cybersecurity

2.1 Introduction: Cybersecurity Fundamentals

In today's digital world, cybersecurity has become a top priority for everyone, not just IT experts. It is essential for families, companies, and governments alike. In this chapter, we will look at the core principles and practices that constitute the basis for sound cybersecurity measures. The CIA Triad—Confidentiality, Integrity, and Availability—which serves as the foundation for all cybersecurity initiatives, is central to this debate. These principles apply universally, whether it is protecting a family's personal information or preserving a country's key infrastructure.

This chapter will explain how the CIA Triad drives our approach to safeguarding digital assets and information using both theoretical ideas and practical examples. We will look at the many stages of data—at rest, in transit, and in use—to gain a thorough knowledge of data security. In addition, we will cover a wide spectrum of cyber risks, from basic hacking tactics to complex malware. This chapter will provide readers with insights into effective defenses against these emerging dangers, ensuring that they are well-equipped to defend their digital interactions and data.

By the end of this chapter, you should have a good understanding of the fundamentals of cybersecurity. You will be equipped with the information necessary to protect your digital presence and the security of your data in an increasingly linked world.

2.2 CIA Triad

The CIA Triad, an underlying approach intended to drive security policies and practices, is central to cybersecurity. The CIA Triad stands for Confidentiality, Integrity, and Availability—three fundamental principles for protecting information and promising secure digital interactions. These concepts are especially applicable to the Wilson family's daily digital activity.

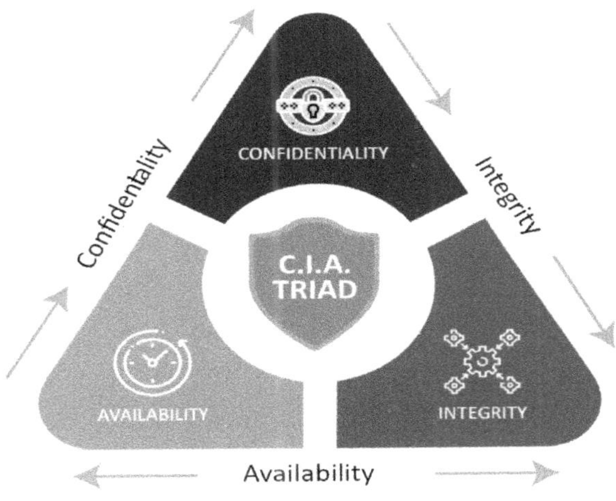

Confidentiality

Confidentiality protects sensitive information, limiting access to authorized individuals. This involves safeguarding the Wilson family's personal information from unwanted access. When Sarah looks up her family's medical data online, confidentiality safeguards ensure that only she and approved healthcare practitioners have access to this sensitive information. Similarly, Emma and Jack's educational information, such as grades and assignments, must be kept private to avoid misuse. Encryption, access controls, and authentication systems all serve to ensure confidentiality and keep the family's sensitive information safe from unauthorized access.

Integrity

Integrity refers to guaranteeing the quality and completeness of data and preventing unauthorized changes. This is important to David, whose firm is based on correct architectural blueprints and customer information. Any unlawful adjustments to his data might have serious professional and financial consequences. For the Wilsons, integrity includes keeping their bank records and other personal information correct and unmodified. Checksums, hash functions, and digital signatures all assist in maintaining data integrity, making sure that the family's information is reliable and correct.

Availability

Availability ensures authorized users may access information and resources as needed. For the Wilsons, availability is critical in their everyday lives. It assures that their internet service, educational platforms, online banking, and other important services are always available and operational. When Jack is unable to access his online lessons, or Sarah is unable to retrieve essential emails, their routines become disrupted and frustrating. Regular maintenance, redundancy, and disaster recovery plans are put in place to prevent downtime and guarantee that these critical services are always available.

Understanding the concepts of the CIA Triad allows the Wilson family—and anybody else—to understand the significance of comprehensive cybersecurity measures better. These principles contribute to addressing major issues of information security, ensuring that personal and professional data remain safe and dependable.

2.3 Data: Storage Locations and Security Measures

In today's digital world, knowing where your data is stored and how to safeguard it is important. Our lives have an unbreakable connection with technology, and our data is spread across several devices and platforms. Let us take a look at the fascinating world of data storage, with the Wilson family as our guide to discovering the secrets of securing your digital life.

Data Explained: A Clear Understanding

Data is at the heart of our digital interactions. It includes personal images, financial details, professional paperwork, and social media posts. David's architectural designs, Sarah's family photographs, Emma and Jack's school assignments, and their combined financial records are all examples of data for the Wilson family. This data, whether personal or professional, requires strong safeguards to maintain its confidentiality, integrity, and availability.

Data Storage: Where Is Your Information Kept?

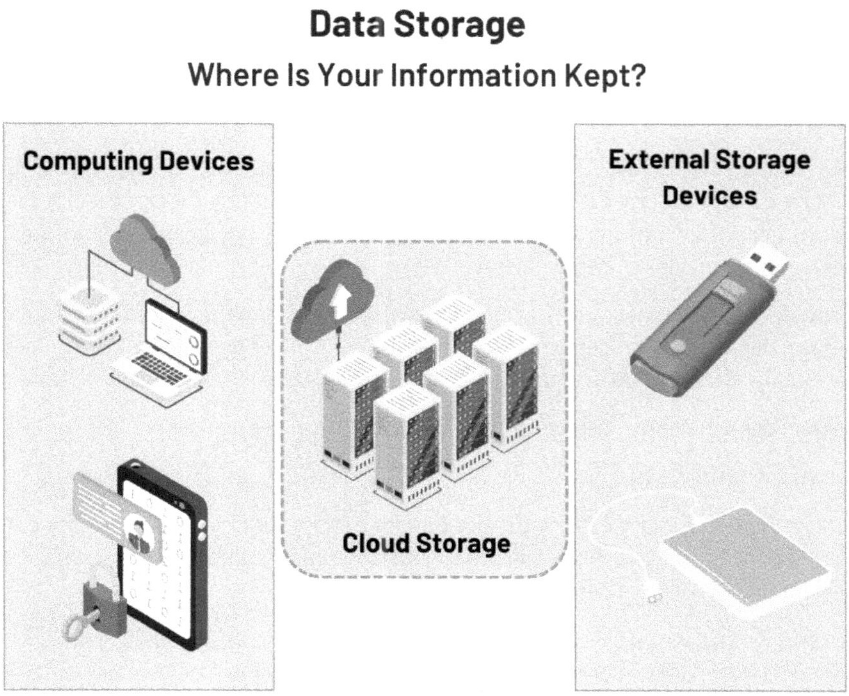

Our Computing Devices:

Data is kept across several computer devices, including desktops, laptops, tablets, and smartphones. David's architectural designs are stored on his work computer, Sarah's family photographs on an external hard drive, and their financial information on a home laptop. Every device has sensitive information that must be kept secure.

Example: David's computer holds sensitive business information, such as customer data and project ideas. If his computer is stolen or hacked, this information may be compromised.

Cloud Storage

Cloud storage is popular due to its convenient and accessible nature. The Wilsons may utilize services such as Google Drive, Dropbox, or iCloud to store and share papers, images, and other items.

Example: Sarah may upload family pictures to a cloud storage service for convenient access and backup. However, without suitable security measures such as strong passwords and encryption, their information may be accessible to unwanted access.

External Storage Devices

External storage devices, including hard drives and USB flash drives, are commonly used for backups and additional storage. The Wilsons utilize an external hard drive to save vital papers and photographs.

Example: While external hard disks are a useful backup option, they can be misplaced or stolen. Encrypting the data on these devices can help prevent unwanted access.

Cyber Threats to Your Finances: Staying Safe

Financial Data

Cybercriminals frequently target financial data for fraud and theft. This includes credit card numbers, bank account information, and internet banking passwords. The Wilsons' financial information is saved on their home computer, online banking accounts, and maybe even cloud services.

Example: If a hacker acquires access to the Wilsons' bank information, they may conduct illicit activities or steal their money. It is critical that their financial information is maintained securely and only accessible using encrypted methods.

Personal Data Security: Shielding Your Identity

Personal Identity Data

Identity theft is a big threat, with hackers targeting personal information such as Social Security numbers, driver's licenses, and birth certificates. This information may be saved digitally on their devices or in cloud storage.

Example: Emma and Jack's school records, which include personal information, are saved online. If these records are hacked, individuals' identities may be stolen and exploited

.Types of Data

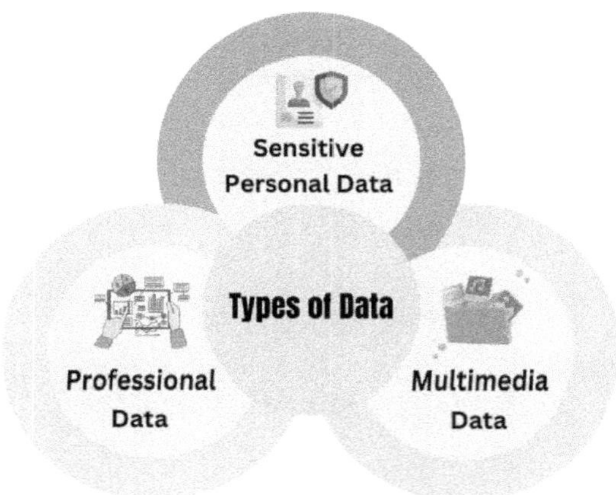

Sensitive Personal Data

Sensitive Personal Data encompasses medical records, personal identifiers, and private correspondence. This category includes Sarah's medical documents and the Wilson family's private correspondence.

Example:

When Sarah accesses her medical records online, ensuring that the connection is encrypted and the data is securely kept protects her sensitive information.

Professional Data

Professional data refers to company paperwork, customer information, and proprietary designs. David's architectural designs and client information are instances of professional data that require security.

Example: To avoid unwanted access and intellectual property theft, David must encrypt and manage access to his company data.

Multimedia Data

Protect multimedia data, including photos, movies, and audio files. The Wilsons' family photographs and movies are valuable memories that must be protected from loss or theft.

Example: By backing up their multimedia files to an encrypted external hard drive and cloud storage, the Wilsons can safeguard their memories against accidental loss or cyber theft.

The Wilson family may take proper cybersecurity measures if they understand where their data is housed and what categories of data need to be protected. To safeguard their data from cyber dangers, they can use encryption, strong passwords, multi-factor authentication, and secure backup solutions.

2.4 Three Stages of Data

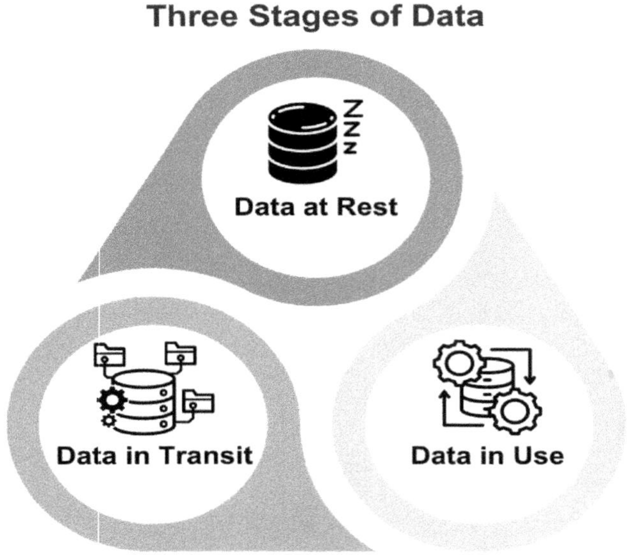

Understanding the three stages of data—data at rest, data in transit, and data in use—is important for adopting successful cybersecurity solutions that adhere to the principles of the CIA Triad. Each step reflects a distinct state of data and necessitates unique safeguards to maintain its security. These stages are particularly significant for the Wilson family as they navigate their digital life.

Data at Rest

Data at rest includes information held on devices such as computers, servers, or external storage. For the Wilsons, this includes David's architectural blueprints on his computer, Sarah's collection of family pictures on an external hard drive, and their financial records. Protecting data at rest is critical for preserving confidentiality and integrity. Encryption, for example, ensures that even if unauthorized persons get access to the storage device, the data will be difficult to read. Strong access controls restrict who has access to this information, and secure backups safeguard against data loss caused by hardware failure or unintentional deletion, ensuring the data's integrity.

Data in Transit

Data in transit refers to information being transported from one point to another. This involves Sarah sending emails, David uploading design files to a customer, and Emma and Jack completing school work online. Protecting data in transit is essential for maintaining confidentiality and integrity. SSL/TLS encryption, secure messaging applications, and virtual private networks (VPNs) maintain data confidentiality and integrity throughout transmission. For example, when the Wilsons utilize online banking, SSL/TLS encryption prevents unauthorized parties from intercepting and tampering with their financial activities.

Data in Use

Data in Use refers to information that is actively handled by applications. This involves Sarah looking at her student's scores on her computer, David updating architectural designs, and Emma and Jack interacting with educational software. Protecting data in use is critical for ensuring its integrity and availability. This includes ensuring that apps are safe and that unauthorized users are unable to access the data being processed. Secure coding methods, frequent software upgrades, and access controls are required. The Wilsons believe that adopting trustworthy software and keeping their devices updated prevents weaknesses from being exploited, making sure that the data is accurate and available when needed.

Individuals and organizations may greatly improve their cybersecurity posture by understanding and safeguarding data at all stages. These safeguards help guarantee that personal and professional information is secure, whether saved on a device, transported over the Internet, or actively employed in apps.

2.5 Hacking

Hacking has developed from its origins in curiosity-driven research to sophisticated and diverse threats in today's digital society. Understanding the concept, typical strategies, and major hacking occurrences is essential for recognizing the significance of cybersecurity.

Definition and Evolution

Originally, hacking was the technique of changing and examining computer systems to understand their functionality better. However, it has subsequently expanded to include illegal access and manipulation of computer systems, networks, and data. Hackers can have a variety of reasons, including financial gain, political action, personal challenge, and malicious intentions. Hacking has evolved into increasingly complex strategies and technologies, posing a substantial threat to individuals, businesses, and governments.

Common Hacking Techniques

- **Phishing:** Phishing is the practice of sending false emails or messages in an attempt to deceive recipients into disclosing sensitive information such as passwords or financial information. For example, David may get an email that purports to be from a customer but is, in fact, a phishing effort to steal his company's data.
- **Malware:** Malware, often known as malicious software, refers to viruses, worms, ransomware, and spyware. These programs have the ability to interrupt operations, steal data, and gain control of systems. Emma and Jack may unintentionally download malware when exploring gaming websites, putting the family's devices in danger.
- **SQL Injection:** SQL Injection is a method in which hackers introduce malicious code into a website's database query, allowing them to access or change the data. If Sarah's school's internet portal is vulnerable to SQL injection, student data may be compromised.
- **Denial of Service (DoS):** Denial of Service (DoS) attacks overload a system with traffic, making it unworkable. A Distributed Denial of Service (DDoS) attack launches from several systems. This could hinder David's architectural firm's website, resulting in commercial disruptions.
- **Man-in-the-Middle (MitM):** MitM attacks occur when a hacker intercepts and possibly modifies communication between two parties without their knowledge. For example, if the Wilsons utilize an unprotected Wi-Fi network, a hacker might get their online banking information.

Famous hacking incidents

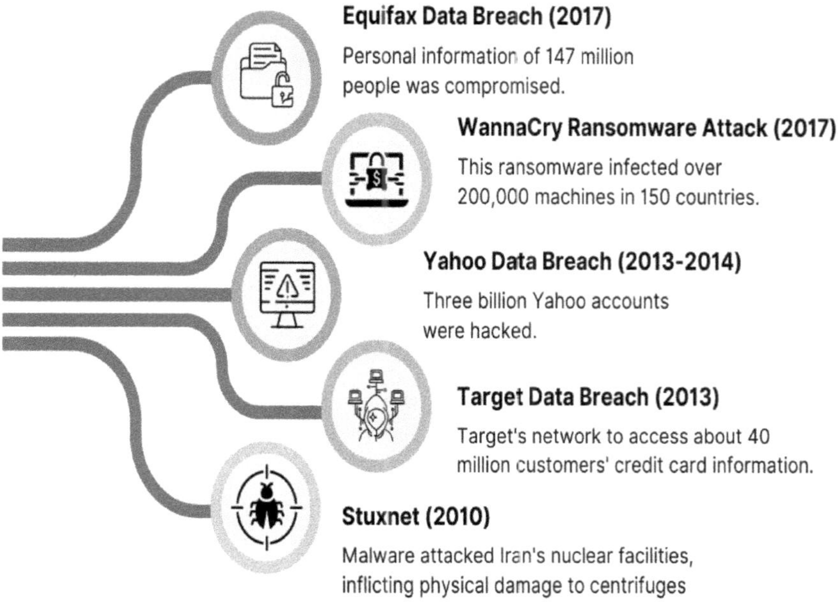

- **Equifax Data Breach (2017):** The personal information of 147 million people, including Social Security numbers and credit card information, was compromised. This event underlined the importance of comprehensive data protection and quick vulnerability patching.
- **WannaCry Ransomware Attack (2017):** This ransomware infected over 200,000 machines in 150 countries, encrypting data and demanding Bitcoin payments. It exploited a vulnerability in Windows computers, emphasizing the significance of frequent software upgrades.
- **Yahoo Data Breach (2013-2014):** In two distinct breaches, all three billion Yahoo accounts were hacked, revealing users' email addresses, phone numbers, and security questions. This event highlighted the huge extent and consequences of data breaches.
- **Target Data Breach (2013):** Hackers exploited flaws in Target's network to access about 40 million customers' credit card information. This intrusion underlined the importance of good network security procedures.
- **Stuxnet (2010):** This sophisticated malware attacked Iran's nuclear facilities, inflicting physical damage to centrifuges. Stuxnet was the turning point in cyber warfare, revealing the ability of cyber-attacks to bring about real-world damage.

Understanding hacking strategies and occurrences emphasizes the importance of robust cybersecurity measures. The Wilson family, like many others, must be watchful and proactive in safeguarding their digital life against these developing threats. In the following parts, we will look at practical actions and best practices for defending against hackers and improving overall cybersecurity.

2.6 Classification of Hackers

Hackers are classified into several sorts, each with their motives, tactics, and purposes. Understanding these classifications helps to understand the different environments of hacking and the significance of specific cybersecurity solutions.

White Hat Hackers

White Hat Hackers, commonly referred to as ethical hackers, assist corporations in identifying and addressing security vulnerabilities. They work within legal restrictions and frequently hold certificates. For example, a white hat hacker may be hired to test David's architectural firm's network's security and ensure it is secure from malicious attacks. Their work is critical in proactively identifying and correcting security vulnerabilities before malicious hackers exploit them.

Black Hat Hackers

Black Hat hackers use unlawful methods to exploit vulnerabilities for personal benefit or malicious purposes. They may steal data, implant malware, or cause system disruptions. If a black hat hacker attacks the Wilson family's internet accounts, they may obtain important data, resulting in financial loss or identity theft. These hackers work outside of the law, posing significant risks to personal and corporate security.

Grey Hat Hackers

Grey hat hackers fall between white and black hats. They may use vulnerabilities without malicious intent but without authority. Their activities may nevertheless create unforeseen harm. For example, a grey hat hacker may find a hole in Emma's social networking platform and broadcast it, potentially allowing unauthorized access before the problem is rectified. While their goals may not be malicious, their behaviors might nonetheless pose security threats.

Script Kiddies

Script Kiddies are those who utilize pre-written scripts or tools to carry out attacks without much technical understanding. They frequently desire attention or excitement rather than substantial financial gain. Jack may come into script kiddies in online gaming groups, who interrupt games with unsophisticated attacks. Despite their limited abilities, they may inflict disruption and harm.

Hacktivists

Hacktivists employ hacking to further political and social goals. They may deface websites, expose sensitive data, or disrupt services to call attention to their problems. For example, if Sarah's school district was targeted by hackers, they may suffer website defacement or data breaches aimed at publicizing specific complaints. Hacktivists frequently target organizations or institutions with whom they disagree in order to make a statement or effect change.

State-Sponsored Hackers

State-sponsored hackers are government-backed and aim to conduct cyber espionage, warfare, or disrupt other nations' operations. They have advanced talents and resources. If state-sponsored hackers target a country's infrastructure, such as power grids or communication networks, the consequences can be extensive and severe, underscoring the importance of strong national cybersecurity measures. These hackers pose the greatest threat because of their ability and the support they receive.

Understanding the various sorts of hackers assists in designing tailored defenses. Recognizing these risks is critical for the Wilson family in order to take suitable protective measures for their digital life. In the following sections, we will go over practical procedures and best practices for defending against various hacking risks and improving overall cybersecurity.

By learning about different hackers' motivations and approaches, the Wilsons may better prepare and implement ways to protect their personal information. This understanding enables students to be cautious and proactive in protecting their digital surroundings, allowing them to traverse the online world securely.

2.7 Malware

Malware, which stands for malicious software, is intended to harm, disrupt, or obtain unauthorized access to computer systems. Understanding the various forms of malware is critical for mitigating these risks. The Wilson family, like many others, must be aware of many sorts of malware to protect their digital lives.

Types of Malware

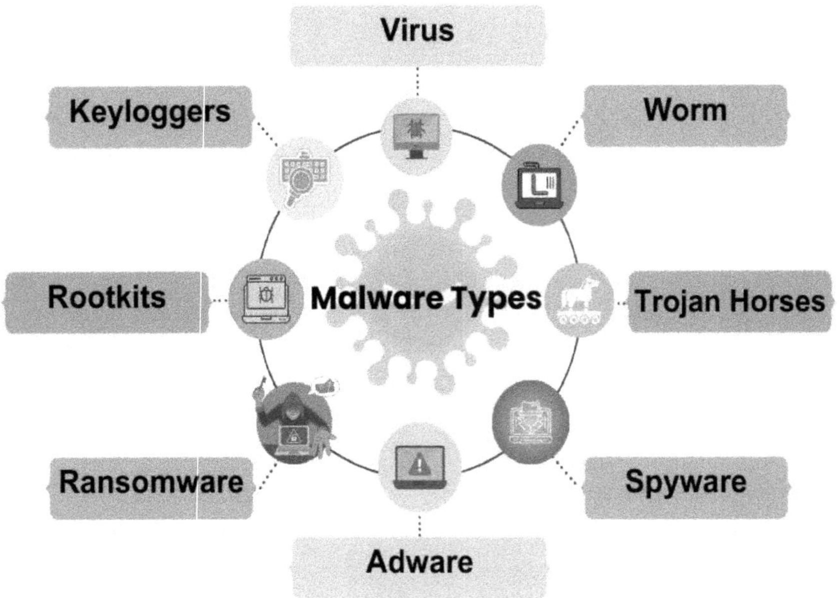

Virus

- **Definition:** A virus attaches to normal applications and multiplies when the infected program is run.
- **Characteristics:** Its characteristics include the ability to destroy or erase data, impede system performance, and spread to other applications and systems.
- **Example:** The ILOVEYOU virus propagated through email and did major harm by overwriting data.

Worm

- **Definition:** A worm is a type of malware that copies itself and spreads to other systems.
- **Characteristics:** It spreads without human participation and may swiftly infiltrate big networks, resulting in extensive harm.
- **Example:** The WannaCry infection, which encrypts data and demands ransom payments.

Trojan Horses

- **Definition:** A Trojan horse pretends to be genuine software but, once installed, executes destructive actions.
- **Characteristics:** It does not reproduce, but it can set up backdoors for other malware, steal data, or disrupt operations.
- **Example:** The Zeus Trojan, which targeted financial information.

Other malware

Spyware

- **Definition:** Spyware stealthily observes user behavior and captures personal information.
- **Characteristics:** It can monitor keystrokes, take screenshots, and steal login information.
- **Example:** Keylogging software may be installed without the user's knowledge in order to harvest passwords.

Adware

- **Definition:** Adware puts unwanted advertisements on a user's device.
- **Characteristics:** It frequently comes packaged with free software and may track browsing patterns to offer customized advertisements.
- **Example:** Adware leads online searches to advertising websites and gathers user preferences.

Ransomware

- **Definition:** Ransomware encrypts a user's data and demands money to recover access.
- **Characteristics:** It can result in considerable financial and data loss, and paying the ransom does not ensure data recovery.
- **Example:** The CryptoLocker ransomware encrypts files and demands Bitcoin payments for decryption keys.

Rootkits

- **Definition:** Rootkits are designed to mask their presence while controlling the infected machine.
- **Characteristics:** They can avoid detection by antivirus software, allowing attackers to gain remote access and control of the machine.
- **Example:** The Sony BMG rootkit, which was inserted on music CDs to prevent piracy, inadvertently exposed security weaknesses.

Keyloggers

- **Definition:** Keyloggers record every keystroke made on a keyboard, typically capturing important information such as passwords.
- **Characteristics:** They can be hardware or software-based and work quietly in the background.
- **Example:** A hardware keylogger, for example, can be plugged into a keyboard port and collect keystrokes without being recognized.

Understanding these sorts of malware enables the Wilson family and other families to take proactive actions to secure their devices and data. To guard against these hazardous attacks, use dependable antivirus software, keep your system up to date, and practice safe browsing habits. These steps help guarantee that their digital environment is secure, allowing them to enjoy the benefits of technology without worry.

2.8 Phishing Attacks

Phishing attacks are fraudulent efforts to gain sensitive information by posing as legitimate companies. These kinds of attacks frequently target individuals using emails, texts, or websites, attempting to steal personal information such as login passwords, credit card numbers, and other sensitive information. Understanding and detecting phishing attempts is critical for the Wilson family's personal and financial security.

Types of Phishing

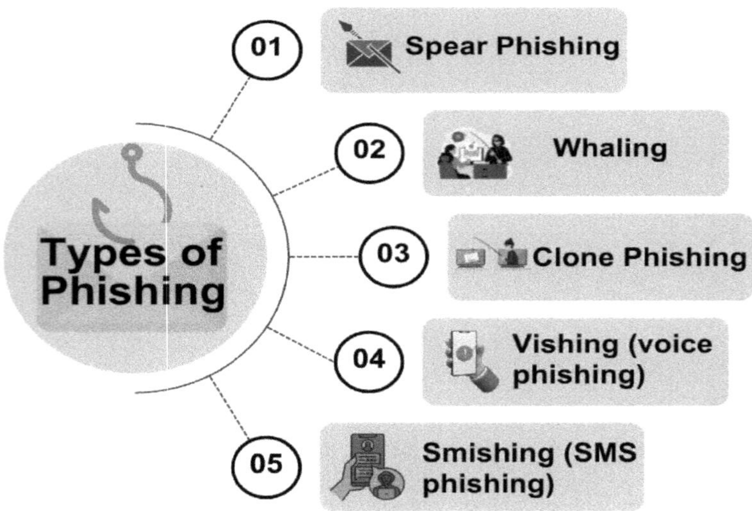

Spear Phishing

- **Definition:** Spear phishing is a targeted assault on a single individual or organization that typically uses personal information to seem authentic.
- **Example:** David may get an email that looks to be from one of his clients requesting that he check architectural designs. However, the email includes a malicious link intended to steal his login information.

Whaling

- **Definition:** Whaling is the practice of targeting high-profile persons, such as executives or senior management, with the purpose of stealing sensitive information or financial assets.

- **Example:** Sarah's school principal may receive an email that appears to be from the school system and requests private personnel or financial information.

Clone Phishing

- **Definition:** Clone phishing is the process of producing a nearly identical clone of a valid email that has already been delivered to the target but contains harmful links or attachments.
- **Example:** Emma may get an email that seems to be from her online school platform, asking her to download an "updated" assignment that includes malware.

Vishing (voice phishing)

- **Definition:** Vishing is the practice of deceiving someone into disclosing personal information over the phone.
- **Example:** Jack may receive a call pretending to be from his bank and requesting verification of his account information.

Smishing (SMS phishing)

- **Definition:** Smishing is the practice of sending text messages to deceive people into clicking on harmful URLs or revealing personal information.
- **Example:** Sarah may receive a text message claiming to be from her healthcare provider, requesting she click a link to confirm her appointment.

How to Identify and Prevent Phishing

Recognizing phishing attempts is the first step towards avoiding them. Here are some advice for the Wilson family to remain cautious:

- **Check the Sender's Email Address:** Examine the sender's email address for any irregularities or strange domain names. For example, an email from David's customer should be sent from a known domain rather than a random or misspelt one.
- **Look for Spelling and Grammatical Mistakes:** Phishing emails frequently include spelling and grammatical errors, as well as general welcomes such as "Dear User" rather than individual names.
- **Beware of Urgent or Threatening Language:** Phishing emails frequently use a feeling of urgency or fear to elicit rapid action. For example, an email informing Sarah that her account would be locked until she rapidly validates her password might arouse suspicion.
- **Hover over Links:** Before clicking on any link, move your cursor over it to reveal the real URL. If it appears strange or does not fit the context of the email, do not click it.

- **Verify Personal Information Requests:** Legitimate companies frequently request sensitive information by email or text message. If David receives an email requesting his login credentials or financial information, he should confirm the request by contacting the sender through a known and trustworthy channel.
- **Use Security Software:** Reputable antivirus and anti-phishing software can help identify and prevent phishing attacks. Updating these programs is critical for maintaining protection against new threats.

By being aware of the many forms of phishing and implementing these preventative methods, the Wilson family may dramatically lower their chances of falling victim to such assaults. Awareness and attentiveness are essential in guarding against phishing efforts.

Understanding and taking these preventative actions enables the Wilsons and other families to secure their personal and financial information from fraudsters. This information enables individuals to move through the digital world securely and confidently, ensuring that their digital lives are secure.

2.9 Advanced Persistent Threats (APTs)

Advanced Persistent Threats (APTs) are a serious problem in cybersecurity. They are extremely sophisticated and focused incidents that enter a network and remain undiscovered for a lengthy period of time, usually to steal data or monitor activity. To protect themselves from these subtle dangers, people, businesses, and governments must first understand APTs.

Features of APTs

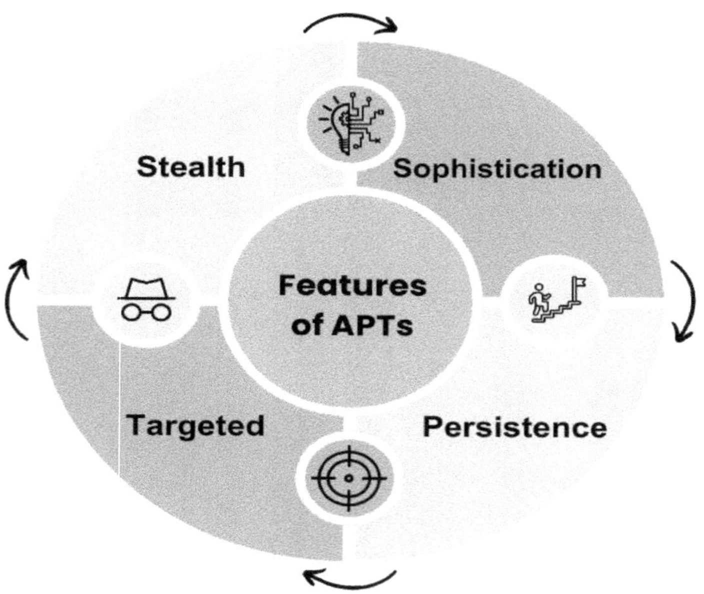

Sophistication: APTs utilize sophisticated tactics and tools to bypass security barriers. They frequently attack zero-day vulnerabilities or previously undisclosed security weaknesses.

Example: An APT may utilize spear phishing emails, malware, and exploit kits to acquire early network access.

Persistence: APTs establish a foothold and gain long-term access to the hacked system. They utilize advanced means to prevent discovery, such as encrypting messages and changing tactics regularly.

Example: An APT may install backdoors and use valid credentials to move laterally throughout a network, making it difficult to detect them.

Targeted: APTs often target certain organizations or sectors for political, economic, or military goals. In order to ensure that their infiltration is successful, the attackers devote a significant amount of time and money to studying their targets.

Example: APTs may target government organizations, financial institutions, or huge enterprises in order to steal critical data or disrupt operations.

Stealth: APTs aim to remain undetected for as long as feasible. They reduce their environmental impact by employing legitimate system tools and processes to avoid generating security alarms.

Example: Attackers may deploy tailored malware that only acts under certain conditions, lowering the likelihood of detection.

Notable APT Groups and Incidents

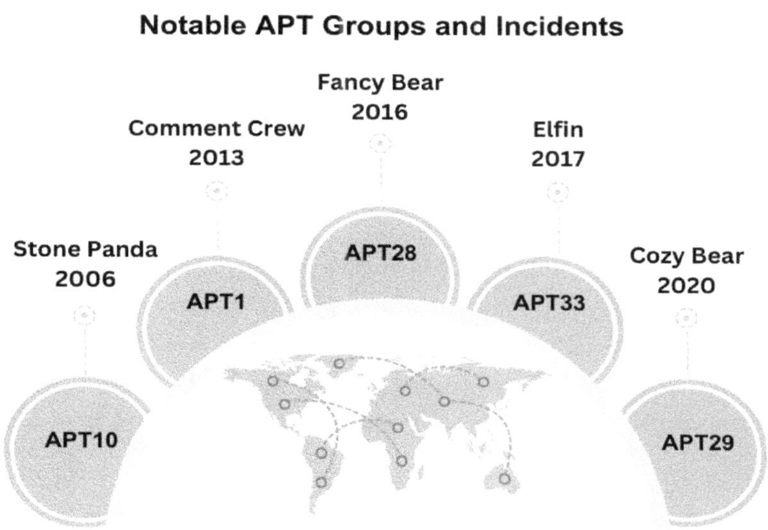

APT10 (Stone Panda)

- **Overview:** APT10, which is linked to Chinese governmental objectives, targets intellectual property and sensitive data from various businesses.

- **Incident:** In 2006, APT10 was part of Operation Cloud Hopper, a massive effort aimed at managed IT service providers to acquire indirect access to their clients' networks.

APT1 (Comment Crew)

- **Overview:** APT1, which is allegedly linked to the Chinese military, has targeted various industries, including aerospace, telecommunications, and energy.
- **Incident:** A 2013 Mandiant study described APT1's broad operations, claiming that the group stole hundreds of gigabytes of data from over 140 businesses.

APT28 (Fancy Bear)

- **Overview:** APT28, which is believed to be linked to the Russian government, has targeted political, military, and security institutions throughout the world.
- **Incident:** In 2016, APT28 was linked to the hacking of the Democratic National Committee (DNC) during the US presidential election, which resulted in the publication of crucial emails.

APT33 (Elfin)

- **Overview:** APT33, which is linked to Iranian governmental objectives, primarily targets the Middle Eastern aerospace and oil markets.
- **Incident:** In 2017, APT33 was connected to a series of assaults against Saudi organizations aimed at disrupting operations and gathering intelligence.

APT29 (Cozy Bear)

- **Overview:** APT29, which is linked to Russian intelligence, has carried out cyber espionage operations targeting government institutions, think tanks, and research groups.
- **Incident:** In 2020, APT29 was linked to efforts to steal COVID-19 vaccination research from organizations in the United States, the United Kingdom, and Canada.

Understanding APTs, including their features and prominent organizations, is critical for developing effective cybersecurity defenses. While such sophisticated dangers do not directly target the Wilson family, the examples provided can help raise awareness and alertness. By following best practices and remaining educated, they may safeguard their digital lives from a variety of cyber risks.

By becoming more aware of APTs, individuals and organizations may strengthen their cybersecurity procedures to guard against these persistent and sophisticated attacks. Understanding how these organizations work and their possible consequences emphasizes the significance of a proactive and educated approach to cybersecurity.

2.10 Emerging Technologies in Cybercrime

Cybercriminals' strategies and tools evolve in parallel with technological breakthroughs. Emerging technologies, although providing various advantages, can also create new vulnerabilities and opportunities for cyberattacks. Understanding these technologies and their potential for exploitation is critical for staying ahead of cyber-attacks.

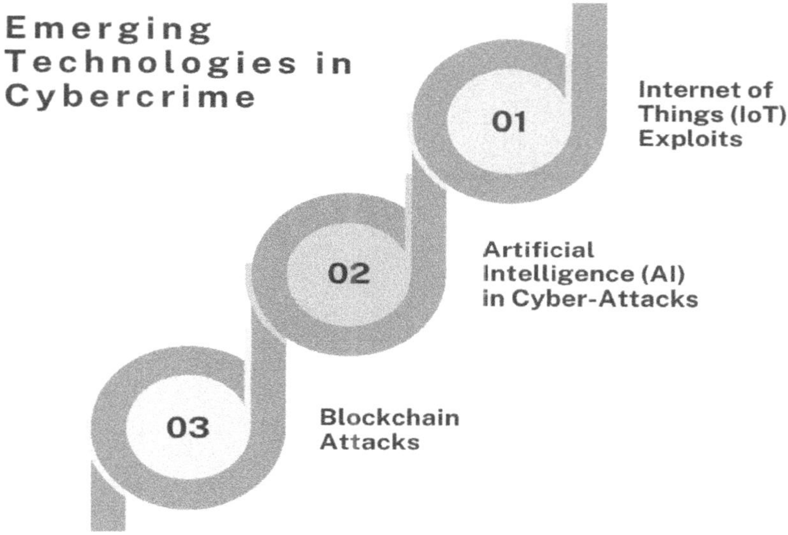

Internet of Things (IoT) Exploits

- **Overview:** The Internet of Things (IoT) connects common things to the Internet, allowing them to gather and share data. This includes smart household appliances, wearable technologies, and industrial equipment.
- **Risks:** Many IoT devices lack adequate security protections, making them accessible targets for attackers. Vulnerabilities in these devices can result in unwanted access, data breaches, or even device control.
- **Example:** The Mirai botnet attack of 2016 used vulnerabilities in IoT devices to build a huge network of hacked devices. This botnet conducted a DDoS attack, briefly disrupting major internet services such as Twitter and Netflix.
- **Impact on the Wilson family:** If the Wilsons employ smart home devices, such as a thermostat or security cameras, fraudsters may use them to obtain access to their home network, endangering their privacy and security.

Artificial Intelligence (AI) in Cyber-Attacks

- **Overview:** Artificial intelligence (AI) and machine learning may be used to improve the capabilities of cyberattacks, making them more complex and difficult to detect.

- **Risks:** AI may be used to automate and enhance phishing attempts, create complex malware, and detect weaknesses more quickly than traditional approaches.
- **Example:** AI-driven phishing attacks can use social network profiles to build highly tailored and convincing phishing emails, boosting the probability of success.
- **Impact on the Wilson Family:** AI-powered attacks might target the Wilsons with highly personalized phishing emails, making it more difficult for them to detect and escape these risks.

Blockchain Attacks

- **Overview:** Blockchain technology, which is widely used in cryptocurrencies, is intended to be safe and tamper-proof. However, it is vulnerable to assaults.
- **Risks:** Blockchain assaults can involve exploiting smart contract weaknesses, launching 51% attacks to acquire control of the blockchain network, and stealing bitcoin from wallets.
- **Example:** In 2016, the DAO, a decentralized autonomous organization on the Ethereum blockchain, was attacked owing to a weakness in its smart contract, resulting in the theft of $50 million in Ether.
- **Impact on the Wilson family:** If the Wilsons invest in cryptocurrencies or utilize blockchain-based services, they may suffer financial losses as a result of these attacks.

Understanding these evolving technologies and their accompanying hazards enables the Wilson family and others to stay informed about potential cyber-attacks. By understanding the risks of IoT devices, the enhanced capabilities of AI in cyber-attacks, and the intricacies of blockchain technology, they may take proactive actions to improve their cybersecurity measures.

By remaining knowledgeable and cautious, the Wilsons can better safeguard their digital life from emerging hazards. This understanding helps people to take necessary security precautions, allowing them to reap the benefits of emerging technology without endangering their safety.

2.11 Cybersecurity Measures

Implementing strong cybersecurity measures is critical for safeguarding personal and professional data against different cyber-attacks. By knowing and implementing these safeguards, the Wilson family and others may build a secure digital environment.

Defense in Depth Concept

Defense in Depth is a layered security approach that incorporates multiple defensive measures to protect data and systems from various threats. Here, we explore the tools and technologies arranged by their respective layers.

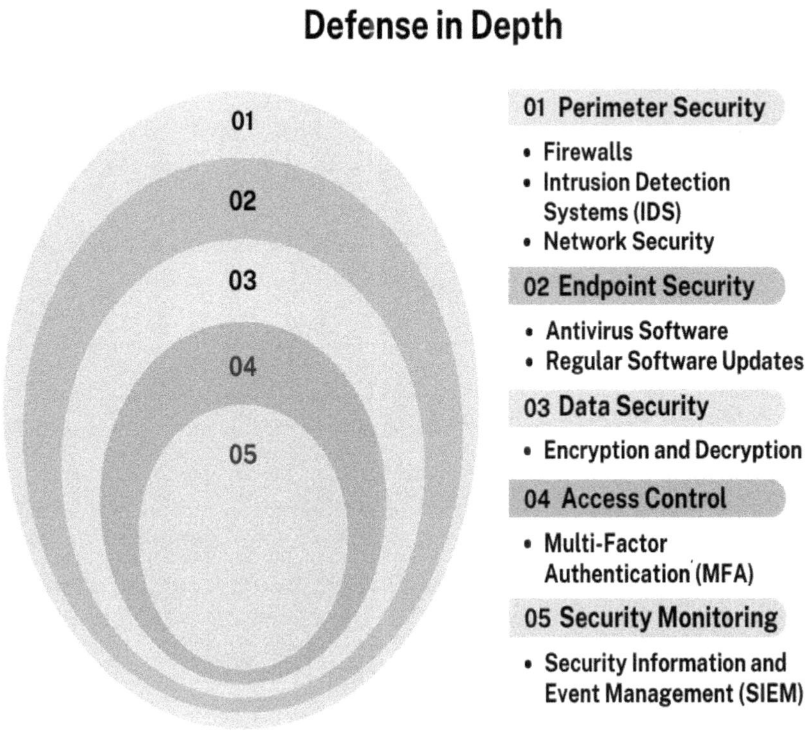

Perimeter Security

Firewalls:

- **Overview:** Firewalls serve as a barrier between trustworthy and untrusted networks, managing incoming and outgoing traffic according to established security rules.
- **Importance:** Firewalls are significant because they safeguard against access and attacks, thereby upholding the security and integrity of the network.
- **Example:** A firewall can prevent unwanted access to David's architectural firm's network by preventing possible attacks.

Intrusion Detection Systems (IDS):

- **Overview:** IDS analyze network traffic for unusual activities and possible threats, notifying administrators to take appropriate action.
- **Importance:** Intrusion Detection Systems (IDS) enhance security by identifying threats and notifying administrators promptly, allowing quick action to mitigate risks effectively.
- **Example:** An IDS can identify odd login attempts on the Wilsons' home network and alert them before a breach happens.

Network Security:

- **Overview:** This involves adopting secure Wi-Fi setups, setting up VPNs for secure remote access, and using network segmentation to restrict access to critical regions.
- **Importance:** Network security measures are essential for safeguarding data during transmission, preventing access attempts and ensuring remote connections.
- **Example:** Using a VPN for remote work protects David's data when he connects to his company's network from outside the office.

Endpoint Security

Antivirus Software:

- **Overview:** These tools detect, block, and remove malware from computers and networks.
- **Importance:** Regular usage of antivirus and anti-malware software protects against a variety of cyber dangers, such as viruses, worms, and ransomware.
- **Example:** By putting antivirus software on their devices, the Wilson family may avoid malware infestations that could endanger their data.

Regular Software Updates and Patch Management:

- **Overview:** Software and systems must be kept up to date with the most recent patches and upgrades to ensure security.
- **Importance:** Updates frequently contain security fixes that address vulnerabilities, lowering the danger of fraudulent individuals exploiting them.
- **Example:** The Wilsons protect themselves against known security problems by routinely updating their operating systems and software.

Data Security

Encryption and Decryption:

- **Overview:** Encryption uses a cryptographic key to convert data into an unreadable format, whereas decryption restores it to its original form when accessed by an authorized user.
- **Importance:** Encryption guarantees that data will remain unreadable and safe even if it is intercepted or viewed by unauthorized parties.
- **Example:** When Sarah sends essential emails, including her family's medical information, encryption assures that only the intended recipient can see them.

Access Control

Multi-Factor Authentication (MFA):

- **Overview:** MFA increases security by requiring two or more verification methods to access an account, such as a password and a fingerprint scan.
- **Importance:** MFA dramatically minimizes the danger of unauthorised access, even if one credential is compromised.
- **Example:** By setting MFA on their online banking accounts, the Wilsons ensure that even if their passwords are compromised, attackers will be unable to access their accounts without the second verification method.

Security Monitoring

Security Information and Event Management (SIEM):

- **Overview:** SIEM systems gather and analyze security-related data from several sources in order to detect, monitor, and respond to possible security risks.
- **Importance:** SIEM delivers real-time insights and extensive analysis of security events, enabling companies to respond quickly to problems.
- **Example:** If David's company deploys an SIEM system, it will be able to swiftly detect and mitigate dangers such as unauthorized access attempts or data breaches.

By implementing these cybersecurity steps in a layered approach, the Wilson family may greatly improve their defenses against cyber threats. These procedures are critical to ensuring the confidentiality, integrity, and availability of their personal and professional data. Understanding and applying these procedures can help them keep their digital life private and their information safe.

2.12 Legal and Ethical Aspects of Cybersecurity

Understanding the legal and ethical aspects of cybersecurity is essential for individuals, businesses, and governments. These features not only establish the bounds of legal activity in the digital environment but also serve as a guide for ethical behaviors that preserve privacy and promote confidence.

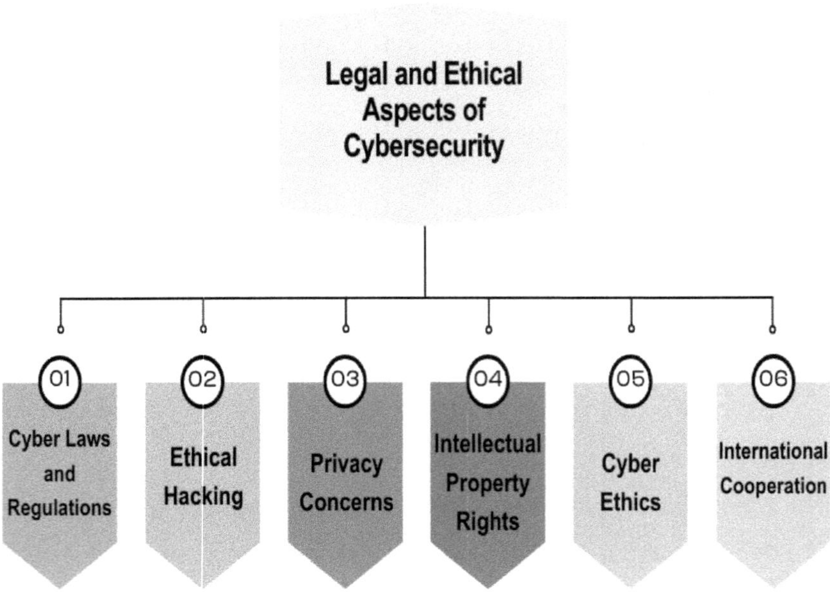

Cyber Laws and Regulations

- **Overview:** Cyber laws and regulations are intended to safeguard people, data, and systems from cyber-attacks. While these laws differ by nation, they often address issues like data protection, privacy, and cybercrime.
- **Importance:** Adhering to Internet laws enables compliance with legal norms and helps to avoid legal consequences.
- **Example:** The European Union's General Data Protection Regulation (GDPR) establishes strong data protection and privacy requirements that influence how corporations manage personal data. David's architectural firm must comply with GDPR if they do business with clients in the EU, ensuring that client data is treated legally and securely.

Ethical Hacking

- **Overview:** Ethical hacking is defined as approved attempts to access systems in order to uncover and fix security issues. Ethical hackers, often known as white hat hackers, contribute to cybersecurity by proactively identifying vulnerabilities before bad hackers exploit them.

- **Importance:** Ethical hacking is an essential component of implementing strong security measures and protecting against cyber threats.
- **Example:** Sarah's school district may engage an ethical hacker to test their internet systems, assuring the security of student data and discovering any weaknesses that need to be rectified.

Privacy Concerns

- **Overview:** Privacy problems in cybersecurity center on the acquisition, use, and exchange of personal information. Ensuring privacy entails safeguarding persons' data against illegal access and exploitation.
- **Importance:** Maintaining privacy promotes trust between individuals and organizations while also meeting legal responsibilities.
- **Example:** The Wilson family should be aware of their social media privacy settings in order to manage who may view their personal information and postings. Organizations, such as David's organization, must create procedures to safeguard customer data, such as encrypting critical information and restricting access to authorized employees only.

Intellectual Property Rights

- **Overview:** Cyber laws safeguard intellectual property (IP), ensuring that creators and corporations retain ownership of their digital goods and inventions.
- **Importance:** Intellectual property rights must be protected in order to stimulate innovation and prevent theft or abuse of digital material.
- **Example:** David's architectural drawings are considered intellectual property, and he must guarantee that they are legally secured against copying or usage without authorization.

Cyber Ethics

- **Overview:** Cyber ethics refers to the moral rules that regulate action in the digital environment. It addresses problems such as digital rights, responsible technology usage, privacy, and intellectual property.
- **Importance:** Adherence to ethical principles fosters a safe and equitable digital environment.
- **Example:** The Wilsons should follow strong cyber ethics by avoiding downloading illicit information, respecting people's online privacy, and utilizing technology responsibly.

International Cooperation

- **Overview:** Cybercrime frequently crosses national borders, necessitating international collaboration to prevent and punish these crimes successfully.
- **Importance:** Collaborative actions improve our ability to combat global cyber threats and bring those responsible to justice.
- **Example:** Governments and organizations throughout the world may collaborate to find and prosecute hackers implicated in global cyber-attacks, ensuring justice is served and comparable risks are prevented.

Understanding the legal and ethical dimensions of cybersecurity enables the Wilson family and others to navigate the digital world ethically and safely. Compliance with laws and ethical norms not only protects individual privacy but also helps to create a safer and more trustworthy online environment.

The consideration of cybersecurity foundations in this chapter emphasizes the crucial significance of proactive security measures in our interconnected society. Understanding the CIA Triad principles, identifying the many phases of data, and becoming familiar with the range of cyber threats will dramatically strengthen our defenses against prospective cyber-attacks. This knowledge is critical not only for IT professionals, but for anybody who interacts with digital technology on a regular basis. As cyber threats grow, remaining knowledgeable and attentive is our best protection against the weaknesses inherent in the digital world. The concepts presented in this chapter serve as the foundation for creating a safe and resilient digital environment for both personal and professional use.

Chapter 3: Everyday Cybersecurity Practices

3.1 Introduction to Everyday Cybersecurity

Understanding and conducting common cybersecurity practices are essential for securing our personal and professional lives in today's increasingly digital environment. Integrating these techniques into the Wilsons' regular routines can dramatically lessen their vulnerability to cyber dangers. This chapter will walk you through some practical cybersecurity strategies you can employ to keep secure online.

Cybersecurity is not only for IT experts; it affects everyone. Whether you are browsing the internet, maintaining your social media accounts, or buying online, you should be aware of possible risks and know how to prevent them. You may secure your personal information and digital privacy by using simple yet effective security behaviors.

Why Everyday Cybersecurity Matters

For the Wilson family, everyday cybersecurity includes protecting their financial data, personal identification, and sensitive information from fraudulent individuals. It is about building a safe digital environment in which they may utilize technology without fear of being compromised.

Practical Cybersecurity Measures

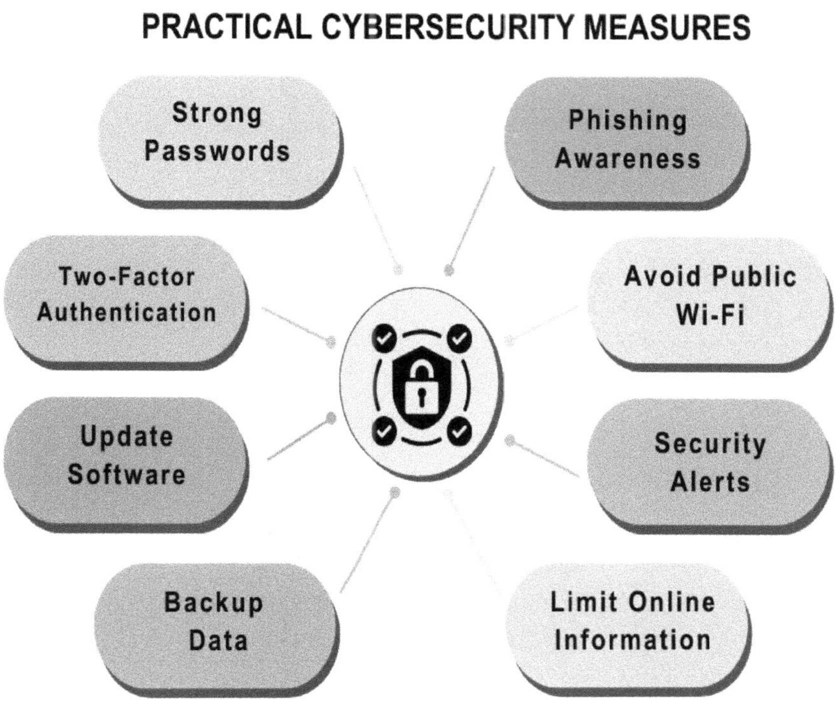

- **Strong Passwords:** Creating complicated passwords is an important step toward securing your online accounts. Use a combination of letters, numbers, and special characters in your passwords, and change them on a frequent basis.
- **Two-factor Authentication**: Two-factor authentication (2FA) increases security by requiring an additional form of verification, such as a code delivered to your phone, in addition to your password.
- **Update Software:** It is crucial to keep your software up to date. To protect yourself against newly identified vulnerabilities, keep your operating systems, programs, and antivirus software updated on a regular basis.
- **Backup Data:** Regularly backing up your vital data can help prevent data loss caused by hardware problems or cyber-attacks. Store copies of your vital information on external drives or in secure cloud storage services.
- **Phishing Awareness:** When it comes to emails, check the sender before clicking on links or downloading files. Phishing efforts sometimes pose as genuine emails to deceive you into disclosing personal information or installing harmful malware.
- **Avoid Public Wi-Fi:** Avoid using unprotected public Wi-Fi networks for important transactions, such as banking, because they are frequently less secure and might expose your data to cybercriminals.
- **Security Alerts:** Pay attention to security notifications from your devices and applications. These notifications frequently signal potential risks and should not be ignored.
- **Limit Online Information:** Limit the amount of personal information you disclose online, particularly on social media platforms, to lessen the likelihood that attackers may acquire information about you.

By incorporating these practical steps into their daily lives, the Wilson family can lay a solid basis for their cybersecurity practices. The following sections will go into further detail on particular topics like safe internet browsing, safeguarding social media accounts, and protecting personal devices, giving you full advice on how to improve your digital security.

3.2 Safe Internet Browsing

In today's digital world, using the internet properly is essential for preserving your personal information and privacy. The Wilsons, like many of us, spend a lot of time online, whether for a job, education, or amusement. Safe internet browsing can help protect against a variety of cyber risks, including malware, phishing, and identity theft.

Understanding Safe Web Browsing

Safe internet browsing is being aware of the risks connected with online activity and adopting preventative measures to reduce them. By adopting sensible browsing habits, you may defend yourself from cyber-attacks and keep your data secure.

Safe Internet Browsing: Do's and Don'ts

What Should You Do?

- **Use Secure Websites**: Before entering any personal information, check for "https" in the URL and a padlock icon in the address bar. These signs indicate that the website employs encryption to secure your information.
- **Keep your browser Updated:** To take advantage of the most recent security updates and features, keep your web browser updated on a regular basis.
- **Use a Reliable Antivirus Program:** Ensure that your antivirus software is up to date and continuously searching for risks as you browse.
- **Enable Pop-up Blockers:** Pop-up advertisements can be a source of malware and phishing attacks. Use a browser that has a built-in pop-up blocker, or download a reliable one.
- **Be Cautious with Downloads:** Only download files and software from reputable sources. Before downloading anything, check the website's validity and read the reviews.

- **Use Strong, Unique Passwords:** Create strong passwords for all of your online accounts and consider using a password manager to keep track of them.
- **Activate Two-Factor Authentication (2FA):** When possible, use 2FA to protect your online accounts.
- **Beware of Phishing Scams:** Avoid unsolicited emails and texts that implore you to click on links or supply personal information. Always check the sender's validity.

What Shouldn't You Do?

- **Do not Ignore Security Warnings:** If your browser alerts you to a potentially harmful website, don't ignore it. These warnings are intended to protect you against dangerous websites.
- **Avoid Using Public Wi-Fi for Sensitive Transactions:** Public Wi-Fi networks are frequently unsafe. Avoid accessing financial information or inputting personal information while linked to them.
- **Do Not Save Passwords on Public Computers:** Never keep your login information on shared or public computers. Always log out and erase your browser history after each usage.
- **Avoid Clicking on Suspicious Links:** Avoid clicking on links in emails or websites that appear suspicious or too good to be true. These may lead to fraudulent websites or malware downloads.
- **Avoid Entering Personal Information on Untrusted Sites:** Never provide personal or financial information on websites you do not trust or recognize.

- **Do Not Use Weak Passwords:** Avoid using simple, easily guessable passwords. Use a mix of letters, numbers, and symbols to create strong, unique passwords for each account.
- **Do Not Ignore Software Updates:** Regularly update your browser, operating system, and security software. These updates often include patches for newly discovered vulnerabilities.
- **Do Not Disable Security Features:** Keep your browser's security settings enabled. Disabling features like pop-up blockers and anti-phishing tools can expose you to more risks.

Practical Tips for Safe Internet Browsing

The Wilson family's secure internet browsing practices can significantly minimize their risk of cyber dangers. Here are some more ways to help them be safe online:

- **Use a Virtual Private Network (VPN):** A VPN encrypts your internet connection, adding an extra layer of privacy and protection, particularly while utilizing public Wi-Fi.

- **Regularly Clear Browsing Data:** To erase cached data that hackers may exploit, clean your browser's cache, cookies, and history on a regular basis.
- **Be Cautious of Pop-ups and Advertisements:** Malware is frequently spread through pop-ups and internet advertisements. Avoid clicking on them, and use an ad blocker if required.
- **Educate Family Members:** Ensure that all family members, particularly youngsters, understand the significance of safe browsing habits and the risks associated with unsafe behaviors.

By adhering to these rules and adopting safe surfing habits into their daily routines, the Wilson family may get the benefits of the internet while reducing their vulnerability to cyber risks. Safe internet browsing is an essential component of everyday cybersecurity, ensuring that personal information is kept private and safe.

3.3 Securing Social Media Accounts

Social media has become an essential part of our everyday lives, giving us a platform for connecting with friends, sharing experiences, and staying informed. However, these platforms represent substantial security threats if not adequately controlled. The Wilson family believes that encrypting their social media accounts is vital for preserving their personal information and online privacy.

Understanding Social Media Security

Securing social media accounts includes taking precautions to avoid unwanted access, data breaches, and identity theft. By taking proactive actions, you can protect your personal information and keep your social network presence secure.

Securing Social Media Accounts: Do's and Don'ts

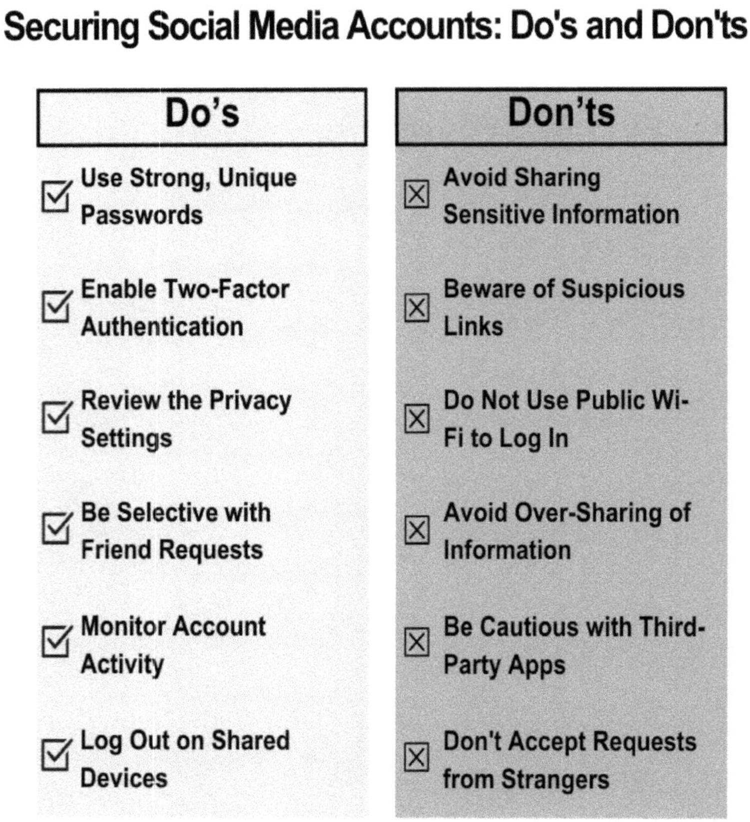

What Should You Do?

- **Use Strong, Unique Passwords:** Set up difficult passwords for each of your social network accounts. Combine letters, numbers, and special characters.
- **Enable Two-Factor Authentication:** Enabling 2FA on your social media accounts provides an added degree of security.

- **Review the Privacy Settings:** Check and change your social media privacy settings on a regular basis to manage who sees your posts and personal information.
- **Be Selective with Friend Requests:** Accept only friend requests from those you know and trust.
- **Monitor Account Activity**: Regularly check your account activity for any unexpected or unauthorized activities.
- **Log Out on Shared Devices:** Always log out of your social media accounts before utilizing shared or public devices.

What Shouldn't You Do?

- **Avoid Sharing Sensitive Information:** Don't share personal information like your address or bank information on social media.
- **Beware of Suspicious Links**: Be wary of links in messages, postings, or emails, even if they look to be from friends.
- **Do Not Use Public Wi-Fi to Log In:** Avoid accessing your social media accounts using unprotected public Wi-Fi networks.
- **Avoid Over-Sharing:** Limit the quantity of personal information you disclose online.
- **Be Cautious with Third-Party Apps:** Only allow access to trusted third-party applications.
- **Do Not Accept Friend Requests from Strangers:** Avoid accepting connection requests from unknown individuals, as they could be fraudulent accounts seeking to access your personal information.

Practical Tips for Securing Your Social Media Accounts

The Wilson family's approach to safeguarding their social media accounts combines attentiveness and practical steps. Here are some more methods to keep children safe:

- **Password Changes:** Change your passwords on a regular basis and avoid using information that is easy to guess.

- **Awareness of Phishing Scams:** Inform family members about typical phishing strategies.
- **Use Privacy Filters:** Use the privacy filters provided by social media companies.
- **Backup Important Data:** You should consider downloading a copy of your social networking data on a regular basis.

- **Report strange Activity:** If you see any strange conduct or communications, please notify the social media network immediately.

The Wilson family can safeguard their social media accounts against unwanted access and cyber dangers by following these simple guidelines. Securing social media accounts is an important part of everyday cybersecurity, as it helps to retain privacy and secure personal information in the digital era.

3.4 Protecting Personal Devices

In today's digital era, personal devices like smartphones, tablets, and laptop computers have become necessary. For the Wilson family, preserving the security of these devices is critical to protecting their personal information and digital privacy. This section outlines practical techniques for protecting personal devices against cyber-attacks.

Understand the Importance of Device Security

Personal devices hold a large quantity of sensitive data, such as emails, images, financial information, and professional papers. Securing these devices helps to avoid unwanted access, data breaches, and malware outbreaks.

Protecting Personal Devices: Do's and Don'ts

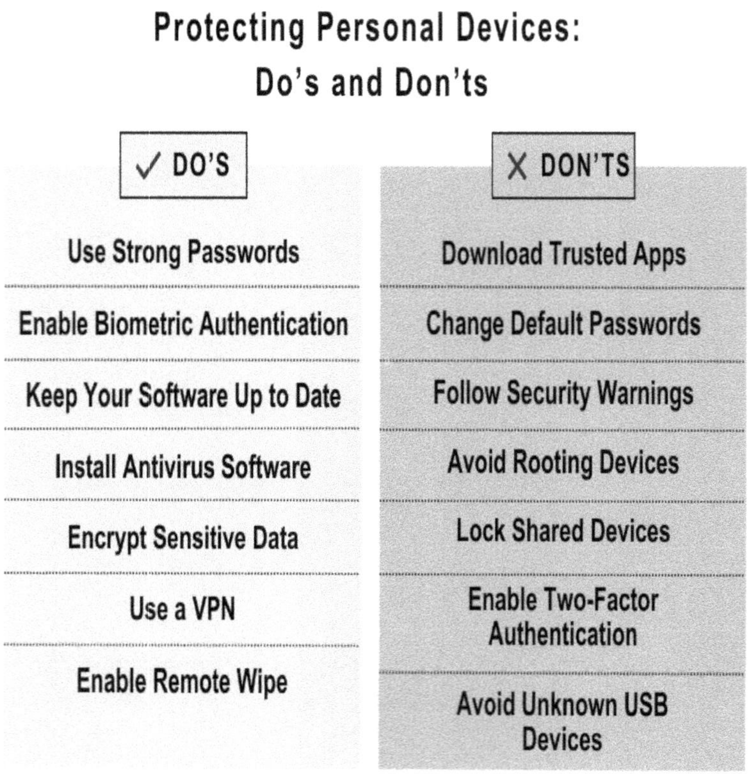

What Should You Do?

- **Use Strong Passwords or Passcodes:** To protect your devices from illegal access, create strong, unique passwords or passcodes.
- **Enable Biometric Authentication**: Use features such as fingerprint scanners or face recognition to increase security.
- **Keep Your Software Up to Date:** Update your device's operating system and applications on a regular basis to address security issues.
- **Install Antivirus Software:** Install trusted antivirus software to safeguard your devices from viruses and other risks.
- **Encrypt Sensitive Data:** Enable encryption to protect data saved on your devices, making it secure even if stolen.
- **Use a VPN:** To secure your internet connection when using public Wi-Fi, connect over a Virtual Private Network.
- **Enable Remote Wipe:** Set up your devices to allow remote wiping in case they are lost or stolen.

What Shouldn't You Do?

- **Change Default Passwords:** Immediately update the default passwords when setting up new devices.
- **Download Trusted Apps:** Only install software from reputable sources, such as legitimate app stores.
- **Follow Security Warnings:** Pay attention to security warnings and notifications from your mobile and computing devices.
- **Avoid Jailbreaking and Rooting Devices:** Modifying the operating system could disable built-in security mechanisms.
- **Lock Shared Devices:** When sharing a device, make sure it is protected and that no personal data is accessible.
- **Do Not Skip Two-Factor Authentication:** Always enable two-factor authentication (2FA) for an added layer of security on your accounts.
- **Avoid Unknown USB Devices:** Do not connect your devices to unfamiliar USB ports or use unknown USB drives, as they may contain malware.

Practical Tips to Protect Personal Devices

The Wilson family secures their personal devices by adopting practical behaviors and exploiting built-in security capabilities.

- **Regular Backups:** Save vital data to secure locations such as external hard drives or cloud services.

- **Secure Network Connections:** Protect your home Wi-Fi network with a strong password and encryption.
- **Monitor Device Activity:** Look for odd activity or unknown applications and report any suspicious conduct.
- **Educate Family Members:** Teach all family members the significance of device security and promote excellent practices.
- **Use the Device Tracking Features:** Enable tracking capabilities such as Find My iPhone or Find My Device to track down misplaced devices and remotely lock or erase them if necessary.

By implementing these security steps, the Wilson family may dramatically improve the security of their devices, keeping sensitive information private and safe from cyber risks.

3.5 Safe Online Shopping

Shopping on the Internet offers both convenience and a broad selection of goods, making it a vital part of daily life. For families like the Wilsons, who frequently make purchases online, it's crucial to maintain vigilant shopping habits to safeguard their financial and personal details against cyber threats.

Understand the Importance of Online Shopping

While convenient, online shopping exposes consumers to risks such as identity theft, fraudulent activities, and data breaches. Cybercriminals often target online shoppers through tactics like phishing, deceptive websites, and insecure payment methods. Adopting prudent online shopping behaviors can greatly mitigate these threats, enhancing the security of your shopping experience.

Safe Online Shopping: Do’s and Don’ts

What Should You Do?

- **Select Established Retailers:** Only make purchases from websites that are well-known and have a good reputation. Verify their legitimacy through customer reviews and ratings.
- **Ensure Secure Website Connections:** Check that the website uses HTTPS, indicated by a padlock symbol in the address bar, which signifies a secure connection.

- **Create Strong, Distinct Passwords:** Develop complex passwords that are unique to each of your shopping accounts.
- **Activate Two-Factor Authentication:** Increase security by enabling two-factor authentication and adding a secondary verification step to your accounts.
- **Prefer Secure Payment Methods**: Choose credit cards or services like PayPal, which provide better protection against fraud.
- **Regularly Monitor Account Statements:** Regularly review statements from your bank and credit card companies for any unauthorized charges.
- **Maintain Updated Security Software:** Ensure that your devices are protected with the latest antivirus software.

What Shouldn't You Do?

- **Refrain from Using Public Wi-Fi:** Avoid conducting transactions over public Wi-Fi networks. If necessary, use a VPN.
- **Access Websites Directly:** Enter the retailer's address directly into your browser instead of clicking on links in emails.
- **Do Not Store Payment Information:** For added security, enter your payment details manually each time you make a purchase.
- **Question Unbelievably Good Offers:** Be wary of deals that seem too good to be true, as they could be bait for scams.
- **Limit Personal Information Shared:** Only provide essential information needed for your transactions.
- **Do Not Use Debit Cards**: Use credit cards or payment services that offer better fraud protection.
- **Do Not Ignore Site Security:** Before entering payment information, ensure the website uses HTTPS and has a valid security certificate.

Practical Tips to Protect Personal Devices

- **Utilize Virtual Credit Card Numbers:** Use virtual numbers provided by your bank for online purchases, which helps protect your real account details.
- **Enable Transaction Alerts:** Set up alerts for new transactions with your bank or credit provider to monitor for unauthorized purchases.

- **Take Advantage of Browser Security Settings:** Use your browser's security settings to block unwanted pop-ups and potential phishing attempts.
- **Review Retailer's Policies:** Familiarize yourself with the retailer's return policies and how they handle your data.

- **Ensure Retailer Contact Information is Authentic**: Verify the authenticity of the retailer's contact details.

By incorporating these measures, the Wilson family can enhance the security of their online shopping experiences. Practicing good online shopping hygiene is an essential component of modern cybersecurity, allowing for safer navigation of digital marketplaces while minimizing risks.

3.6 Email Security Basics

Emails are a central communication tool in our personal and professional spheres, and cybercriminals often target them. For families like the Wilsons, understanding the basics of email security is crucial to guarding sensitive data and mitigating cyber threats like phishing, malware, and identity theft.

Understanding Email Security

Email security refers to practices and technologies that aim to keep email accounts and communications safe from unauthorized access, breaches, and malicious attacks. By implementing robust email security strategies, you can shield your personal and professional data from online threats.

Email Security: Do's and Don'ts

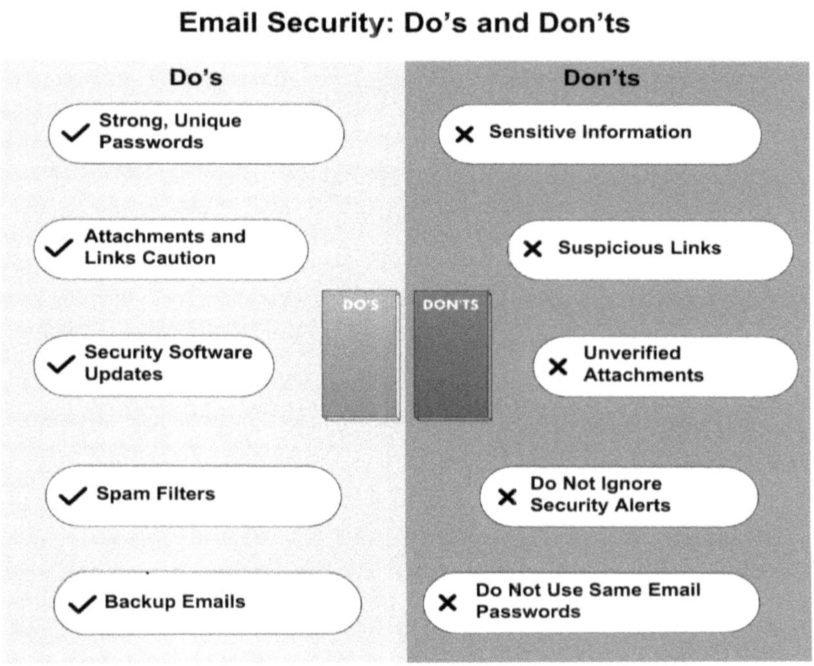

What Should You Do?

- **Strong, Unique Passwords:** It is important to devise robust, unique passwords for your email accounts and update them periodically.

- **Two-Factor Authentication (2FA):** Strengthen your security by activating 2FA on your email accounts.
- **Attachments and Links Caution:** Open attachments and click on links only from trusted sources. Always confirm the sender's identity before engaging with the content of the email.
- **Security Software Updates:** Regularly update your antivirus software, email client, and operating system to fend off emerging threats.
- **Spam Filters:** Activate and configure spam filters to lessen the chance of phishing and other harmful emails landing in your inbox.
- **Backup Emails:** Frequently backup crucial emails and attachments to a secure storage solution to prevent data loss.

What Shouldn't You Do?

- **Sensitive Information:** Avoid sending sensitive information such as passwords and credit card numbers through email.
- **Suspicious Links:** Avoid links in unsolicited emails, particularly those that request personal or financial information.
- **Unverified Attachments:** Do not download attachments from unknown or suspicious sources, as they could contain malware.
- **Do Not Ignore Security Alerts:** Do not ignore security alerts, and pay attention to any security alerts from your email provider which might signal potential threats or suspicious activities.
- **Do Not Use Same Email Passwords:** Do not use the same passwords, and employ distinct passwords for different accounts to decrease the risk of multiple services being compromised by a single breach.

Practical Tips for Email Security

For the Wilson family, embedding email security practices into their daily routine can drastically lower their risk of encountering cyber threats. Some additional tips include:

- **Verify Email Senders:** Always double-check the sender's email address and remain wary of emails from unfamiliar sources.
- **Phishing Signs:** Watch for typical phishing indicators such as urgent language, strange links, and requests for personal details. Report any dubious emails to your email provider.
- **Use Encryption:** If you are sending sensitive information via email, consider employing encryption tools.
- **Email Recovery Options:** Set up account recovery options to restore access should your account become compromised.

- **Monitor Account Activity:** Monitor your email account activity for signs of unauthorized access or unusual actions.

Example for the Wilson Family:

David can secure his professional interactions by using strong passwords and enabling 2FA. Sarah can dodge phishing attempts by being vigilant with unexpected emails and checking the sender's credentials. Emma and Jack should understand the risks of sharing sensitive data through email and how to spot suspect emails.

Through these security practices, the Wilson family can ensure their email communications are protected from unauthorized access and cyber threats. Email security is an essential element of daily cybersecurity, vital for keeping personal and professional data private and secure.

3.7 Identifying Assets and Threats

To properly defend your digital life, you must first understand what you need to protect and the potential risks you may encounter. Identifying significant digital assets and understanding possible cyber threats are essential stages for the Wilson family in developing a strong cybersecurity plan.

Understanding Assets and Threats

Personal data, financial information, professional papers, and digital identities are all examples of valuable assets that must be protected. Threats are prospective occurrences or acts that might affect these assets, such as hacking, malware, and phishing attempts.

Identify Your Digital Assets

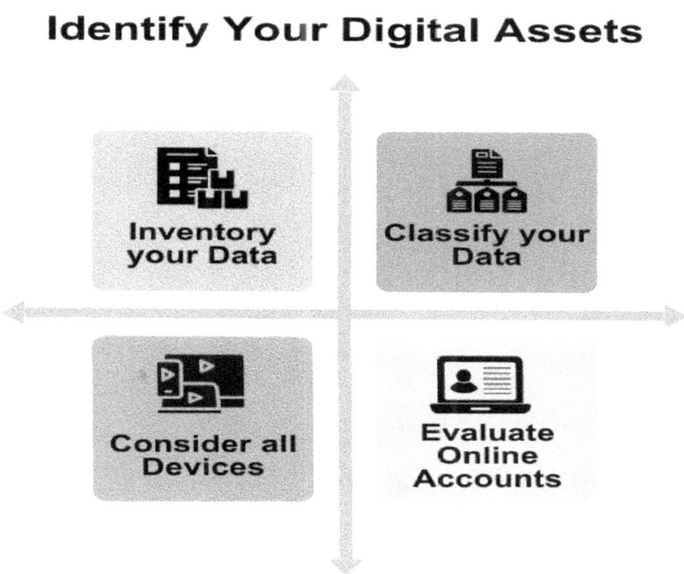

- **Inventory your Data:** Create a list of any digital assets that require security, such as personal information, financial data, professional papers, and personal recollections.
- **Classify your Data:** Sort assets according to their relevance and sensitivity, with financial information and professional papers taking precedence.
- **Consider all Devices:** Include all types of storage devices, such as laptops, cellphones, tablets, external hard drives, and cloud accounts.
- **Evaluate Online Accounts:** List all internet accounts, including email, social media, banking, and shopping sites, and make sure they are secure.

Recognize Potential Threats

- **Stay Informed About Common Threats:** Be aware of typical cyber risks such as phishing, malware, ransomware, and identity theft.
- **Monitor Cybersecurity News:** Stay updated on the latest cybersecurity news and trends to prepare for new attacks.
- **Evaluate your Risk Exposure:** Assess each asset's vulnerability to possible threats, with an emphasis on high-risk activities such as online banking.
- **Implement Threat Detection Tools:** Monitor and prevent threats through antivirus software, firewalls, and intrusion detection systems.

Practical Tips for Identifying Assets and Threats

Recognizing their digital assets and the challenges they face requires practical efforts integrated into the Wilson family's everyday routines:

- **Regular Security Evaluations:** Schedule regular evaluations of digital assets and security measures, including inventory updates and threat assessments.
- **Educate Family Members:** Ensure that all family members understand the worth of their digital assets and the significance of cybersecurity measures.
- **Use Strong, Unique Passwords**: To protect accounts, use strong, unique passwords and activate multi-factor authentication wherever possible.
- **Backup Important Data:** Regularly back up vital data to external drives or secure cloud services, ensuring that backups are encrypted and securely stored.
- **Be Cautious of Public Wi-Fi**: Avoid accessing sensitive information using public Wi-Fi networks, and use a VPN if required.

By identifying their digital assets and understanding the dangers they face, the Wilson family can put in place effective cybersecurity measures to secure their precious information. Recognizing these components is essential for creating a safe digital environment and maintaining peace of mind in their daily activities.

3.8 Creating and Managing Strong Passwords

Passwords are the first line of defense for safeguarding your online accounts and personal information. The Wilson family believes that knowing how to generate and maintain secure passwords is critical to protecting themselves against illegal access and cyber dangers.

The Importance of Strong Password

Strong passwords are important because they make it far more difficult for fraudsters to get access to your accounts. A weak password is readily guessed or cracked, putting your personal and financial data in danger.

Characteristics of a Strong Password

A secure password should be:

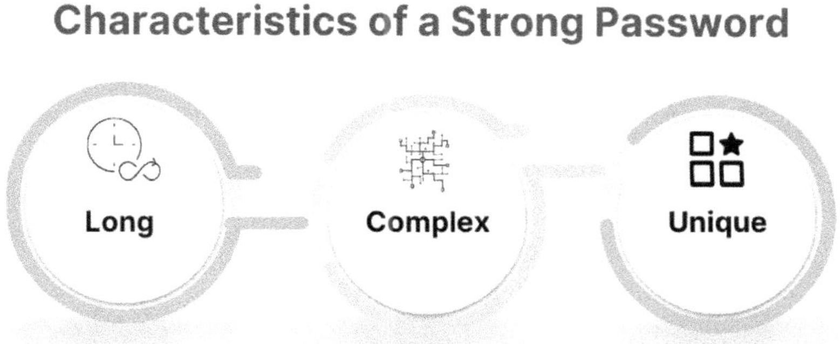

- **Long:** Aim for at least 12 characters.

- **Complex:** Combine capital and lowercase letters, digits, and special characters.
- **Unique:** Avoid repeating passwords across multiple sites.

Creating Strong Password

There are a few ways that can help you create strong passwords:

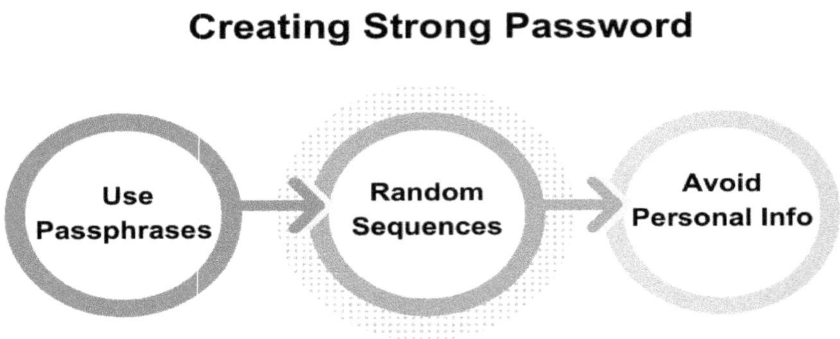

- **Use Passphrases:** Combine random words into a phrase that is simple to remember but difficult to guess.
- **Incorporate Randomness:** Use random character sequences and technologies such as password generators.
- **Avoid Personal Information:** Do not utilize widely available information such as your name or birthday.

Managing Passwords

Managing many strong passwords might be difficult. Here are a few strategies:

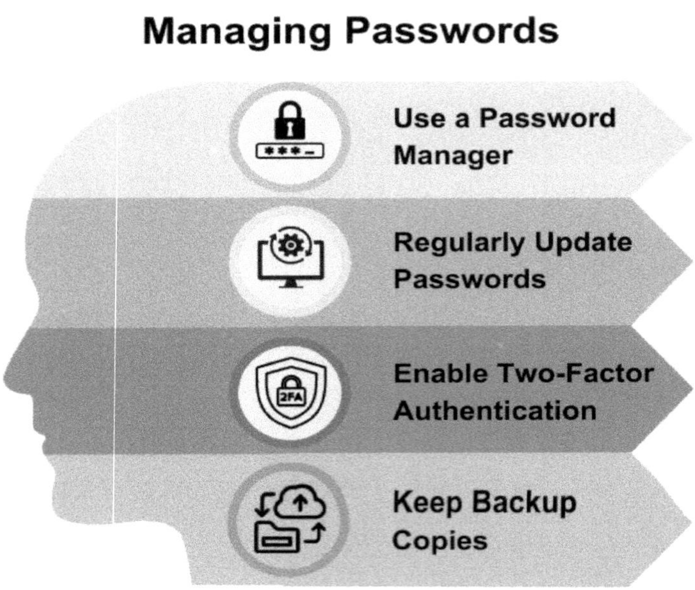

- **Use a Password Manager:** It will securely store and manage your passwords while also generating strong passwords for you.
- **Regularly Update Passwords:** Change your passwords on a regular basis, especially if you suspect a breach.
- **Enable Two-Factor Authentication:** Add another layer of security to your accounts.
- **Keep Backup Copies:** Make sure you have a safe mechanism to retrieve your passwords, such as using secure physical backups or recovery keys.

Example of the Wilson Family

David may use a password manager for his business accounts, whilst Sarah can generate a memorable yet safe password for her email. Emma and Jack should create complicated passwords for their social media and school accounts to avoid illegal access.

The benefit of Strong Passwords:

Implementing good password habits improves security and lowers the likelihood of illegal access. These practices provide the Wilson family with a safer digital environment for both personal and professional pursuits.

The Wilson family's cybersecurity posture may be dramatically improved by appreciating the value of strong passwords and implementing good management practices. Creating and preserving strong passwords is an important step in everyday cybersecurity, ensuring that their digital lives are safe and secure.

3.9 Recognizing and Avoiding Scams

Scams are deceptive schemes designed to trick individuals into providing personal information, financial details, or other valuable assets. For the Wilson family, learning how to recognize and avoid scams is crucial to protecting their personal and financial information.

Understanding Common Scams

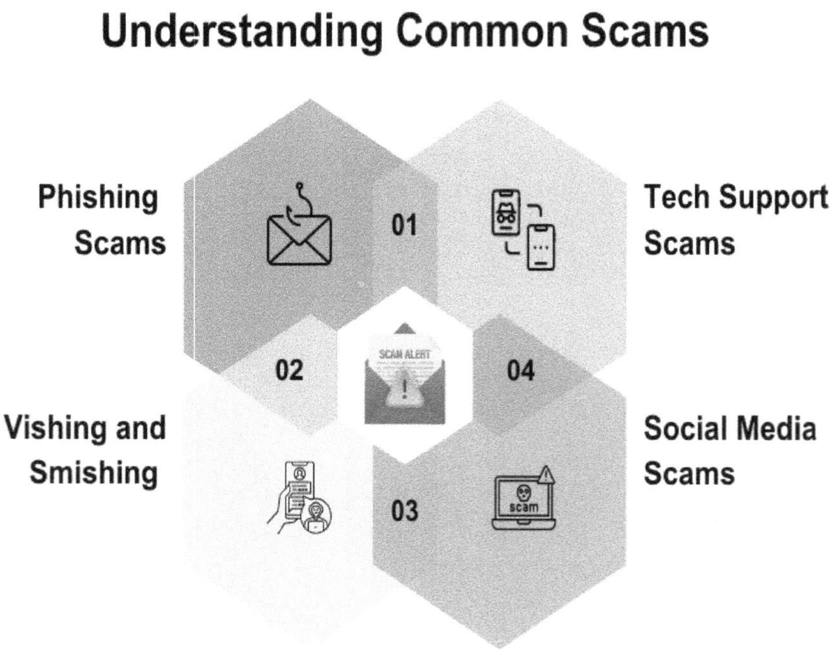

Phishing Scams

- **Overview:** Fraudulent emails or messages appear to come from legitimate sources, asking for sensitive information.
- **Example:** David receives an email from a fake bank website asking for his login credentials.

Vishing and Smishing

- **Overview:** Scam phone calls and text messages attempting to collect personal information or payments.
- **Example:** Sarah gets a call from someone claiming to be from her bank, asking for her account details.

Social Media Scams:

- **Overview:** Fake giveaways, fraudulent friend requests, and malicious links on social media platforms.

- **Example:** Emma receives a message claiming she won a prize, asking for personal information.

Tech Support Scams:

- **Overview:** Scammers posing as tech support to fix non-existent issues, asking for remote access or fees.
- **Example:** Jack gets a pop-up message claiming his computer has a virus, urging him to call for help.

Recognizing Scam Indicators

- **Urgent or Threatening Language:** Scammers create a sense of urgency or fear.
- **Unsolicited Requests for Personal Information:** Be cautious of unexpected requests via email, phone, or text.
- **Spelling and Grammar Errors:** Many scam messages contain mistakes.
- **Generic Greetings:** Scammers often use generic greetings like "Dear User."
- **Suspicious Links or Attachments:** Hover over links to check URLs, and avoid unknown attachments.

Avoiding Scams

- **Verify the Source:** Contact the organization directly using known methods.
- **Use Security Software:** Protect your devices with up-to-date antivirus and anti-malware software.
- **Educate yourself and Family Members:** Stay informed about common scams and teach family members to recognize them.
- **Report Scams:** Report scams to authorities like the Federal Trade Commission (FTC) or the Internet Crime Complaint Center (IC3).

Example of the Wilson Family

David can verify unexpected emails by contacting his bank directly. Sarah should be cautious of unsolicited calls and verify them independently. Emma should avoid suspicious social media links and report fraudulent accounts. Jack can ignore unexpected pop-up messages and run security scans on his computer.

Benefits of Recognizing and Avoiding Scams

By learning to recognize and avoid scams, the Wilson family can protect their personal and financial information from cybercriminals, maintaining their digital security and avoiding potential financial losses and identity theft.

3.10 Regular Audits and Updates

Maintaining cybersecurity is an ongoing process that requires regular audits and updates. For families like the Wilsons, this ensures their personal and professional information remains secure against evolving cyber threats.

Understanding the Importance of Regular Audits and Updates

Regular audits identify vulnerabilities and gaps, while updates protect against the latest threats. This proactive approach is crucial for maintaining a secure digital environment.

Conducting Regular Security Audits

A security audit systematically evaluates your digital assets, security measures, and practices:

- **Inventory Your Digital Assets:** List all digital assets, including devices, online accounts, and sensitive data.
- **Assess Current Security Measures:** Evaluate existing security measures, such as antivirus software, firewalls, and encryption.
- **Check for Vulnerabilities:** Use security tools to scan for weak passwords, outdated software, and other risks.
- **Review Account Activity:** Regularly check online account activities for suspicious actions.

- **Evaluate Access Controls:** Ensure only authorized individuals have access to sensitive information.

Implementing Updates and Patches

Keeping software and systems up-to-date is crucial for protection:

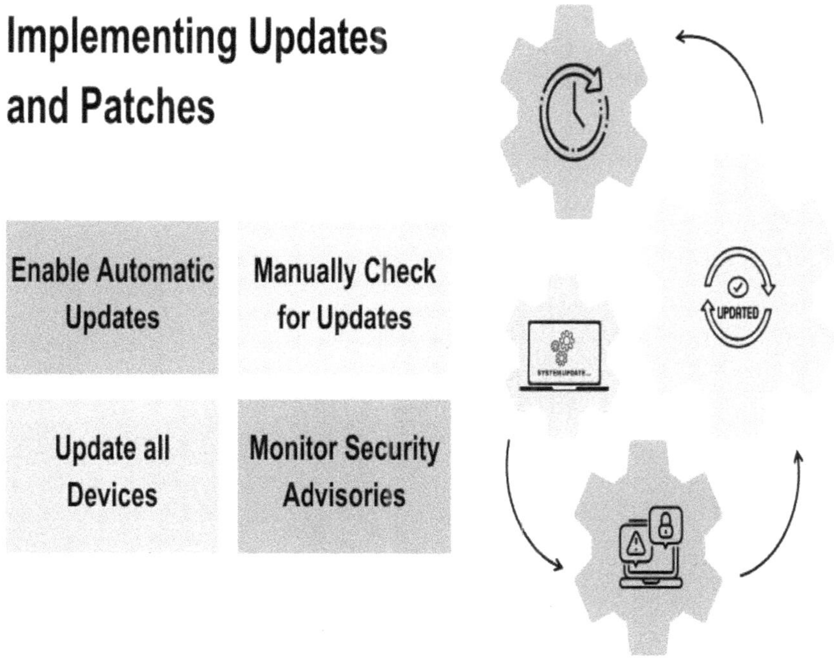

- **Enable Automatic Updates:** Enable automatic updates for operating systems, applications, and antivirus software.
- **Manually Check for Updates:** Regularly check and install updates for systems that do not offer automatic updates.
- **Update all Devices:** Keep all devices, including computers, smartphones, and network equipment, updated with the latest firmware and software.
- **Monitor Security Advisories:** Stay informed about security advisories and updates from software vendors and cybersecurity organizations.

Example of the Wilson Family

David can schedule monthly security audits for his firm's network, Sarah can enable automatic updates on her devices, and Emma and Jack can learn to update their apps regularly to stay protected.

Benefits of Regular Audits and Updates

Regular audits and updates help maintain a strong cybersecurity posture, addressing vulnerabilities and keeping security measures current. This reduces the risk of cyber-attacks and ensures information remains protected.

By incorporating everyday cybersecurity practices, the Wilson family can enhance their digital security. From safe internet browsing and securing social media accounts to creating strong passwords and conducting regular audits, these practices provide comprehensive protection. Proactive measures, staying informed, and continuously updating security practices are key to a secure digital environment. Following the guidance in this chapter ensures a safer and more secure digital experience for you and your family.

Chapter 4: Cybersecurity Tools and Technologies

4.1 Overview of Cybersecurity Tools

In the current digital age, it is crucial to protect personal and professional data from cyber threats. Cybersecurity technologies play a pivotal role in safeguarding information, blocking unauthorized access, and ensuring safety online. Grasping the function and importance of these technologies is vital for the Wilson family, and indeed any family, to maintain a secure digital environment.

Understanding Cybersecurity Tools

Cybersecurity tools are specialized software designed to identify, prevent, and counter cyber threats. These tools employ multiple security layers to protect devices, networks, and data from malicious activities. Ranging from basic antivirus solutions to advanced intrusion detection systems, each tool plays a specific part in an overarching cybersecurity strategy.

Primary Types of Cybersecurity Tools

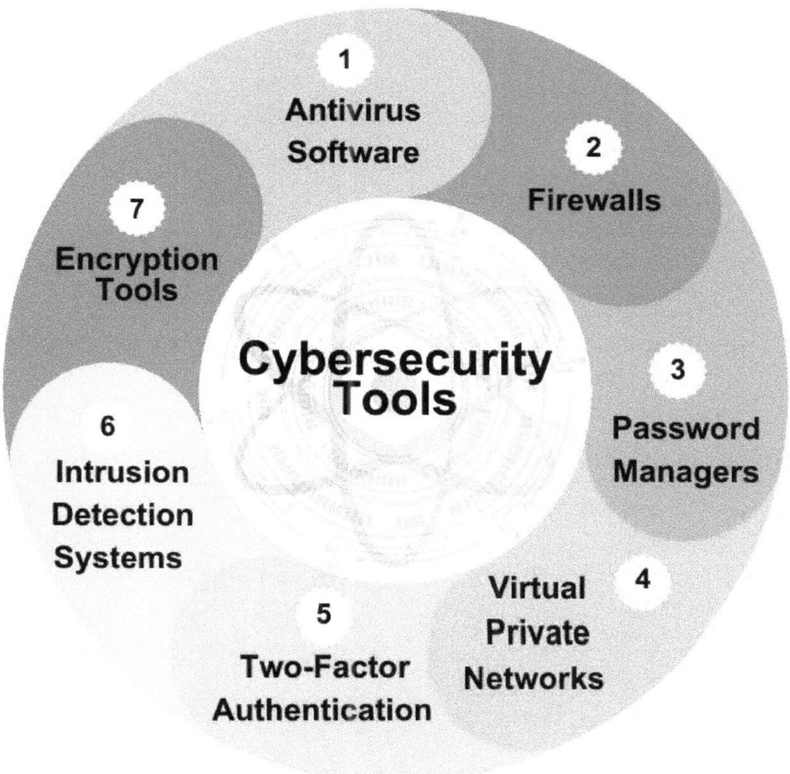

1. **Antivirus Software:** Antivirus programs act as the first defense against malware, detecting and removing harmful software like viruses, worms, and trojans, thus keeping devices safe from attacks. For instance, Sarah, who manages family finances, relies on antivirus software to protect her computer from spyware that could compromise sensitive financial data.
2. **Firewalls:** Firewalls function as barriers between trusted and untrusted networks, regulating network traffic based on set security rules. David, who runs his architecture business from home, uses a firewall to defend his business network against external threats and unauthorized access.
3. **Password Managers:** These tools securely store and manage passwords, allowing users to employ complex and unique passwords for different accounts without needing to remember each one. Emma and Jack, who engage in online learning and social interactions, utilize a password manager to secure their accounts easily.
4. **Virtual Private Networks (VPNs):** VPNs encrypt and secure internet connections, shielding them from snooping and interception. Whenever Sarah and David engage in online banking or remote work, they use a VPN to maintain the privacy and security of their internet activities.
5. **Two-Factor Authentication (2FA):** 2FA enhances security by requiring not just a password but also a code sent to a user's phone, ensuring that access is blocked even if a password is compromised. For example, David employs 2FA for his email and professional accounts, adding an extra layer of security.
6. **Intrusion Detection Systems (IDS):** IDS monitor network traffic for unusual activities and potential threats, alerting users to any suspicious actions. This proactive monitoring allows the Wilson family and others to respond swiftly to potential security breaches, keeping their network secure.
7. **Encryption Tools:** Encryption software converts sensitive information into a code that only authorized users can decode, securing personal data like medical records and personal documents stored on Sarah's computer.

The Role of Cybersecurity Tools

For families like the Wilsons, cybersecurity tools are indispensable for protecting their digital lifestyle. These tools prevent data breaches, identity theft, and financial losses by enforcing robust security measures. By understanding and implementing these tools, families can ensure their data remains safe from cyber threats.

4.2 Antivirus Software

In our digital-centric world, antivirus solutions are essential for keeping personal and professional information secure from harmful attacks. It is critical for families like the

Wilsons, and indeed any household, to understand the role and mechanics of these tools to ensure their digital spaces remain protected.

Understanding Antivirus Solutions

Antivirus programs are engineered to spot, intercept, and eradicate harmful software, known as malware, on various devices. This category of software includes viruses, worms, trojans, ransomware, and spyware, all of which can damage or corrupt data, steal personal details, or degrade system performance.

Operational Insights of Antivirus Tools

- **Detection:** These applications examine files and observe system behaviors to pinpoint harmful entities. They apply signature-based detection, aligning files with a database of known malware signatures, alongside heuristic detection, which identifies abnormal patterns of behavior.
- **Prevention:** After detecting malware, the software either isolates or deletes the compromised files to prevent further harm. Real-time defenses constantly monitor the system to intercept newly emerging threats.
- **Mitigation:** If malware manages to infiltrate, antivirus and anti-malware tools can thoroughly remove it. This often involves erasing infected files or quarantining them to avert additional problems.

Choosing Effective Software

When selecting antivirus software, important factors to consider include:

- **Broad Spectrum Defense:** Choose software that offers protection from a wide range of threats, including viruses, spyware, ransomware, and phishing schemes.
- **Real-Time Scanning:** Ensure the software is capable of detecting and neutralizing threats as they appear.
- **Regular Updates:** Choose programs that automatically update their databases to stay ahead of the newest threats.
- **Intuitive Interface:** Select software with a straightforward and easy-to-use interface that accommodates all family members.

Example of the Wilson Family

David protects his sensitive business data using advanced antivirus tools, safeguarding his architectural designs. Sarah employs anti-malware programs to secure the family's financial records and personal details. For Emma and Jack, real-time scanning and automatic updates are invaluable in keeping their online educational and social activities secure.

Staying Secure with Regular Maintenance

To maintain their effectiveness, antivirus and anti-malware applications should be routinely scanned and updated:

- **Scheduled Scans:** Regularly scanning your systems helps detect and remove hidden threats, thus maintaining device health and security.
- **Ongoing Updates:** Enable automatic updates to ensure your security software is equipped with the most up-to-date malware definitions and capabilities, protecting against both known and novel threats.

Understanding and effectively using antivirus and anti-malware tools are crucial for families to protect their digital realms. By making informed choices about security software and keeping it updated, the Wilson family—and any family—can ensure their data is safeguarded against cyber threats, allowing them to navigate the digital world securely and confidently.

4.3 Encryption Technologies

In today's interconnected society, securing sensitive data is essential. Encryption technologies shield information from unauthorized access and cyber threats. For families like the Wilsons, understanding and implementing encryption is key to maintaining the privacy of their personal and professional information.

Understanding Encryption

Encryption transforms readable data into a secure format that only those with the appropriate decryption key can access, effectively making the data unreadable to unauthorized users.

Types of Encryption

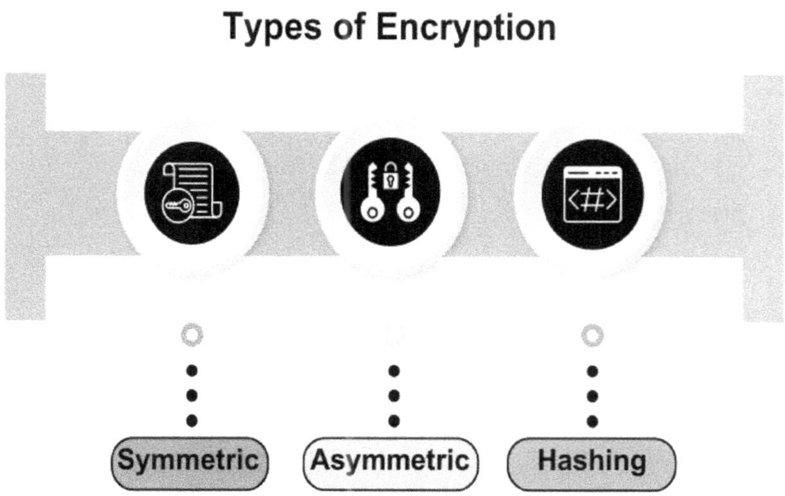

Symmetric Encryption

- **Concept:** Utilizes the same key for both encrypting and decrypting data.
- **Example:** David uses a symmetric key to both secure and access his architectural blueprints.
- **Application:** Efficient for encrypting large data volumes quickly.

Asymmetric Encryption

- **Concept:** Employs a public key for encryption and a private key for decryption.
- **Example:** Sarah employs this method for her secure email communications, using a public key to encrypt messages and a private key for decryption.
- **Application:** Suitable for secure communication over the Internet.

Hashing

- **Concept:** Converts data into a non-reversible, fixed-length string of characters.
- **Example:** Emma and Jack use hashing for their passwords, ensuring their actual passwords remain secure, even in a data breach.
- **Application:** Used for verifying data integrity and secure password storage.

Implementing Encryption Technologies

Device Encryption

- **Overview:** Encrypting an entire device ensures all stored data is protected.
- **Example:** David encrypts his laptop's hard drive to secure business documents and client information.

Communication Encryption

- **Overview:** Encrypted communication tools protect data sent over the internet.
- **Example:** Sarah uses encrypted messaging to discuss family medical details securely with her healthcare provider.

Cloud Storage Encryption

- **Overview:** Encrypting data stored in the cloud prevents unauthorized access, safeguarding the data even if the cloud service is compromised.
- **Example:** The Wilsons encrypt their cloud storage to store and share family photos and vital documents safely.

Key Management in Encryption

Proper management of encryption keys is crucial to ensure data remains secure. Important practices include:

- **Secure Storage:** Encryption keys should be stored securely, such as in hardware security modules or encrypted databases.
- **Key Rotation:** Regularly updating encryption keys can help prevent unauthorized access.
- **Access Control:** Limit access to encryption keys to only those who require it.

Example of the Wilson Family

David securely transmits architectural plans to clients using asymmetric encryption, ensuring only intended recipients can view them. Sarah protects her bank details and personal files through encryption on her computer and cloud services. Emma and Jack ensure their communications are secure using encrypted messaging apps.

By understanding and applying various encryption strategies, the Wilson family, like any other, can safeguard their sensitive information from cyber threats. Effective encryption and key management enhance security, providing peace of mind in the digital age.

4.4 Firewalls and Intrusion Detection Systems

In the World of digital security, safeguarding networks against unauthorized access and cyber threats is crucial. Firewalls and Intrusion Detection Systems (IDS) are essential tools for securing networks and preventing cyber-attacks. For the Wilson family, as well as any other household, grasping the functionalities of these technologies is key to maintaining a secure digital space.

Understanding Firewalls

Firewalls serve as protective barriers between trusted and untrusted networks, regulating incoming and outgoing traffic based on established security rules. They can be implemented as hardware, software, or a combination of both.

Diverse Types of Firewalls

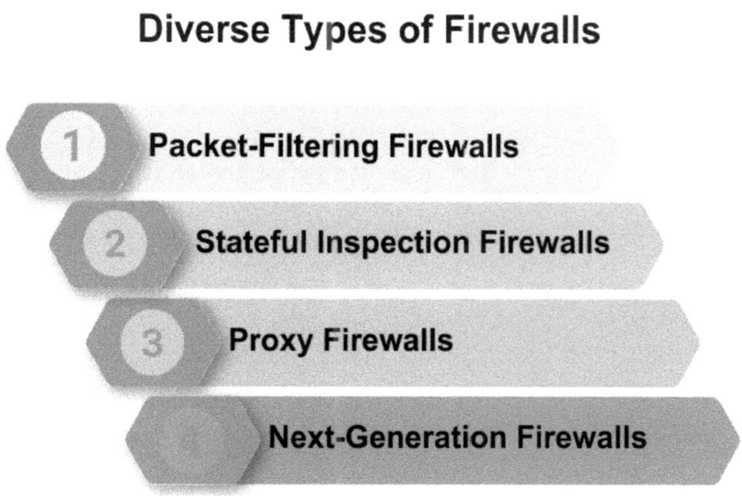

Packet-Filtering Firewalls

- **Function:** These firewalls examine each packet of data against a series of filters, deciding whether to allow passage or blockage based on IP addresses, ports, and protocols.
- **Example:** David's home network is safeguarded by a packet-filtering firewall, shielding his architectural firm's data.

Stateful Inspection Firewalls

- **Function:** These firewalls track the state of network connections and base decisions on the traffic's context rather than isolated packets.
- **Example:** Sarah's firewall employs stateful inspection to allow only legitimate traffic, enhancing security.

Proxy Firewalls

- **Function:** Acting as intermediaries, these firewalls filter internet requests and responses between users and the web.
- **Example:** Emma and Jack's school network employs a proxy firewall to ensure their internet access is secure and appropriate.

Next-Generation Firewalls (NGFW)

- **Function:** NGFWs merge traditional firewall capabilities with advanced features such as intrusion prevention and application awareness.
- **Example:** The Wilson family's home network is protected by an NGFW, offering robust defense against modern threats.

Understanding Intrusion Detection Systems (IDS)

IDS monitor for suspicious network activities and potential threats, alerting administrators to unusual patterns that may indicate a breach.

Types of Intrusion Detection Systems

Network-Based IDS (NIDS)

- **Function:** Positioned at strategic points within a network, NIDS monitor traffic to and from all connected devices.
- **Example:** David uses a NIDS to oversee his business network, ensuring no unauthorized access occurs.

Host-Based IDS (HIDS)

- **Function:** Installed directly on devices, HIDS monitor system operations, log files, and application activities for signs of intrusion.
- **Example:** Sarah's laptop is equipped with HIDS to detect any signs of compromise or malicious activity.

Implementing Firewalls and IDS

Setting up Firewalls

- **Approach:** Configure firewalls with specific rules to block unauthorized activities while allowing valid traffic.
- **Example:** David customizes his firewall settings to restrict incoming traffic to essential business interactions only.

Deploying IDS

- **Approach:** Install and set up IDS to continuously monitor network and system activities, configured to alert upon detecting suspicious behavior.
- **Example:** Sarah's home network includes an IDS system to actively monitor and counteract potential threats.

Maintenance of Security Systems

Regular Updates and Maintenance

- **Importance:** Continually updating firewalls and IDS with the latest security patches and threat data is crucial for maintaining effectiveness.
- **Example:** The IT department at Emma and Jack's school regularly updates their security systems to guard against new cyber threats.

Example of the Wilson Family

David secures his business communications with an NGFW, while Sarah's laptop is protected by HIDS against intrusions. Emma and Jack's school experience is safeguarded by a proxy firewall, while their home network benefits from a comprehensive NIDS setup.

For families like the Wilsons, understanding and deploying firewalls and IDS are critical for network protection. Regular updates and vigilant maintenance of these systems are essential to defend against evolving cyber threats, ensuring a secure digital environment for all.

4.5 Virtual Private Networks (VPNs)

In today's interconnected society, securing online privacy and safe internet connections are essential. Virtual Private Networks (VPNs) serve as crucial tools in this regard by establishing a secure, encrypted pathway across the internet. It is vital for households like the Wilsons to grasp the advantages and proper application of VPNs to protect their digital activities.

Understanding VPNs

A VPN constructs a protected channel between your device and the internet, encrypting all data that passes through. This encryption helps keep your online actions confidential and safe from prying eyes, whether you are surfing the internet, accessing private information, or using public Wi-Fi.

Advantages of Utilizing a VPN

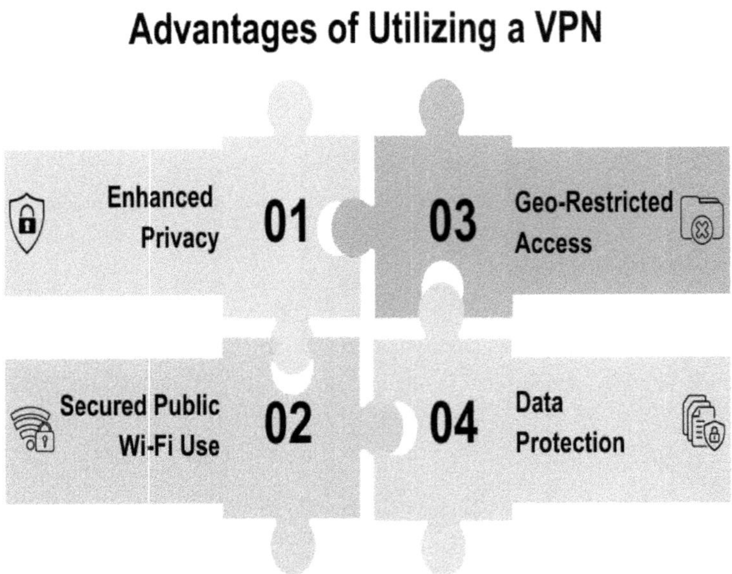

Enhanced Privacy:

- **Overview:** VPNs hide your IP address, complicating efforts by websites and online services to track your activities.
- **Example:** Sarah employs a VPN to keep her browsing data private and avoid online tracking.

Secured Public Wi-Fi Use:

- **Overview:** VPNs encrypt your internet connection, safeguarding your data on public Wi-Fi networks.
- **Example:** While working remotely from a cafe, David uses a VPN to secure his business communications and client interactions.

Access to Geographically Restricted Content:

- **Overview:** VPNs allow you to bypass geographical limitations and access content unavailable in your area.
- **Example:** Emma and Jack use a VPN to access educational materials and streaming services otherwise inaccessible in their region.

Data Protection:

- **Overview:** VPNs prevent sensitive data from being intercepted by cybercriminals, particularly during financial transactions or while accessing personal accounts.
- **Example:** The Wilsons rely on a VPN for their online banking to keep their financial information secure against threats.

Selecting the Right VPN

Choosing a trustworthy VPN service is crucial for achieving the best security and performance. Key considerations include:

- **Strong Encryption:** Choose a VPN with solid encryption protocols like OpenVPN or WireGuard.
- **No-Logs Policy:** Select a VPN provider that does not keep records of your online activities.
- **Server Locations:** Choose a VPN with a broad selection of server locations to access various regional content.
- **Speed and Performance:** Confirm that the VPN provides quick and dependable connections to prevent browsing or streaming disruptions.

Example of the Wilson Family

David enhances the security of his remote work sessions with a VPN, safeguarding his business communications. Sarah uses a VPN for added privacy while shopping or managing family finances. Emma and Jack access educational resources safely, even on public Wi-Fi, thanks to their VPN.

Setting Up and Using a VPN

Select a VPN Provider: Investigate and choose a VPN service that meets your privacy and security requirements.

- **Install VPN Software:** Download and install the VPN app on your devices, including computers, smartphones, and tablets.

- **Connect to a VPN Server:** Launch the VPN app and connect to your chosen server. This connection will encrypt your internet link and disguise your IP address.
- **Activate Auto-Connect:** Configure your VPN to connect automatically each time you access the internet, ensuring ongoing protection.

VPNs are invaluable for enhancing online privacy and securing internet connections. By comprehending their benefits and proper use, families like the Wilsons can shield their online activities from cyber threats and preserve their digital privacy. Carefully choosing and setting up a reliable VPN provider on all devices guarantees thorough security, enabling confident navigation of the digital world.

4.6 Multi-Factor Authentication (MFA)

In the modern digital landscape, relying only on a password for online security is insufficient. Multi-factor authentication (MFA) introduces an additional layer of protection, significantly restricting cybercriminals' ability to access accounts unauthorized. It's crucial for the Wilson family, and indeed any family, to grasp and deploy MFA to strengthen their digital safety.

How Multi-Factor Authentication Functions

MFA generally incorporates a mix of the following elements:

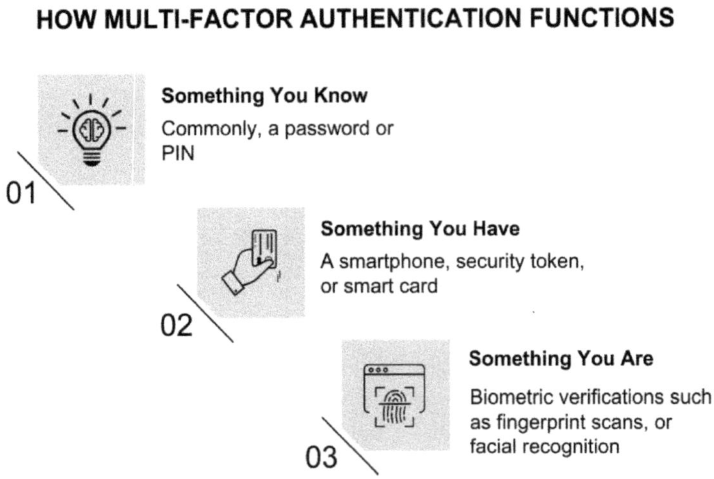

Something You Know:

- **Details:** Commonly, a password or PIN.
- **Example:** David inputs his password to access his email.

Something You Have:

- **Details:** This might be a smartphone, security token, or smart card.
- **Example:** Following his password entry, David receives a verification code on his smartphone.

Something You Are:

- **Details:** This factor includes biometric verifications such as fingerprint scans, facial recognition, or voice recognition.
- **Example:** Sarah employs fingerprint verification to open her banking app after entering her password.

Advantages of Utilizing MFA

Enhanced Security:

- **Details:** MFA significantly elevates account security by demanding multiple authentication forms.
- **Example:** Even if Emma's social media password gets exposed, a potential intruder would still require her smartphone to breach her account.

Protection against Phishing:

- **Details:** MFA aids in blocking unauthorized access even if login details are stolen through phishing.
- **Example:** Jack's school account is safeguarded with MFA, ensuring that even if he inadvertently discloses his password through a phishing scam, the attacker cannot gain access without the second factor.

User-Friendliness:

- **Details:** Contemporary MFA solutions are straightforward to use and integrate seamlessly with most devices and applications.
- **Example:** The Wilson family utilizes MFA applications like Google Authenticator or Authy effortlessly, ensuring quick and secure account access.

Deploying MFA

Activating MFA on Vital Accounts:

- **Details:** Begin by enabling MFA on sensitive accounts, including email, banking, and social media.
- **Example:** David activates MFA on his business email and financial accounts to secure critical client and financial data.

Choosing Verification Methods:

- **Details:** Pick the most convenient and secure verification methods, such as SMS codes, authentication apps, or biometric elements.
- **Example:** Sarah prefers biometric verification for fast and secure account access on her smartphone.

Educating Family Members:

- **Details:** Make sure all family members understand the significance of MFA and know how to configure it on their devices and accounts.
- **Example:** Emma and Jack familiarize themselves with using an authentication app for their school and social media accounts, elevating their digital protection.

Example of the Wilson Family

David employs an authentication app to receive verification codes on his business accounts, adding a crucial security layer. Sarah utilizes biometric authentication for her smartphone to access her banking and healthcare applications securely. Emma and Jack implement MFA for their school and social media accounts, safeguarding their online interactions.

Multi-factor authentication (MFA) is an effective tool for enhancing online account security. By requiring multiple verification forms, MFA significantly lowers unauthorized access risks and protects against various cyber threats. By implementing MFA on all critical accounts, families like the Wilsons can achieve a higher security level, providing peace of mind in their digital engagements.

4.7 Password Manager

In today's digital era, creating solid and distinct passwords for each online account is essential for security. However, memorizing numerous complex passwords can be daunting. Password managers offer a feasible solution by securely storing and handling passwords. For families like the Wilsons, adopting a password manager can significantly strengthen their cybersecurity.

Understanding Password Managers

A password manager is a digital tool designed to assist users in generating, storing, and managing their passwords securely. It safeguards stored passwords through encryption, allowing access only through a master password.

Advantages of Using a Password Manager

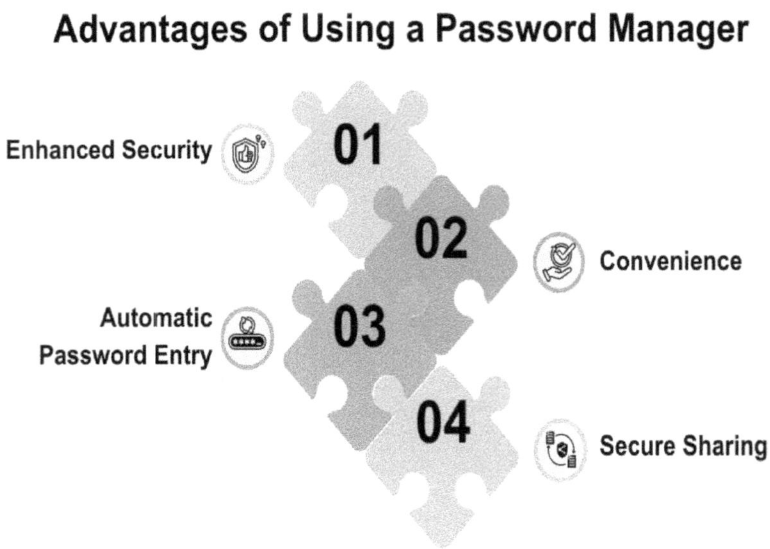

Enhanced Security:

- **Detail:** Password managers create strong, unique passwords for each account, minimizing the risk of password-related security breaches.
- **Example:** David utilizes a password manager to devise and maintain complex passwords for his business accounts, enhancing their security.

Convenience:

- **Detail:** Users need to remember only one master password, simplifying the management of various accounts.

- **Example:** Sarah appreciates being able to access her multiple online accounts easily without the need to recall distinct passwords, thanks to her password manager.

Automatic Password Entry:

- **Detail:** Password managers can auto-fill login credentials on websites and apps, saving time and mitigating phishing risks.
- **Example:** Emma and Jack employ a password manager for quick and secure login into their school accounts without manually entering passwords.

Secure Sharing:

- **Detail:** Password managers enable the safe sharing of passwords with trusted individuals without revealing the actual passwords.
- **Example:** David securely shares business tool credentials with his team via the password manager.

Implementing a Password Manager

Choosing a Password Manager:

- **Detail:** Choose a reputable password manager with strong security features like robust encryption, cross-device compatibility, and two-factor authentication (2FA).
- **Example:** The Wilsons select a password manager that supports all their devices and offers top-tier encryption for their passwords.

Setting Up the Password Manager:

- **Detail:** Install the password manager across all devices and create a strong, memorable, but hard-to-guess master password.
- **Example:** Sarah establishes her password manager with a master password that blends random words and characters for optimal security and memorability.

Migrating Existing Passwords:

- **Detail:** Import or update existing passwords to stronger versions created by the password manager.
- **Example:** David updates all his business passwords within the password manager, enhancing their strength.

Using the Password Manager:

- **Detail:** Utilize the password manager to generate new passwords, securely store them, and use auto-fill for logging in.

- **Example:** Emma and Jack rely on the password manager to generate and secure passwords for their social media and educational accounts, ensuring robust protection.

Example of the Wilson Family

David, who manages sensitive business data, depends on a password manager to create and keep complex passwords for his various accounts secure. Sarah leverages the password manager to protect her personal and financial information, facilitating easy and secure account access. Emma and Jack enjoy the convenience and safety provided by the password manager for their school and social interactions, safeguarding their online activities.

Password managers are indispensable tools for enhancing cybersecurity through the management of strong, unique passwords. For the Wilson family and others, using a password manager offers convenience and security, shielding their online accounts from unauthorized access and cyber threats. By adopting a password manager, families can maintain the security of their digital lives and ensure their personal information remains protected.

4.8 Mitigating Cyber Risks with Technology

In today's networked world, individuals encounter numerous cyber threats that can endanger their personal and digital security. It is vital for families like the Wilsons to understand these threats and apply effective cybersecurity measures. This discussion outlines various cyber threats and how the right tools and strategies can reduce these risks, helping families maintain a safe digital environment.

Current Cyber Threats

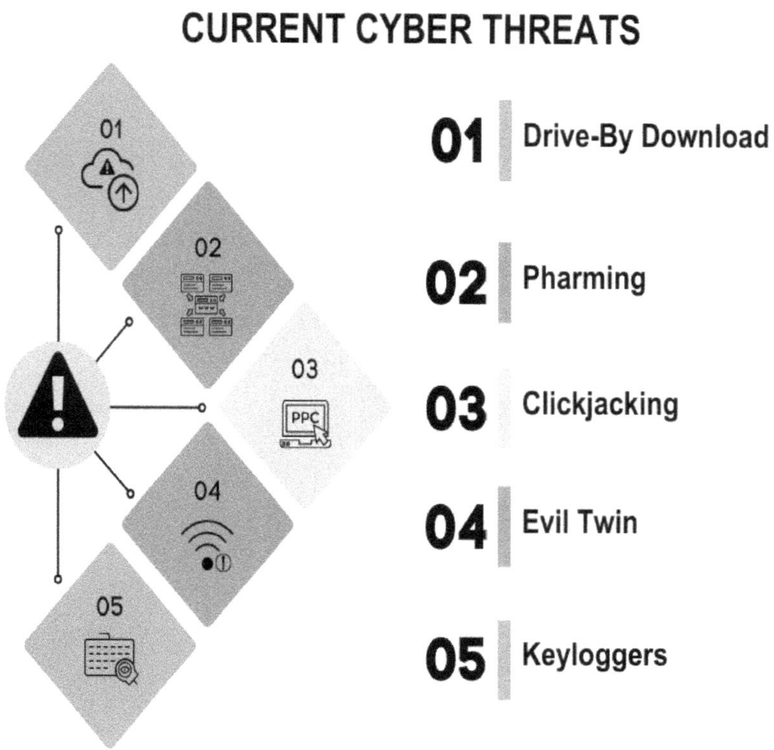

Drive-By Download Attacks:

- **Description:** This occurs when visiting a compromised website, which can lead to downloading malware due to vulnerabilities in web browsers or plugins.
- **Example:** Emma accesses a site for educational content, which secretly downloads malware onto her device.

Pharming:

- **Description:** Users are redirected from legitimate websites to fraudulent ones through DNS poisoning or malware.
- **Example:** David enters his bank's URL, but malware redirects him to a fraudulent website that mimics the original.

Clickjacking:

- **Description:** Users are tricked into clicking on hidden elements overlaid on legitimate web pages.
- **Example:** Sarah intends to click a video play button but instead clicks a hidden element that compromises her social media credentials.

Evil Twin Attacks:

- **Description:** Hackers create a deceivingly legitimate-looking Wi-Fi network to intercept data from users.
- **Example:** Jack connects to what he thinks is the school's Wi-Fi, but it is a hacker's setup stealing his credentials.

Keyloggers:

- **Description:** Malicious programs that record every keystroke to capture sensitive information like passwords and credit card numbers.
- **Example:** A keylogger on David's laptop records his email and banking passwords, sending this sensitive information to cybercriminals.

Technological Strategies for Mitigating Cyber Risks

Antivirus Software:

- **Action:** These tools detect and remove malicious software, addressing threats from drive-by downloads and keyloggers.
- **Example:** Emma's device is protected as her antivirus software detects and eradicates the malware she unknowingly downloaded.

Firewalls and Intrusion Detection Systems (IDS):

- **Action:** Firewalls prevent unauthorized access, and IDS monitor for suspicious activities, protecting against pharming and clickjacking.
- **Example:** David's firewall stops the redirection to a fraudulent site, and the IDS alerts him to the attempted redirection.

Virtual Private Networks (VPNs):

- **Action:** VPNs encrypt internet connections, securing data from interception, which is particularly effective against evil twin attacks.
- **Example:** Jack's internet connection is encrypted through a VPN, safeguarding his data from the counterfeit Wi-Fi network.

Multi-Factor Authentication (MFA):

- **Action:** MFA requires additional verification factors, greatly improving security even if login details are compromised.
- **Example:** Despite clickjacking attempts, Sarah's accounts are secure because her MFA prevents access without the second verification.

Password Managers:

- **Action:** These tools generate and securely store complex passwords, decreasing the risk of security breaches.
- **Example:** David uses a password manager to generate and manage strong passwords, ensuring security across his accounts.

By recognizing these cyber threats and implementing strategic tools like antivirus software, firewalls, VPNs, MFA, and password managers, families can significantly improve their digital safety. These technologies are crucial for protecting personal information and creating a secure online environment, enabling families to navigate the digital world with confidence and knowing their data and privacy are protected.

Chapter 5: The Human Element in Cybersecurity

5.1 Introduction to Human Factors

Cybersecurity discussions often highlight the importance of sophisticated technologies and tools as the frontline defense against digital threats. But, it is critical not to overlook the human side of security. Individual choices, actions, and habits are fundamentally important in shaping the security landscape. Exploring human factors in cybersecurity means understanding the interaction between people and technology, pinpointing frequent user errors, and examining the psychological and sociological influences on behavior.

Cybersecurity: Tools and Human Factors

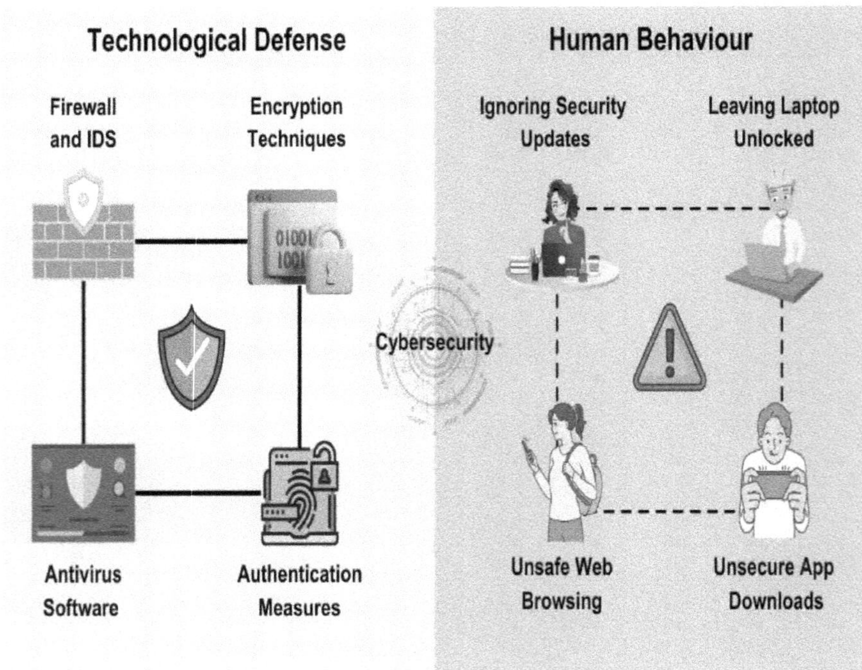

Incorporating Human Insights into Cybersecurity Strategies

For any family similar to the Wilsons, understanding the importance of human behavior in cybersecurity is essential. Effective cybersecurity is more than just about deploying the most advanced software or crafting unbreakable passwords. It revolves around how these tools are employed and adherence to security best practices. Human actions can serve as both a challenging defense and a significant weak point. When people are educated, aware, and proactive, they strengthen their defense against digital threats. Conversely, a lack of awareness or indifference can inadvertently lead to security breaches.

Real-life Examples of Human Influence on Cybersecurity

The significance of human involvement in cybersecurity can be illustrated through daily life examples. Consider the case of Sarah, a diligent high school teacher who regularly accesses sensitive student information online. Although she uses a robust password, her habit of leaving her computer unlocked while away poses a security risk. Similarly, David, who operates a small architectural firm, tends to dismiss update notifications for his software, viewing them as bothersome interruptions. This procrastination exposes his business to avoidable cyber risks due to unaddressed vulnerabilities.

Teenagers like Emma and Jack, who are quick to embrace new technologies and platforms, exemplify another aspect of human factors. Their interest in new apps and games often leads them to unsafe downloads or risky clicks on questionable links, potentially compromising their devices with malware.

The Broad Impacts of Human Behavior on Cybersecurity

These instances clearly demonstrate the impact of human behavior on cybersecurity. The key to mitigating these risks starts with raising awareness and promoting education about cybersecurity. It is crucial for every individual to recognize the potential consequences of their digital habits and adopt a proactive security-conscious approach.

Promoting a Culture of Security Awareness

In cybersecurity, everyone has a role to play. Technologies are crucial, but their effectiveness is significantly determined by how they are used by individuals. For families like the Wilsons, promoting a culture of security awareness is crucial. This involves educating each member about the significance of protecting personal information, identifying common online threats, and recognizing their part in ensuring collective digital safety.

Further in this chapter, we will focus on specific human behaviors that affect cybersecurity. We will explore common errors, the psychology behind cyber threats, and effective strategies to enhance security awareness and responsible online behavior. Understanding these human factors enables families to safeguard themselves better and nurture a more secure digital environment.

5.2 Cybersecurity Awareness and Training

Understanding the human aspect of cybersecurity starts with developing awareness and providing training. Establishing a strong foundation in cybersecurity knowledge is essential for safeguarding personal details and ensuring digital safety for any family, including the Wilsons.

The Vital Role of Cybersecurity Awareness

Understanding cybersecurity awareness means being mindful of the risks and threats in the digital world. It encompasses knowledge of how cyber-attacks are executed, identifying signs of an attack, and knowing the preventative measures necessary. Awareness serves as the frontline defense against digital threats. When individuals recognize the threats and are equipped with protective strategies, they can bypass many typical security errors.

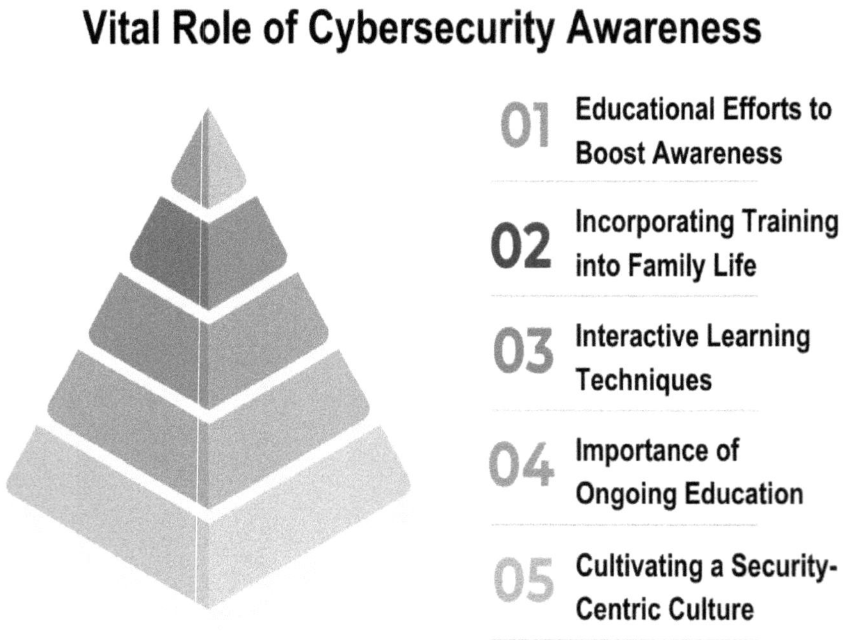

Educational Efforts to Boost Awareness

Education is key in promoting cybersecurity awareness. Various settings such as schools, workplaces, and community centers can introduce educational initiatives that inform about cybersecurity fundamentals. For instance, Emma and Jack's school could integrate lessons on recognizing phishing attempts, setting strong passwords, and securing personal devices into their curriculum. Similarly, David's architectural practice could host regular training sessions to stress the importance of updating software, maintaining secure communication, and protecting data.

Incorporating Training into Family Life

Training should not be limited to official environments but should also be provided to families. The Wilsons could benefit from regular family discussions on cybersecurity topics, such as the dangers of sharing passwords, the risks associated with unknown links, and managing social media privacy settings. Regular dialogues help embed awareness of potential threats and best practices in handling them.

Interactive Learning Techniques

Adopting interactive learning methods like quizzes, workshops, and simulated scenarios can make cybersecurity education more captivating. Sarah could employ interactive online quizzes and engaging lessons to teach her students cybersecurity principles in an active manner. Likewise, David's firm might use simulation drills to train employees on responding to cyber-attacks swiftly and efficiently.

The Importance of Ongoing Education

With cyber threats continually evolving, maintaining up-to-date awareness and training is crucial. The Wilsons can stay informed by subscribing to cybersecurity newsletters, following reputable blogs, and participating in forums. Regular updates are critical in keeping attentive and ready to tackle new cyber threats.

Cultivating a Security-Centric Culture

Building a culture of security involves integrating cybersecurity practices into everyday routines and prioritizing them. For the Wilsons, this means encouraging one another to adhere to security best practices, remaining alert to new threats, and supporting ongoing education about cybersecurity. By creating an environment that values and actively engages in cybersecurity, the entire family contributes to a more secure digital sphere.

Cybersecurity awareness and training are critical in shielding against digital threats. Through educational efforts, practical training, and continuous learning, families like the Wilsons can forge formidable defenses against potential attacks. By embedding cybersecurity into their daily lives and fostering a security-focused culture, they can protect their personal information effectively in a dynamic digital landscape.

5.3 Social Engineering Attacks

Social engineering attacks harness human psychology to manipulate individuals into disclosing confidential information or performing actions that threaten their security. These tactics are notably dangerous as they bypass technical safeguards, directly targeting the most vulnerable aspect of security infrastructure: human behavior. For families like the Wilsons, a deep understanding of these methods is crucial for robust protection against such deceptive approaches.

Understanding Social Engineering Attacks

These attacks primarily utilize psychological manipulation instead of conventional technical hacking techniques. Attackers often disguise themselves as trusted entities or individuals to trick victims into exposing sensitive data or allowing access to protected systems.

Frequent Variants of Social Engineering Attacks

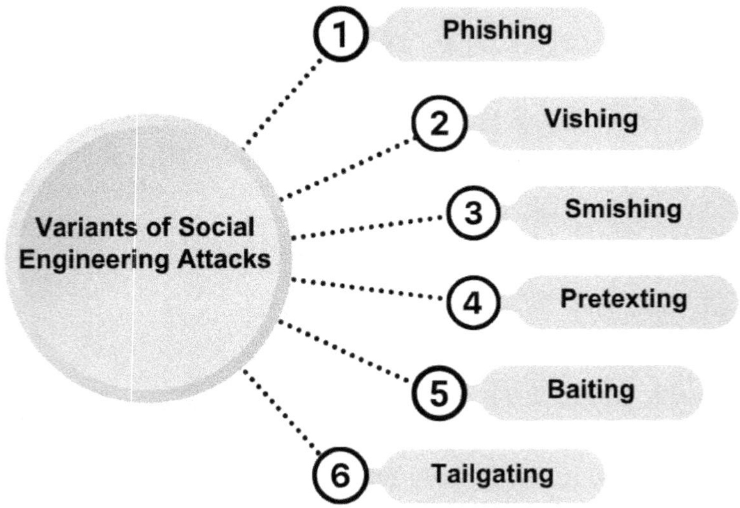

Phishing:

- **Overview:** Fraudulent emails or messages mimic reputable sources like banks to deceive individuals into providing personal details or clicking dangerous links.
- **Example:** Sarah gets an email that seems to be from her bank, encouraging her to verify her account details through a provided link, which actually directs to a fraudulent website.

Vishing (Voice Phishing):

- **Overview:** Here, attackers impersonate credible organizations through phone calls to request private information or financial dealings.

- **Example:** David gets a call from someone claiming to represent his credit card company, discussing supposed suspicious charges and requesting his account information.

Smishing (SMS Phishing):

- **Overview:** Similar to phishing, this involves sending deceitful text messages purporting to be from well-known organizations, pushing recipients to act on malicious links.
- **Example:** Emma gets a text announcing she's won a prize and must click a link to claim it, which is actually a trap to harvest her data.

Pretexting:

- **Overview:** Attackers simulate scenarios to gain access to information or systems.
- **Example:** Jack receives a call from a person pretending to be a school official needing his student ID and password for verification.

Baiting:

- **Overview:** This involves leaving physical media containing malware, like USB drives, in places where they can tempt the curious.
- **Example:** David finds a USB labelled "Confidential" and, driven by curiosity, plugs it into his computer, unwittingly triggering a malware installation.

Tailgating:

- **Overview:** Attackers physically follow someone with legitimate access into secured areas, exploiting social hesitation to confront or stop them.
- **Example:** Sarah holds the door open for what seems to be a colleague but is actually an unauthorized intruder.

Strategies to Prevent Social Engineering Attacks

- **Identity Verification:** Always confirm the identity of anyone requesting sensitive information using contact details obtained from reliable sources rather than those provided in suspicious communications.
- **Caution with Unsolicited Contacts:** Maintain a healthy suspicion of unexpected requests via email, calls, or texts that seek personal information or immediate action.
- **Educational Initiatives:** It is crucial that all family members are educated about the tactics employed in social engineering and how to effectively identify and counteract them.
- **Utilization of Security Software:** Implement comprehensive security solutions that can identify and neutralize phishing attempts and other related threats.

- **Enforcement of Multi-Factor Authentication (MFA):** Enhance account security by enabling MFA, which provides an additional verification step, making unauthorized access considerably more challenging.

Practical Application for the Wilson Family

With a proper understanding of social engineering, the Wilson family can proactively safeguard themselves. David ensures he independently verifies any unexpected financial communications by using known and trusted contact routes. Sarah empowers her students with the knowledge to examine seemingly harmless emails, and Emma and Jack remain vigilant against misleading text messages and links.

Social engineering schemes cleverly play on human vulnerabilities to compromise security. By recognizing these strategies and adopting preventive measures, families like the Wilsons can shield themselves from these cunning threats. Ongoing awareness and education are fundamental in mitigating the risks associated with social engineering, encouraging a safer digital landscape for all.

5.4 Insider Threats

Insider threats are cybersecurity challenges originating from individuals within an organization or a family who have access to important information and operational systems. These threats might be either deliberate or accidental, but both have the potential to inflict significant damage. For families like the Wilsons, understanding insider threats is pivotal for the safeguarding of their personal and work-related data.

Understanding Insider Threats

Such threats manifest when insiders exploit their legitimate access in destructive ways. Activities might range from the outright theft of data to the accidental exposure of sensitive details through careless handling.

Different Faces of Insider Threats

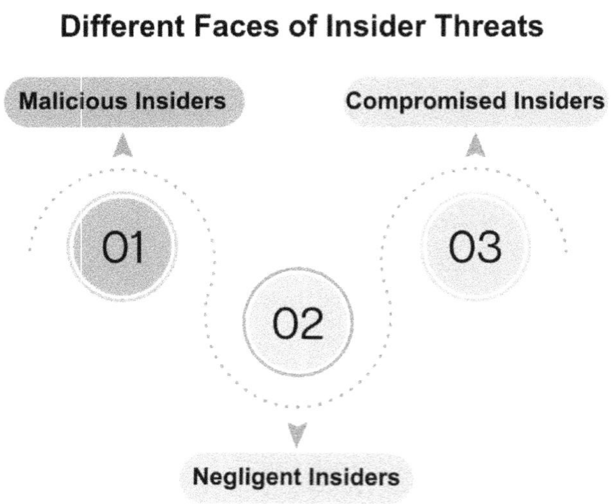

Malicious Insiders:

- **Definition:** Individuals intentionally leveraging their access for destructive purposes.
- **Example:** After his dismissal, a dissatisfied David's ex-employee deletes essential files from the architectural projects database.

Negligent Insiders:

- **Definition:** Those who unintentionally trigger security breaches due to their careless behavior.
- **Example:** Sarah sends an email meant for internal use containing student data to an unintended external recipient.

Compromised Insiders:

- **Definition:** Insiders whose accounts have been taken over by external threats.
- **Example:** An external hacker gains control over Jack's email and conducts a phishing campaign against his contacts.

Spotting Insider Threats

- **Behavioral Red Flags:** Observing actions such as irregular system access times or unusual data inquiries.
- **Example:** Emma notices her colleague accessing confidential financial records well beyond normal working hours, prompting concerns.
- **Unauthorized Attempts:** Monitoring any access to restricted data or physical areas without the requisite permissions.
- **Example:** An alert for unauthorized file access is triggered in David's firm, concerning files typically irrelevant to the employee's duties.
- **Suspicious Data Movements:** Watching for unexpected large-scale data movements that might suggest an attempt to extract data covertly.
- **Example:** The IT department at Sarah's school detects an unusual upload of large student databases to an unknown external server.

Mitigating Insider Threats

- **Controlled Access:** Implementing rigid access protocols to ensure that sensitive data is accessible only to those with a direct need.
- **Example:** David institutes a system of role-based access, restricting data touch points according to specific job requirements.
- **Routine Surveillance:** Implementing systematic checks of all access logs and user activities to pinpoint potential security setbacks.

- **Example:** Quarterly system reviews at Sarah's school aim to catch any unauthorized or abnormal access patterns.
- **Awareness and Training:** Regularly educating all members of an organization or family about the perils of insider threats and promoting adherence to security practices.
- **Example:** The Wilsons periodically review security protocols during family meetings, emphasizing the criticality of maintaining robust password hygiene and recognizing anomalies.
- **Rapid Response Protocols:** Establishing quick-response mechanisms to address and neutralize threats as they arise.
- **Example:** A swift incident response strategy at David's office involves immediate access cancellation followed by a thorough investigation if an insider threat is suspected.

Practical Steps for the Wilson Family

By thoroughly understanding insider threats, the Wilsons can proactively shield themselves. David ensures that only authorized staff can access sensitive client information. Sarah keeps a watchful eye on who accesses educational records, ensuring all protocols are followed. Emma and Jack remain attentive in their online interactions to prevent their accounts from being compromised.

Insider threats are a challenging risk due to the inherent trust and access granted to insiders. Recognizing these threats and deploying a suite of defensive measures allows families and organizations like the Wilsons to protect their valuable data effectively. Ongoing vigilance, continuous education, and strict security practices are essential for mitigating the inherent risks of insider threats, thereby creating a secure and trustworthy digital atmosphere.

5.5 Developing a Security Habits

For any family, like the Wilsons, developing strong security routines is essential to defend against cyber threats and protect both personal and professional data. These routines play a critical role in strengthening their cybersecurity posture and minimizing the incidence of digital breaches.

The Significance of Sound Security Practices

Adopting regular security practices is key to maintaining a secure digital environment. These habits are crucial in shielding against cyber-attacks and ensuring that preventive measures are consistently applied to reduce the potential for human errors.

Crucial Security Measures to Implement

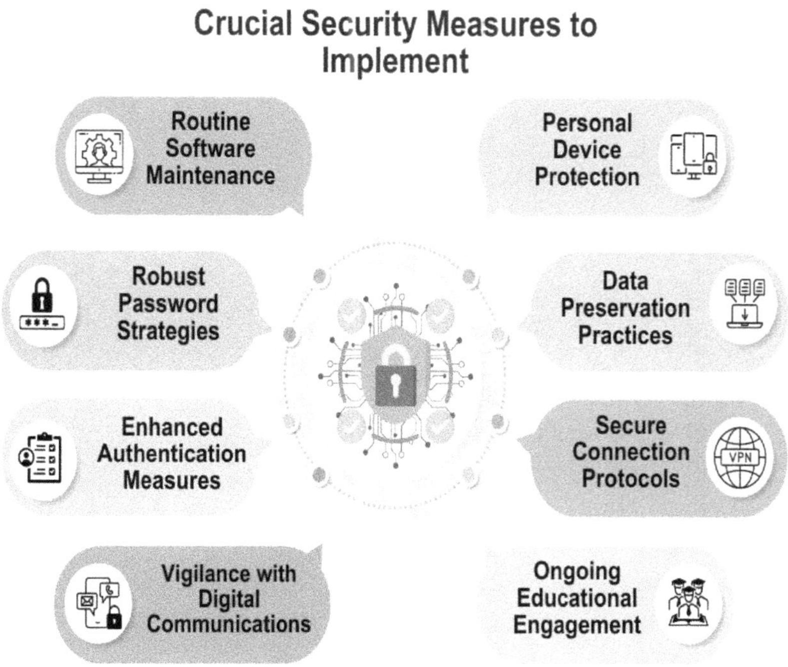

Routine Software Maintenance:

- **Overview:** Ensure continuous updates for all systems and applications to mitigate vulnerabilities.
- **Example:** David has automated his systems to apply security updates as soon as they are available, keeping his protections current.

Robust Password Strategies:

- **Overview:** Craft and manage distinct, complex passwords for each account, utilizing a password manager for efficiency.
- **Example:** Sarah uses a password manager to handle her diverse set of strong passwords, enhancing her online security.

Enhanced Authentication Measures:

- **Overview:** Implement Multi-Factor Authentication (MFA) for an added layer of security on all accounts.
- **Example:** Emma strengthens her accounts with MFA, adding a critical layer of defense against unauthorized access.

Vigilance with Digital Communications:

- **Overview:** Exercise caution when dealing with links and attachments from unknown sources to avoid phishing and malware.

- **Example:** Jack meticulously verifies the authenticity of each email attachment he considers opening, particularly those from unfamiliar senders.

Personal Device Protection:

- **Overview:** Apply rigid security measures like biometric authentication and encryption to personal devices.
- **Example:** Sarah ensures her devices are both encrypted and secured with a strong biometric lock.

Data Preservation Practices:

- **Overview:** Consistently back up essential data to reliable external or cloud storage solutions.
- **Example:** David maintains regular backup control, securing his critical business files offsite.

Secure Connection Protocols:

- **Overview:** Choosing protected network connections, especially when handling sensitive transactions, and employing VPN services when necessary.
- **Example:** While travelling, Emma relies on a VPN to maintain a secure connection, safeguarding her data transfers.

Ongoing Educational Engagement:

- **Overview:** Stay informed about the latest cybersecurity threats and protective strategies, sharing insights with family and colleagues.
- **Example:** The Wilson family engages in frequent discussions about new cybersecurity practices and potential threats.

Benefits of Solid Security Routines

Minimized Threat Exposure:

- **Overview:** By adhering to established security measures, the risk of cyber-attacks is substantially reduced.
- **Example:** The Wilsons' consistent use of comprehensive passwords and MFA drastically lowers their vulnerability to hacks.

Enhanced Data Integrity:

- **Overview:** Regular system updates and backups ensure the safety and availability of important data.
- **Example:** Sarah's active backups of her photos and documents mean she is well-prepared against data loss.

Increased Vigilance:

- **Overview:** Keeping up-to-date with the latest security trends allows for quick identification and mitigation of threats.
- **Example:** David's routine review of security updates enables him to promptly adapt to new cybersecurity challenges.

Practical Implications for the Wilson Family

By embracing strict security practices, the Wilsons can effectively shield their digital activities from a range of cyber threats. David's thorough update schedule ensures his business data remains protected, while Sarah's use of advanced password management guards her sensitive information. Similarly, Emma and Jack's cautious approach to online interactions and their proactive use of enhanced security settings strengthen their digital presence against potential breaches.

Adopting dynamic security habits is vital for averting cyber threats. These habits, when consistently practiced, provide a solid foundation for cybersecurity, significantly reducing breach risks and safeguarding both personal and professional data. For families like the Wilsons, these practices are fundamental to navigating the digital realm safely, ensuring ongoing security and peace of mind.

5.6 Leading Cybersecurity for Your Family

In the modern, interconnected world, carrying the role of cybersecurity leader within the family unit is more vital than ever. As cyber threats evolve with increasing complexity, it is crucial for families like the Wilsons to develop a solid digital environment that safeguards all members. Taking a forward-thinking approach to cybersecurity is imperative to ensure a comprehensive understanding and adherence to online safety protocols.

Framework Development for Family Cybersecurity

The first step in strengthening family cybersecurity involves constructing a solid framework based on clear, actionable guidelines that everyone, from young to old, can follow. Begin by determining the essential focus areas—such as device security, online behavior regulation, and data protection. From there, establish a tailored set of rules and routines that are straightforward and practicable.

Educational Outreach within the Family

At the heart of strong cybersecurity leadership lies the commitment to education. It is crucial that each family member, irrespective of age, gains a firm understanding of basic cybersecurity principles and the types of threats they might face. For children, employ easy-to-understand language and relatable scenarios to explain secure online practices like creating strong passwords and the pitfalls of indiscriminate information sharing. For adolescents and adults, delve into more intricate topics, such as the mechanics of social engineering and the critical importance of keeping software updated.

Take initiatives like David and Sarah alternating as instructors during family meetings to teach about cybersecurity topics, perhaps demonstrating how to activate two-factor authentication, spot phishing scams, or effectively manage passwords with digital tools. Involving everyone in these educational moments encourages a collective responsibility toward maintaining cybersecurity.

Implementation and Continuous Monitoring of Cybersecurity Measures

After establishing an educational foundation and a strategic framework, the next step is the consistent application of these protocols. Encourage family members to adopt and maintain strong, distinctive passwords, updating them regularly. Make sure that all family devices are equipped with the latest antivirus software and that updates are applied as soon as they become available.

Periodically evaluate the family's cybersecurity approach to identify any vulnerabilities or areas needing enhancement. This can be achieved through regular security audits—check for software that is out of date, passwords that are too weak, and any unusual activity across family devices and accounts. These audits serve not only as maintenance checks but also as educational sessions to underscore the value of vigilant security practices and to resolve any questions.

Cultivating a Cybersecurity-Aware Household

Building a culture of cybersecurity awareness means embedding it into the fabric of everyday life. Promote regular discussions on the latest threats and updates in the cybersecurity landscape, sharing tips and resources to strengthen the family's online defense. Lead by example: exhibit diligent cybersecurity habits and maintain alertness to potential risks.

For instance, David can demonstrate the importance of secure connections, especially when working remotely, by consistently using a VPN and regularly backing up his data. Sarah can highlight cautious behavior with emails and links by double-checking the sources of unexpected communications. Emma and Jack can play their part by ensuring they log out of accounts after use and stay updated on the newest security settings for social media platforms.

Evolving With the Cybersecurity Landscape

As digital threats and technologies develop, it is crucial to stay flexible and willing to update your family's cybersecurity strategies. Encourage an environment where continuous learning and adaptation are valued, ensuring that the family remains well-equipped to face new and emerging threats.

Leading a family's cybersecurity initiatives is a dynamic and ongoing process that requires informed leadership, constant vigilance, and adaptability. By developing a comprehensive cybersecurity framework, continuously educating family members, implementing and reviewing security practices regularly, encouraging an aware household, and adjusting to technological shifts, families like the Wilsons can secure a protective digital environment. This proactive stance not only guards against cyber threats but also provides confidence as family members navigate the digital world.

Understanding the human elements in cybersecurity and integrating educational, preventative, and adaptive measures are crucial for a resilient defense against digital risks. By promoting cybersecurity awareness and adapting to evolving threats, families can navigate digital challenges more safely and securely. Cybersecurity is about more than just technological defenses; it is about empowering individuals with the knowledge and tools to make safe choices online, thus creating a secure environment for everyone.

Chapter 6: Cybersecurity and Privacy

6.1 Introduction to Privacy in Cybersecurity

In our increasingly digital world, the concepts of privacy and cybersecurity are deeply interconnected, serving as dual shields for both personal and professional data. Cybersecurity focuses on defending data against unauthorized access and various cyber threats, whereas privacy is about the rights and expectations people have concerning their personal information usage and security. It is crucial for families like the Wilsons to grasp these concepts to navigate the digital world with assurance and safety.

The Significance of Privacy

Privacy stands as a cornerstone right that grants individuals the power to manage their personal data. This covers information ranging from names and addresses to financial and medical records and web activities. Ensuring the security of such data involves proper handling, storage, and usage, safeguarding against unauthorized access or misuse. Given the frequency of data breaches and identity theft today, the importance of privacy has increased.

Cybersecurity Role in Maintaining Privacy

Effective cybersecurity measures are essential in upholding privacy as they protect the infrastructure and databases that store sensitive data. Through solid cybersecurity practices, both individuals and corporations can prevent unauthorized entries, data leaks, and other digital threats that endanger privacy. Techniques like encryption, robust authentication processes, and secure communication methods are key cybersecurity tools aiding in the defense of personal information.

Daily Privacy Issues

Daily life brings various privacy issues for many families, including the Wilsons. David, who owns an architectural business, must protect his client's sensitive data from both competitors and hackers. Sarah, an educator, is responsible for keeping her students personal and educational details confidential. Meanwhile, their children, Emma and Jack, who are active on social media and online gaming, should be cautious about the personal information they broadcast.

Challenges in Preserving Privacy

The digital age presents numerous obstacles to privacy preservation. The universal use of online platforms and social media means personal details are always collected and stored, often raising privacy concerns. Moreover, businesses accumulate large data volumes for marketing, heightening privacy risks. The growing sophistication of cyber threats also poses a significant challenge, potentially compromising even the most secure systems.

Maintaining a Balance between Privacy and Convenience

A key challenge in privacy management is maintaining a harmony between privacy and the convenience digital technology offers. While sharing personal data can improve user experiences and provide service access, it elevates the risk of data mishaps and exploitation. For the Wilsons, it is about weighing the benefits against the privacy risks of the information they disclose online.

Proactive Privacy Safeguards

The Wilson family can implement several proactive strategies to shield their privacy. Strong, unique passwords and multi-factor authentication are fundamental in securing online accounts. Exercising caution with the information shared on digital platforms can mitigate identity theft risks. Additionally, regularly updating privacy settings on devices and applications ensures that personal data remains limited to intended parties.

For families like the Wilsons, understanding the integral role of privacy within cybersecurity is vital for safeguarding both personal and professional data. By acknowledging the associated challenges and taking active steps, families can maintain privacy and foster a secure digital environment. Staying informed and attentive and making educated decisions about data security are indispensable practices in the face of evolving digital threats.

6.2 Data Protection Laws

In our modern digital landscape, rising concerns about privacy have encouraged governments globally to establish laws aimed at protecting personal data. These legal frameworks dictate organizations' collection, utilization, and storage practices, thereby preserving individual privacy rights. Families like the Wilsons can benefit from understanding these laws, which illuminate governmental strategies for data protection and clarify citizens' rights concerning their personal information.

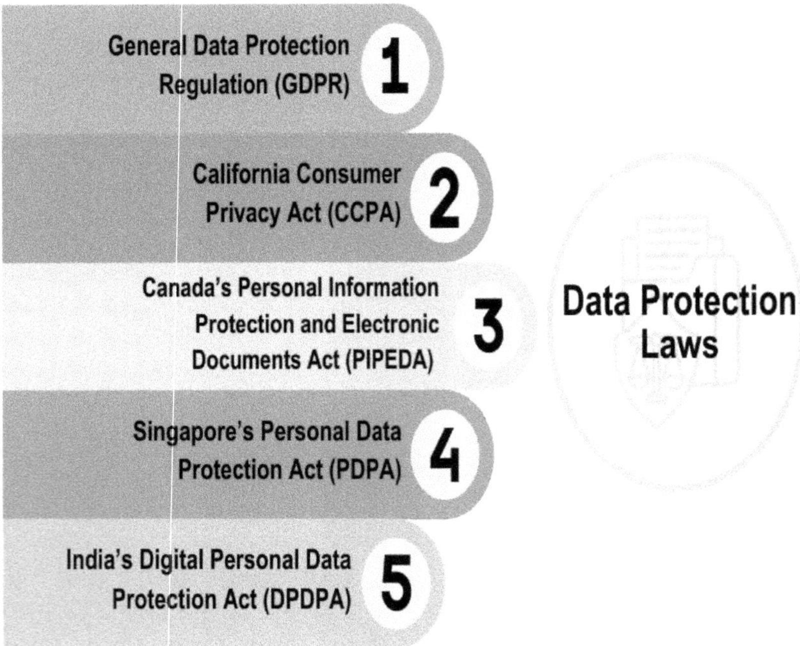

General Data Protection Regulation (GDPR)

The General Data Protection Regulation, or GDPR, was implemented by the European Union in May 2018 and stands as a standard of data protection laws. It governs the handling of personal data and affects entities both within and outside the EU that deal with the data of EU residents.

- **Goals:** The GDPR is primarily prepared to enhance individuals' control over their personal data and standardize privacy regulations throughout Europe.
- **Principal Rules:** Organizations must obtain explicit consent to gather data, protect stored data, and enable individuals to access, amend, or remove their information. Crucially, this requires organizations to notify authorities of data breaches promptly, within 72 hours.
- **Effects on Individuals:** The GDPR mandates that the Wilson family, and particularly David's architectural business, handle client data from the EU with utmost responsibility, ensuring transparency and accountability.

California Consumer Privacy Act (CCPA)

Since January 2020, the CCPA has been a landmark privacy regulation in the United States, augmenting privacy rights for Californians.

- **Goals:** The CCPA seeks to strengthen transparency and give consumers more control over how businesses use their personal information.
- **Principal Rules:** Californians are granted the right to inquire about the data businesses collect and can request data deletion or withdrawal of its sale. Businesses are obligated to reveal their data collection methods and include a "Do Not Sell My Personal Information" option on their websites.
- **Effects on Individuals:** For the Wilsons, residing in California means benefiting from the CCPA's strict privacy provisions. Sarah, involved in education, can check how student data is handled, while teenagers Emma and Jack can withdraw data sales on social platforms.

Survey of Global Data Protection Measures

Many countries have passed their data privacy laws, reflecting a growing global emphasis on personal data security:

- **Singapore's Personal Data Protection Act (PDPA):** This act ensures that personal data is managed responsibly by Singaporean entities, focusing on transparent data handling.
- **Canada's Personal Information Protection and Electronic Documents Act (PIPEDA)** Governs data use in private sectors and emphasizes informed consent and clear data management practices.
- **India's Digital Personal Data Protection Act (DPDPA):** This act of 2023 in India establishes a detailed structure for managing data protection. It safeguards personal information by mandating legal and secure processing, highlighting the importance of user consent and the responsibility of data handlers.

Worldwide Privacy Advancements

With the increasing importance of data security, these legislations signify a strong commitment by governments to address privacy concerns, reassuring citizens that their data is treated with care and respect.

Understanding laws like the GDPR and CCPA enables families to appreciate the extensive efforts undertaken by governments to safeguard personal data. These regulations mandate responsible data management by organizations, providing enhanced control and transparency to individuals. As we continue to engage with the complexities of cybersecurity and privacy, recognizing the critical role of these legal structures is essential for promoting a secure digital environment.

6.3 Building Strong Privacy Habits

In our current digital generation, the boundaries protecting personal privacy seem thinner than ever. Every day, a vast amount of personal data is shared online, necessitating that families like the Wilsons—and indeed, anyone—develop attentive privacy habits. By embracing proactive measures and consciously managing their digital footprints, individuals can ensure their private information remains just that—private.

Emphasizing Privacy in Daily Habits

Promoting strong privacy habits is close to maintaining a healthy lifestyle; it requires consistent and dedicated effort. Such habits form a shield against potential threats like identity theft and data breaches. For the Wilson family, these habits are not just routines but a way of life that keeps their personal and professional lives secure.

Essential Privacy Habits Everyone Should Adopt

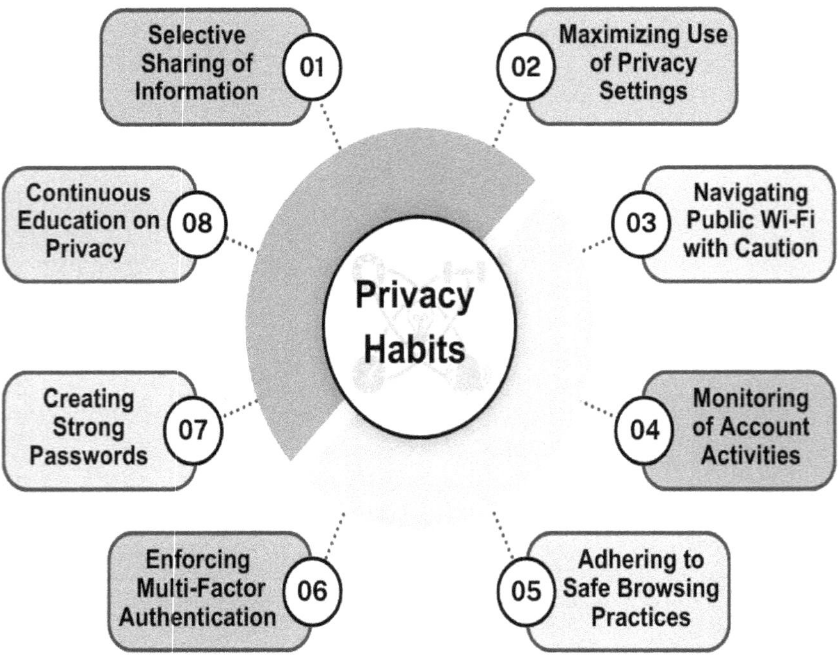

Selective Sharing of Information:

A crucial habit is being selective about what personal information to share online. Details such as home addresses, personal phone numbers, and sensitive financial information should be guarded enthusiastically, much like one would protect a family antique. Sarah, for instance, continuously educates Emma and Jack on the importance of sensibleness in their online interactions, advising them against oversharing on social platforms.

Maximizing Use of Privacy Settings:

Utilizing available privacy settings on social media and other online platforms is a proactive way to manage who can view personal information. David, who manages his firm's online presence, regularly audits these settings to ensure they are at their most strict, thus safeguarding client information from prying eyes.

Navigating Public Wi-Fi with Caution: The convenience of public Wi-Fi can be a double-edged sword, as these networks are often not secure. The Wilsons use VPNs (Virtual Private Networks) to encrypt their internet connection whenever they access the internet from public spots like coffee shops or libraries, ensuring their online actions remain confidential.

Monitoring of Account Activities:

Keeping an eye on signs of unusual activities within online accounts is crucial for spotting potential breaches early. Sarah has set up notifications for any strange transactions within her online banking apps, allowing her to react swiftly to any unauthorized actions.

Adhering to Safe Browsing Practices:

Safe browsing habits include using secure, encrypted connections and being cautious about engaging with unknown links or downloading suspicious attachments. Jack, an internet user, employs browser extensions that provide an additional layer of protection against malicious websites and phishing attempts.

Enforcing Multi-Factor Authentication (MFA):

MFA adds a significant barrier to unauthorized access, combining something known (a password) with something possessed (a verification code sent to a device). David has implemented MFA across all his business-related accounts, providing an extra layer of security to protect sensitive client information.

Creating and Managing Strong Passwords:

It is essential to compose strong, unique passwords for each account. The Wilsons use a password manager to generate and store complex passwords, ensuring that each password is as impregnable as possible. Sarah makes it a point to discuss with Emma and Jack the dangers of using the same password across different sites.

Continuous Education on Privacy and Security:

Regular discussions on the latest in privacy and cybersecurity keep the Wilson family informed and prepared. They share updates on recent security breaches and emerging threats, encouraging a culture of awareness and proactive defense.

Benefits of Active Privacy Practices

The benefits of maintaining rigid privacy habits are various, including reduced risks of identity theft and data breaches and a greater sense of control over one's personal information. For the Wilsons, these habits are essential in creating a secure digital environment where they can confidently engage with the digital world without fear.

Establishing and maintaining strong privacy habits is fundamental in the digital age. The Wilson family shows that thoughtful practices like limiting personal information sharing, utilizing robust privacy settings, practicing safe browsing, enabling MFA, and educating all family members can significantly strengthen one's privacy defenses. For the Wilsons, and indeed for any family, these habits are not just recommendations but necessities for ensuring a safer online existence and peace of mind.

6.4 Data Minimization and Anonymization

In their journey to protect their personal privacy in our digital world, the Wilson family, like many others, turns to the crucial strategies of data minimization and anonymization. These methods are vital in reducing the amount of personal information collected and ensuring that any data possessed remains secure from unauthorized access.

Understanding Data Minimization

Data minimization is about gathering only the essential personal information needed for a specific purpose. This approach limits the risk of data breaches by reducing the volume of data sensitive to attacks.

Best Practices for Data Minimization

- **Evaluate the Need for Data:** Before inputting personal information, it is wise to consider its necessity. For instance, when the Wilsons sign up for new online services, they fill out only the mandatory fields, skipping optional ones to keep extra personal details private.

- **Conduct Regular Data Audits:** It is beneficial to periodically check the data you have accumulated. David takes time every quarter to filter through his architectural firm's client data, removing anything outdated or irrelevant.
- **Set Data Retention Limits:** It is crucial to define clear policies on how long to keep personal information. Once its purpose is served, the data should be securely destroyed. Sarah, who handles educational records, ensures that student information is discarded securely after graduation.
- **Leverage Minimal Data Collection Tools:** Using tools that support minimal data collection, like privacy-centric browsers and search engines, can enhance online privacy. Emma and Jack make it a habit to use these tools to safeguard their activities on the internet.

Understanding Data Anonymization

Data anonymization alters personal information so it cannot lead back to an individual, ensuring that even if the data is stolen, it lacks value to an attacker.

Best Practices for Data Anonymization

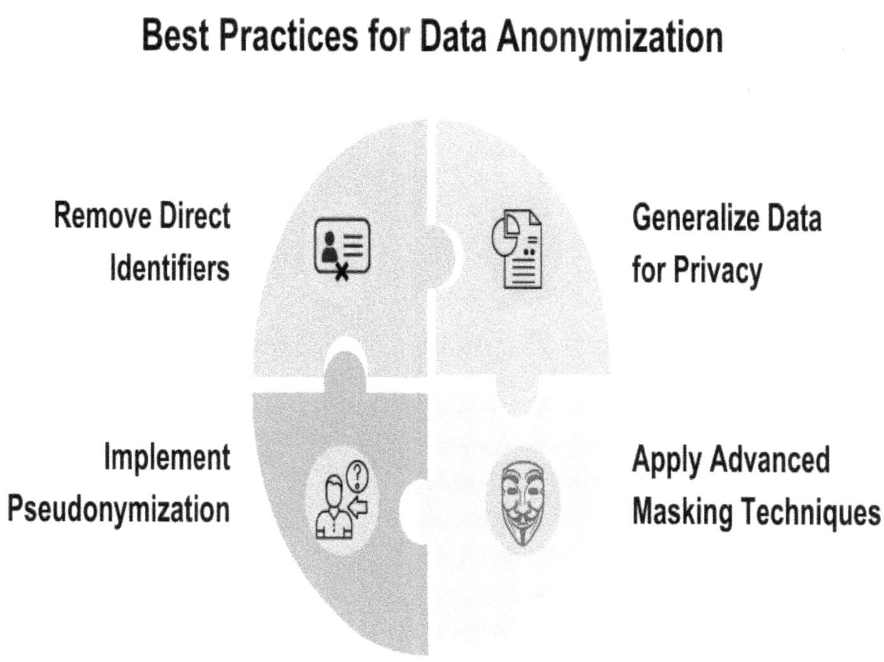

- **Remove Direct Identifiers:** This involves stripping away details such as names and addresses. When David shares project details with collaborators, he anonymizes any client-specific data to maintain confidentiality.

- **Generalize Data for Privacy:** Instead of precise details, use broader categories—for instance, categorizing ages or locations more generally to unknown specific identities but still provide useful data.
- **Implement Pseudonymization:** This technique involves substituting identifiers with pseudonyms that do not hold value without a key. Sarah applies this method to student data for academic studies, ensuring the student's identities remain protected.
- **Apply Advanced Masking Techniques:** Data masking can alter datasets subtly, ensuring personal data is hidden while the overall data remains useful for analysis. These techniques are helpful when sharing information for broader analytical purposes.

Advantages of Embracing Data Minimization and Anonymization

By adopting these privacy-preserving strategies, the risk of data breaches decreases, compliance with privacy laws increases, and client trust grows. These practices assure the Wilsons—and any other cautious family—that their private information stays private.

Practical Applications for the Wilsons

David ensures only necessary client information is collected and old files are securely deleted after projects. Sarah anonymizes student data before it is used in research. Emma and Jack are careful about the personal details they share online, using privacy-focused tools and keeping unnecessary data sharing to a minimum.

For families like the Wilsons, data minimization and anonymization are not just strategies but necessities in maintaining privacy and security in the digital age. By understanding and implementing these practices, they can ensure a secure digital environment for themselves and maintain control over their personal information.

6.5 Privacy Breach Handling: Key Measures

In our digital world, despite careful efforts to safeguard personal data, privacy breaches can still occur. It is vital for families like the Wilsons, and indeed all families, to be equipped with a rich plan to manage such incidents effectively. Knowing what steps to take in the event of a privacy breach can significantly reduce the damage and help in swiftly restoring security.

Understanding Privacy Breaches

A privacy breach occurs when personal information falls into unauthorized hands, which could be due to cyber-attacks, human errors, or weaknesses in system security. The repercussions of such breaches are severe, potentially leading to identity theft, significant financial loss, and a profound weakening of trust.

Strategic Measures for Managing Privacy Breaches

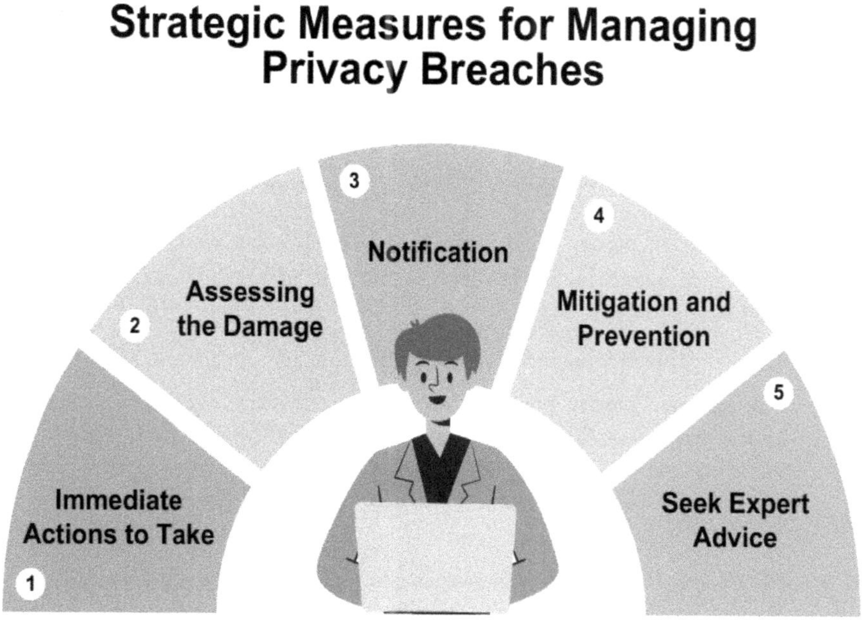

Immediate Actions to Take

- **Identify the Incident:** It is critical to recognize a breach swiftly. Signs to watch for include unusual account behavior, unexpected notifications, or warnings from antivirus programs. For example, if David spots strange transactions on his business ledger, he should immediately consider a breach.
- **Contain the Situation:** Act quickly to stop the breach. This might mean disconnecting affected systems from the internet, updating passwords, or shutting down compromised accounts. Sarah, for example, might change her email password and activate two-factor authentication upon detecting suspicious activity.

Assessing the Damage

- **Scope of the Breach:** Determine the extent of the breach by identifying which data was accessed and the number of people impacted. This step is crucial for understanding the potential damage and directing an adequate response. If Emma and Jack's educational accounts are breached, Sarah needs to figure out what specific data was compromised.
- **Risk Evaluation:** Assess how sensitive the exposed data is and the risks associated with it. Information like Social Security numbers or bank details carries higher risks compared to less sensitive data. David needs to evaluate how the breach could affect his clients and their confidential data.

Notification and Open Communication

- **Inform Those Impacted:** It is important to alert anyone affected by the breach rapidly. Share details about the nature of the breach, which data was compromised, and how they can protect themselves. The Wilsons would need to communicate with their bank, internet service providers, or schools, depending on who is affected.
- **Clear Communication:** Maintain transparency in your communications about the breach. Clear information helps rebuild trust and guides impacted individuals in taking protective measures. Sarah should ensure that she explains the breach clearly to Emma and Jack, helping them understand how to secure their accounts.

Mitigation and Future Prevention

- **Strengthen Security Posture:** After a breach, it is essential to strengthen your security defenses to prevent future incidents. This could involve updating antivirus software, patching vulnerabilities, or improving overall security practices. David could collaborate with IT specialists to strengthen the defenses of his architectural firm.
- **Continuous Monitoring:** Monitor accounts and systems closely for signs of further unauthorized actions. Ongoing vigilance helps ensure that all aspects of the breach have been addressed. Sarah could set up ongoing alerts for unusual activities across all family devices.

Seek Expert Advice

- **Engage with Professionals:** For significant breaches, it might be necessary to consult with cybersecurity experts or legal advisors who can offer specialized advice on mitigating the breach and meeting legal obligations. David might consider hiring a cybersecurity firm to review and enhance his firm's digital defenses.
- **Legal Compliance:** Be aware of and adhere to any legal requirements related to the breach, which might include notifying authorities and adhering to specific data protection laws. Sarah should stay informed about the legal protocols for handling breaches involving her school's data.

Example of the Wilson Family

Should the Wilsons face a privacy breach, their immediate steps would include:

- Identifying and containing the breach.
- Evaluating its impact.
- Notifying relevant parties.
- Taking action to mitigate and recover from the incident.

For instance, if their online banking details are compromised, quick actions like contacting the bank, changing passwords, enabling additional security measures, and closely monitoring their accounts would be crucial.

Effectively managing a privacy breach involves prompt identification, immediate containment, thorough impact assessment, transparent communication, and active mitigation efforts. By learning these critical measures, families like the Wilsons can significantly reduce the impact of privacy breaches and swiftly restore their digital safety. Being well-prepared and knowledgeable about responding to such incidents is indispensable for maintaining privacy in our digital age.

In this digital age, where personal data is always vulnerable, learning vital privacy practices is essential for safeguarding our digital existence. This chapter has underscored the critical nature of privacy within the domain of cybersecurity, explored the impact of data protection lawmaking, and discussed the advantages of strategies like data minimization and anonymization. It also outlined critical approaches for managing privacy breaches effectively. For families like the Wilsons—and indeed, any family—embracing these practices is crucial for keeping both personal and professional information secure against the backdrop of ever-evolving cyber threats.

By staying up-to-date on the latest developments, developing solid privacy habits, and preparing to tackle privacy breaches head-on, individuals can foster a more secure digital environment. As we navigate the complexities of the digital world, placing a high priority on privacy, hand-in-hand with cybersecurity measures, is crucial. This strategic focus will enable us to shield our most precious assets: our personal information and, ultimately, our peace of mind.

Chapter 7: Cybersecurity Careers and Future Opportunities

7.1 Introduction to Cybersecurity Careers

In today's tech-driven world, the urgency for skilled cybersecurity professionals is more prominent than ever. As the landscape of cyber threats continues to evolve with increasing complexity, there is an increased demand for talented individuals who can robustly defend our digital world. This field offers a productive ground for students, career transitioners, or anyone curious about the domain, presenting a career path packed with diverse opportunities and tough challenges.

Why Cybersecurity?

In our digital age, where daily life is inseparably linked with digital technologies, cybersecurity has become a cornerstone of modern existence. Protecting personal details to securing critical infrastructures, professionals in cybersecurity are the unsung heroes who ensure our digital interactions remain secure. For families like the Wilsons, this translates into having trusted experts who protect their online activities and personal information from potential digital attackers.

Range of Career Opportunities

The field of cybersecurity is rich with diverse career paths, catering to a wide range of interests and skill sets, promising a fit for virtually anyone drawn to this field. Highlighted roles include:

- **Security Analyst:** Security analysts are the observant caretakers of an organization's digital boundaries. They monitor networks for anomalies, resolve security breaches, and strengthen defenses against future threats.

For someone like Jack, who thrives on solving puzzles and staying one step ahead of cyber adversaries, this role is a perfect match.

- **Penetration Tester (Ethical Hacker):** Ethical hackers, or penetration testers, are creative minds who test and secure systems by simulating attacks. This role is suited for individuals who enjoy technical challenges and creative solutions, much like Emma, who has always been fascinated by understanding and dismantling systems.
- **Security Consultant:** As advisors, security consultants assess and enhance organizations' security strategies. This role is ideal for those like Sarah, who excel in roles that involve guidance and strategic planning, helping businesses shield themselves against digital threats.
- **Incident Responder:** These professionals are the rapid response forces of the cybersecurity world. In the event of a breach, they are the first on the scene, working swiftly to mitigate damage and strategize recovery. David, known for his cool head in crises, would find this role highly fulfilling.
- **Security Architect:** These architects design the blueprint of an organization's network security. This role demands a deep understanding of cybersecurity principles and a skill for developing strategic, robust network solutions, making it an excellent path for those inclined towards comprehensive planning and execution.

Educational Pathways and Skills

Entering the cybersecurity world typically involves a combination of academic education and hands-on experience. Degrees in computer science, information technology, or related fields lay the foundation, supplemented by certifications like CompTIA Security+, CISSP, and CEH that validate expertise.

Essential skills in this field include analytical thinking, keen attention to detail, and solid technical understanding. Equally important are communication skills, as explaining complex security issues to non-experts is often part of the job.

Employment Landscape

The job market for cybersecurity experts is rich and expected to grow. Industry analysts predict a continued rise in demand for these professionals, noting a persistent shortage. This gap in the workforce presents a unique opportunity for job security and competitive gain.

For the Wilsons and any family considering this path, cybersecurity offers not just career stability but a chance to contribute meaningfully to societal safety. Whether at the beginning of a career journey or shifting to a new field, cybersecurity stands as a promising and rewarding effort.

7.2 Essential Skills and Qualifications

Undertaking a cybersecurity career involves combining a unique set of skills and qualifications. This path is well-suited not only for students but also for professionals considering a career shift or those merely curious about the field. This section will explain what it takes to succeed in this dynamic domain, making it approachable even for newcomers.

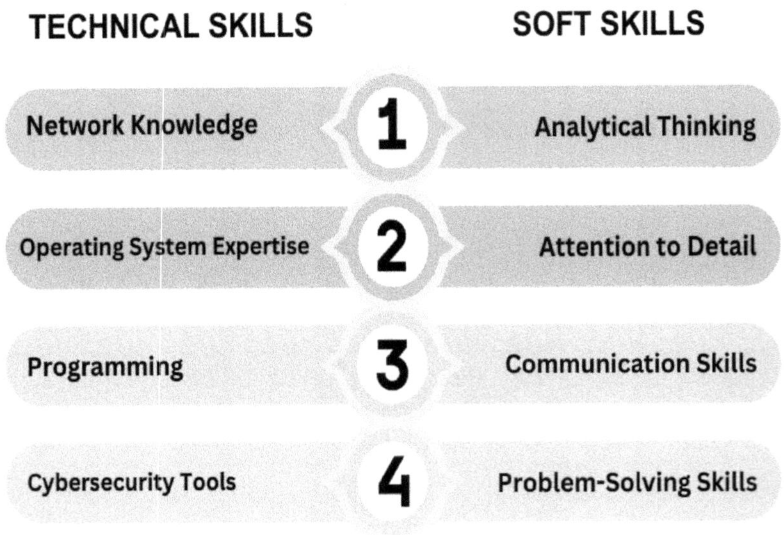

Technical Skills You Will Need

- **Network Knowledge:** Understanding how networks function is linked to understanding the concepts of the digital world—vital for understanding how data moves and spotting potential cyber threats. This includes a solid foundation in network protocols, IP addressing, and the flow of data across the Internet.
- **Operating System Expertise:** Proficiency in various operating systems, from Windows to Linux and macOS, is crucial. Each system has its strengths and vulnerabilities, and knowing these can be particularly advantageous for securing systems.
- **Programming:** Not all cybersecurity roles demand deep programming knowledge, but having a grasp of basic coding in languages like Python, JavaScript, and SQL is beneficial. These skills enable you to automate tasks, analyze threats, and deeply understand the cyber-attacks.
- **Mastering Cybersecurity Tools:** Familiarity with essential tools—antivirus software, firewalls, intrusion detection systems, and encryption technologies—is essential. These tools form the frontline defense against cyber threats.

Soft Skills That Make a Difference

- **Analytical Thinking:** The essence of cybersecurity lies in tackling complex problems and producing effective solutions. It requires a sharp analytical mind capable of identifying patterns and anomalies that may indicate security issues, such as unexpected login activities.
- **Attention to Detail:** In cybersecurity, a minor oversight can lead to major vulnerabilities. Precision in tasks, from monitoring security logs to setting up firewalls, is important.
- **Communication Skills:** The ability to convey complex security issues clearly to those not knowledgeable in technical-speak is invaluable. Whether explaining the necessity of a security measure to a non-technical manager or outlining a breach's implications, clear communication is key.
- **Problem-Solving Skills:** Cybersecurity professionals are essentially digital detectives who solve puzzles under pressure. Quick, creative thinking is crucial, especially when responding to security incidents.

Educational Qualifications and Pathways

Formal Education: Typically, a foundational degree in computer science, information technology, or related fields lays the groundwork for a career in cybersecurity. Yet, many professionals successfully enter the field from other areas through dedicated self-study and obtaining certifications.

Industry Certifications: Certifications can strengthen a resume and demonstrate specialized knowledge:

- **CompTIA Security+:** Great for beginners, covering basic security principles.
- **Certified Information Systems Security Professional (CISSP):** Ideal for seasoned professionals, encompassing a broad range of security topics.

- **Certified Ethical Hacker (CEH):** Focuses on penetration testing and ethical hacking techniques.
- **Certified Information Security Manager (CISM):** Developed for those managing enterprise information security.

Continual Learning: With cybersecurity's fast-evolving nature, staying updated through online courses, workshops, and industry conferences like DEF CON and Black Hat is essential. Regular reading and research also keep one ahead of emerging trends and threats.

Example of the Wilson Family

David could enhance the security of his architectural firm by embracing basic cybersecurity principles. Sarah might integrate cybersecurity awareness into her teaching, equipping her students with early skills. Meanwhile, Emma and Jack can learn about cybersecurity through online learning and practical experimentation, laying a solid groundwork for potential future careers.

Developing a successful career in cybersecurity requires an understanding of technical skills and soft skills and a commitment to continuous learning. Understanding these essential elements prepares you for a rewarding journey in this dynamic field.

7.3 Certifications and Training Programs

Considering a cybersecurity career involves navigating a landscape rich with educational paths and certifications, each designed to build foundational skills and advance knowledge. Whether you are just starting or seeking to escalate your career, a domain of certifications caters to every skill level, this section outlines some of the most respected certifications and training programs, starting from beginner options and moving to more specialized, advanced certifications.

Beginning with Entry-Level Certifications

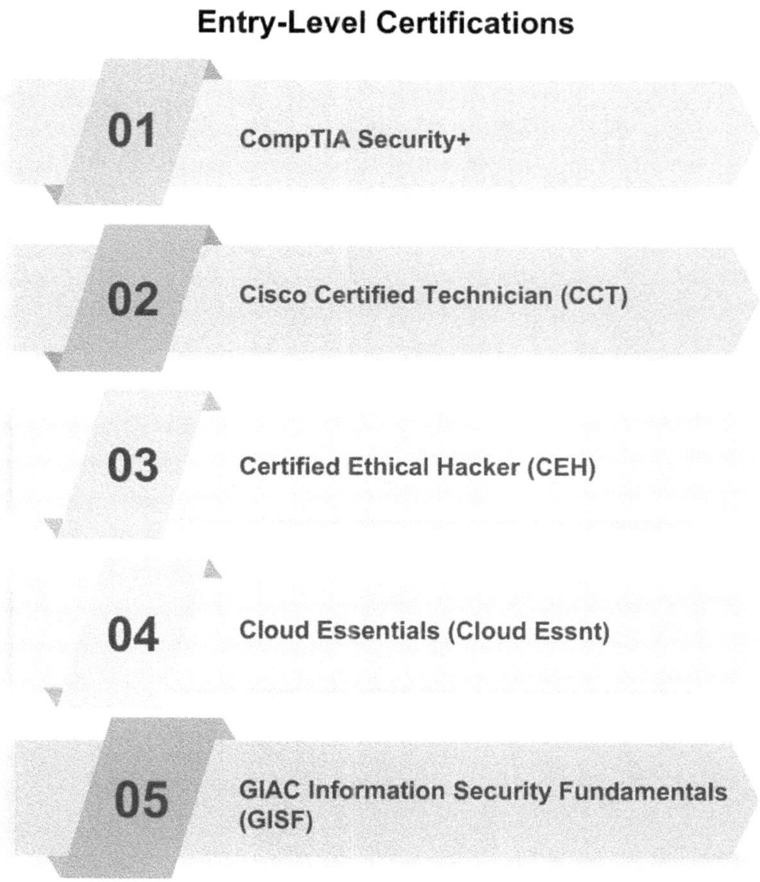

- **CompTIA Security+:** This certification offers an excellent introduction to cybersecurity for beginners. It covers fundamental topics such as network security, compliance, operational security, threats, vulnerabilities, and access control. Recognized widely across the industry, this certification lays the foundation for a solid understanding of core cybersecurity principles.
- **Cisco Certified Technician (CCT):** This Certification is ideally suited for those at the beginning of their journey in cybersecurity and networking. It concentrates on equipping individuals with the necessary skills to

troubleshoot, restore, repair, and replace essential Cisco network and system devices, setting a vital technical base.

- **Certified Ethical Hacker (CEH):** For those fascinated by the hacker mindset, CEH is a perfect fit. This certification trains you to think and act like a hacker to better defend against threats, making it ideal for problem-solvers and those curious about cyber attacker tactics.
- **Cloud Essentials (Cloud Essnt):** This certification introduces the basic principles of cloud computing and its impact on both business and IT sectors. It's ideal for beginners, helping them to comprehend the workings of the cloud environment, its advantages, and the associated security issues.
- **GIAC Information Security Fundamentals (GISF):** This certification is a valuable asset for newcomers in cybersecurity. It addresses fundamental topics such as networking, cryptography, and defensive measures. GISF aids professionals in establishing a foundational knowledge of information security principles and best practices.

Advanced Certifications for Specialized Skills

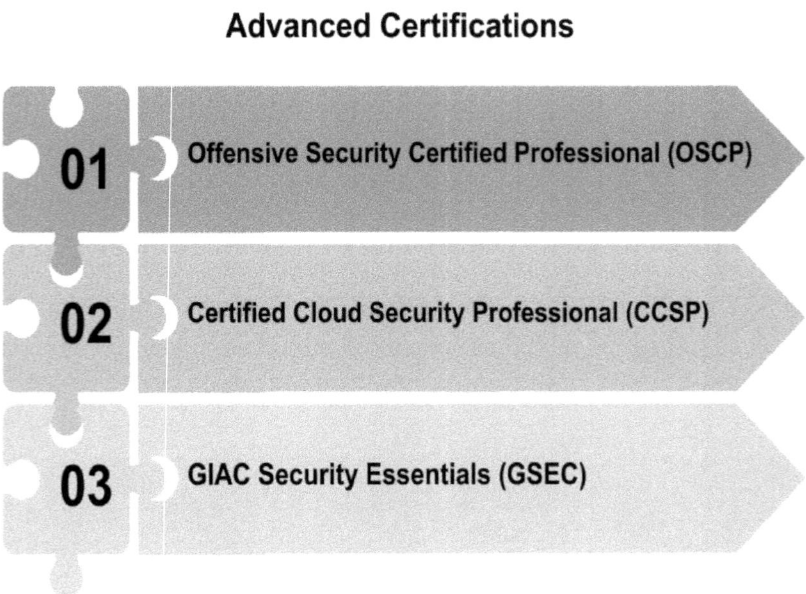

- **Offensive Security Certified Professional (OSCP):** Respected among ethical hackers and penetration testers, OSCP challenges candidates to exploit vulnerabilities as proof of their skills in a strict, hands-on exam. It is a standard certification for those dedicated to the offensive side of cybersecurity.
- **Certified Cloud Security Professional (CCSP):** As cloud technologies become universal, the CCSP is crucial for those specializing in cloud security. It delves

into cloud architecture, operations, and security management, which are critical for safeguarding cloud-based environments.

- **GIAC Security Essentials (GSEC):** GSEC is designed for IT professionals seeking to validate their hands-on skills in handling fundamental security functions. Topics covered include cryptography, network security, and incident handling, ideal for those looking to solidify their technical cybersecurity capabilities.

Exploring Training Programs and Learning Platforms

- **Online Learning:** Platforms like Coursera, Udemy, and LinkedIn Learning provide extensive courses across all cybersecurity levels, from introductory to advance. These are fantastic starting points for foundational learning or touching up on new advancements.
- **Bootcamps:** Intense and focused cybersecurity boot camps like those offered by Cybrary or General Assembly are perfect for practical training and appeal to those who wish to start their careers quickly.
- **Academic Programs:** For a more traditional educational path, many universities now offer dedicated undergraduate and graduate programs in cybersecurity. These comprehensive courses prepare students for a variety of roles in the sector.

Example of the Wilson Family:

David could strengthen his architectural firm's defenses by starting with CompTIA Security+. Sarah might integrate basic cybersecurity principles into her high school curriculum through a beginner's course on Coursera. Meanwhile, Emma and Jack could get into this field by engaging in online courses or a local boot camp, laying a strong foundation for future exploration.

Navigating the collection of certifications and training programs is crucial for anyone serious about a cybersecurity career. They not only offer structured learning paths and skill validation but also keep you up-to-date on the latest industry trends and threats. With options available for every level, these educational resources are invaluable for both beginners and seasoned professionals looking to advance.

7.4 Career Pathways in Cybersecurity

Exploring the various career pathways in cybersecurity reveals a rich field packed with opportunities for diverse interests and skill sets. Whether you are initiating your career journey or aiming to escalate your professional life, the field of cybersecurity presents a number of roles, ranging from foundational positions for beginners to specialized, technical slots for the more experienced.

Introductory Career Pathways for Beginners

Career Pathways for Beginners

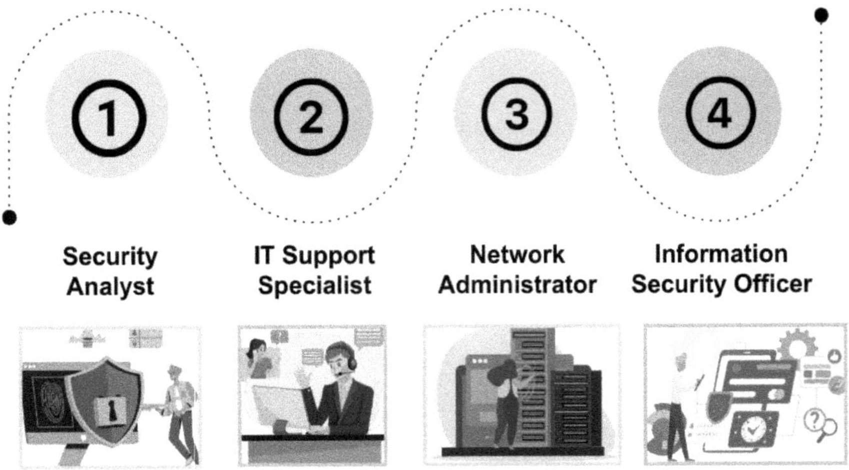

- **Security Analyst:** Often a gateway role into cybersecurity, Security Analysts are fundamental in monitoring and protecting an organization's networks and systems. They identify security breaches, investigate incidents, and deploy measures to defend the organization's data. For someone like Jack, who prospers in solving complex problems and understanding how systems operate, this role could be a perfect fit.
- **IT Support Specialist:** These specialists provide essential technical support within an organization, handling issues related to software, hardware, and network connectivity while ensuring compliance with security protocols. This role is perfect for individuals like Emma, who naturally excel in assisting others with technical challenges and enjoy making technology more accessible to everyone.
- **Network Administrator:** Network Administrators ensure that an organization's network infrastructure is secure, efficient, and reliable. This role demands a solid understanding of networking concepts and security practices, making it ideal for someone like David, who would appreciate ensuring his architectural firm's network is both secure and perfectly functioning.
- **Information Security Officer:** This strategic role leads the organization's entire information security strategy and policies, focusing on risk assessment, security measure implementation, and compliance adherence. Sarah, with her leadership abilities and keen interest in security, would find this role fulfilling as it merges technology management with protective strategy implementation.

Advanced and Specialized Career Pathways

- **Penetration Tester (Ethical Hacker):** Penetration Testers, or Ethical Hackers, simulate cyber-attacks to identify and fix system vulnerabilities before they are exploited maliciously. This role suits those who think creatively and possess an in-depth understanding of hacking techniques. Emma, known for her love of challenges and talent for deconstructing systems, would likely excel in this dynamic role.
- **Security Architect:** Responsible for designing and implementing secure network solutions, Security Architects play a critical role in safeguarding an organization's data and systems. The role demands a strategic approach and a comprehensive understanding of cybersecurity principles, which could be a perfect match for David as he seeks to enhance his firm's security protocols.
- **Incident Responder:** These professionals are crucial during a security breach. They are tasked with responding swiftly to mitigate damage and investigate the root causes to prevent future incidents. For Jack, whose strengths lie in maintaining composure under pressure and swiftly navigating complex situations, this role could be highly suitable.
- **Security Consultant:** Security Consultants evaluate and enhance organizational security strategies, making recommendations to strengthen security postures. Sarah, with her adeptness at guiding and teaching, could leverage her skills to assist various organizations in strengthening their defenses against cyber threats.
- **Forensic Analyst:** Specializing in the investigation of cybercrimes, Forensic Analysts gather and analyze digital evidence, often collaborating with law enforcement to trace cybercriminals and understand breach

methodologies. This role, blending cybersecurity knowledge with investigative skills, could fascinate someone deeply interested in the intersection of technology and law enforcement.

Example of the Wilson Family:

The Wilson family could greatly benefit from exploring these diverse cybersecurity roles. David might consider starting with the fundamentals of a Security Analyst to strengthen his business's defenses. Sarah could find her place as a Security Consultant, applying her educational skills in a new context. At the same time, Emma and Jack could pursue their technological passions through roles like Penetration Tester or Incident Responder, aligning with their love for problem-solving and technology.

Cybersecurity careers offer a broad range of opportunities that cater to various interests and expertise levels. From entry-level positions to specialized roles, there's a pathway for everyone in this dynamic field. By exploring these options, you can identify a career that not only matches your skills and passions but also contributes to securing the digital landscape.

7.5 Emerging Job Roles and Opportunities

As technology advances, so too do the career opportunities in the cybersecurity sector. This field continuously gives rise to new roles designed to counteract the latest digital threats and challenges. For anyone inclined toward cybersecurity, whether they are just beginning their career journey or looking to advance, these emerging roles offer exciting opportunities to be at the cutting edge of technological progress. Here is an easy-to-understand guide on some of the most interesting new job roles in cybersecurity, developed for everyone, including families exploring future possibilities like the Wilsons.

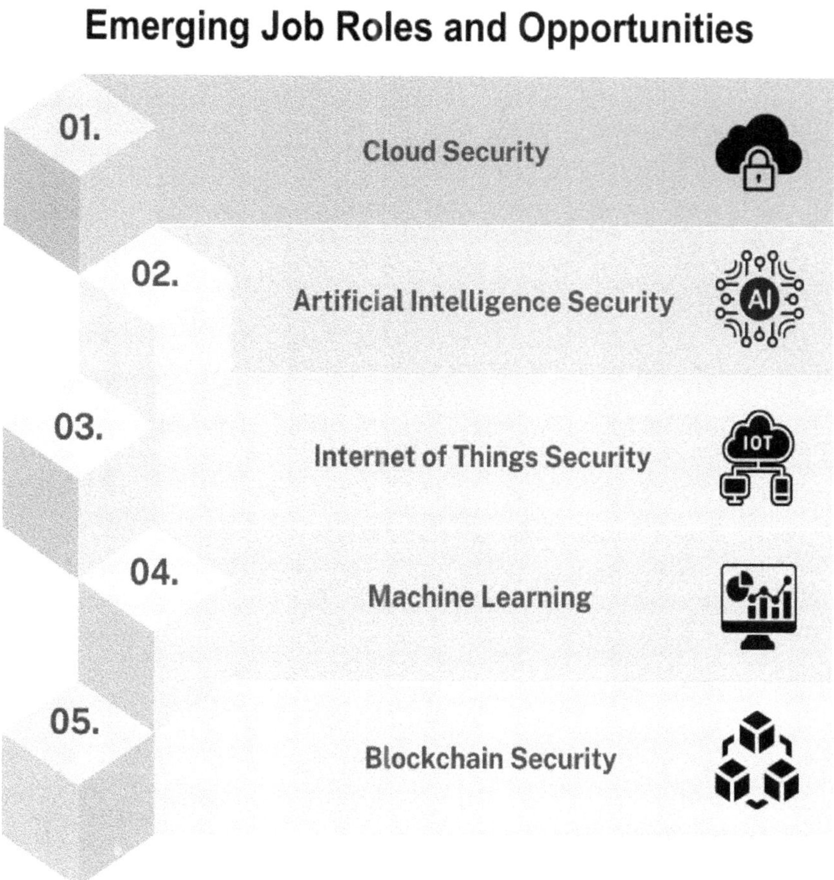

Cloud Security:

The shift towards cloud computing has developed the demand for Cloud Security Specialists. These professionals are crucial in ensuring that cloud platforms—where both personal and professional data like family photos and business operations reside—are robustly secured against unauthorized access and cyber threats.

- **Why It Matters:** As cloud platforms become integral to storing our most precious and critical data, securing these platforms is vital for personal and professional peace of mind.
- **What They Do:** These specialists craft and implement security frameworks for cloud platforms, sharply monitor for any suspicious activities, and strictly ensure adherence to security regulations.

Artificial Intelligence Security:

In an era where AI is revolutionizing industries, AI Security Specialists focus on safeguarding AI systems and utilizing AI to enhance cybersecurity defences.

- **Why It Matters:** AI's role in cybersecurity is becoming increasingly crucial, improving threat detection and response capabilities. However, the security of AI systems themselves is critical to prevent them from becoming cybercriminals' next target.
- **What They Do:** Tasks include developing security protocols for AI systems, employing AI to identify threats, and ensuring AI is used responsibly and securely.

IoT Security:

With the Internet of Things connecting everything from kitchen appliances to industrial equipment to the Internet, securing these devices is more critical than ever.

- **Why It Matters:** As homes and businesses increasingly rely on these connected devices, they also become prime targets for attacks. Adequate security measures are essential to protect against breaches that could invade personal privacy or disrupt business operations.
- **What They Do:** Specialists in this area focus on developing security measures for IoT devices, finding and fixing vulnerabilities, and collaborating with manufacturers to embed security into the design of new devices.

Machine Learning:

Cybersecurity Data Scientists using Machine Learning analyze vast amounts of data to uncover patterns that predict and mitigate cyber threats.

- **Why It Matters:** In a data-driven world, these scientists play a critical role by using big data to predict and prevent attacks before they happen, enhancing proactive security measures.
- **What They Do:** Their work involves analyzing cyber threat data, creating predictive models, and offering insights that help shape more effective security strategies.

Blockchain Security:

As blockchain technology finds its way into various sectors beyond cryptocurrency, securing these systems becomes crucial.

- **Why It Matters:** While blockchain naturally offers certain security advantages, it is not immune to threats. Ensuring the security of blockchain applications is crucial for their adoption and trustworthiness.
- **What They Do:** These professionals are tasked with creating and maintaining the security of blockchain applications, constantly monitoring for potential vulnerabilities, and safeguarding transaction integrity.

Example of the Wilson Family:

For the Wilsons, these emerging roles open doors to exciting and relevant opportunities. David could look into how IoT Security Specialists might secure his firm's smart devices. Sarah, with her analytical skills, might find a new role as a Cybersecurity Data Scientist. At the same time, Emma and Jack could delve into roles like AI Security Specialists or Blockchain Security Specialists, matching their tech-savvy interests with impactful careers.

The field of cybersecurity is dynamic and evolving, offering a range of opportunities for every skill level and interest. From foundational roles to specializations, there is a path for everyone in this dynamic field. Understanding these roles not only helps align one's career aspirations with one's skills and interests but also contributes to a safer digital world.

Navigating the changing landscape of cybersecurity reveals a wealth of opportunities, for those to delve into this field. From entry-level positions like Security Analysts and IT Support Specialists to roles such as Penetration Testers and AI Security Specialists, cybersecurity offers a diverse range of career paths. Each role plays a part in strengthening our world protecting personal, professional and national data from constantly evolving threats.

The Wilson family serves as an example for those considering an experience in cybersecurity. David could improve security measures at his architecture firm by taking on roles tailored to cybersecurity, while Sarah's background makes her well-suited to promoting cybersecurity awareness through education. For enthusiasts like Emma and Jack, the field presents a range of opportunities, from ethical hacking to mastering cloud security.

Embarking on a career in cybersecurity involves acquiring skills and certifications. It begins with certifications like CompTIA Security+ and progresses to ones such as CISSP or CEH, each building upon the previous one to establish a strong knowledge base and demonstrate expertise to potential employers. In this field, ongoing learning and staying up to date with trends and threats are essential for professional development and success.

Furthermore, the rise of roles like Cloud Security Experts, IoT Security Specialists, and Blockchain Security Professionals highlights the importance of adapting to technologies and evolving security threats. These positions not only offer challenges but also play a crucial role in shaping the future landscape of cybersecurity.

To sum up, choosing a path in cybersecurity offers both fulfilment and is essential in our technology-driven society. By exploring career options, acquiring the required skills and certifications, and keeping up with emerging opportunities, individuals can establish an impactful career in this field. Looking ahead, there is a growing demand for cybersecurity experts, ensuring a promising career trajectory for those willing to undertake this journey.

Chapter 8: Cybersecurity Professions and Certifications

8.1 Introduction to Cybersecurity Professions and Certifications

As digital landscapes expand, so too does the need for competent cybersecurity professionals. This field provides a wealth of career possibilities suitable for individuals at any point in their career pathway, from beginners to seasoned experts. This chapter is designed to offer a thorough overview of the range of opportunities in cybersecurity, detailing both the roles available and the certifications that can speed up success in this industry.

For households like the Wilsons, gaining an understanding of the diverse pathways within cybersecurity can lead to productive and prosperous career options. Whether you are a student mapping out your future, a professional, or someone keen on widening your cybersecurity understanding, this chapter will accompany you through the fundamental roles and requisite certifications in the industry.

- CompTIA Security+
- GIAC Information Security Fundamentals (GISF)
- Certified in Cybersecurity (CC)
- eLearnSecurity Junior Penetration Tester (eJPT)
- Certified Ethical Hacker (CEH) ANSI
- CompTIA Cybersecurity Analyst (CySA+)
- Cisco CyberOps Associate (CBROPS)
- Blue Team Level 1 (BTL1) Junior Security Operations
- GIAC Security Essentials (GSEC)
- Google Cybersecurity Professional Certificate

The Vital Role of Cybersecurity Experts

Professionals in cybersecurity are essential in maintaining the security of our digital frameworks. They shield sensitive data, counteract cyber threats, and maintain the integrity and accessibility of information. As cyber threats grow in complexity, the urgency for proficient cybersecurity experts becomes more evident. These experts are often the unsung champions who ensure the safety of our digital domains.

Understanding Cybersecurity Certifications

In the world of cybersecurity, certifications are critical. They act as approvals of your skills and knowledge, validating your expertise, underscoring your dedication to the field, and supporting your standing with prospective employers. These certifications vary from entry-level to advanced, helping in the enhancement of your career opportunities and keeping you up-to-date on the latest cybersecurity evolutions.

Example of the Wilson Family

Consider David, who manages an architectural firm, and his interest in how diverse cybersecurity roles could strengthen his business operations. Sarah, a teacher, might investigate how certain certifications could allow her to incorporate cybersecurity fundamentals into her teachings, thereby preparing her students for future industry roles. Meanwhile, young Emma and Jack could start with basic certifications and gradually move towards more complex ones as they refine their skills.

Throughout this chapter, we will learn about the variety of professions within the cybersecurity landscape and the certifications that support these careers. We will explore the skills and qualifications necessary for each role, the routes to obtaining these certifications, and the career opportunities they unlock. By the chapter's end, you will possess a comprehensive understanding of the diverse career options in cybersecurity and the actionable steps you can undertake to either start or advance your career in this dynamic, rapidly evolving sector.

8.2 Entry-Level Cybersecurity Professions

For those undertaking a cybersecurity career, entry-level positions present an ideal starting opportunity. These roles lay the foundation with essential experience and knowledge, preparing individuals for further advancement. This section will explain some general entry-level cybersecurity roles, emphasizing the skills required, job duties, and how to begin your career.

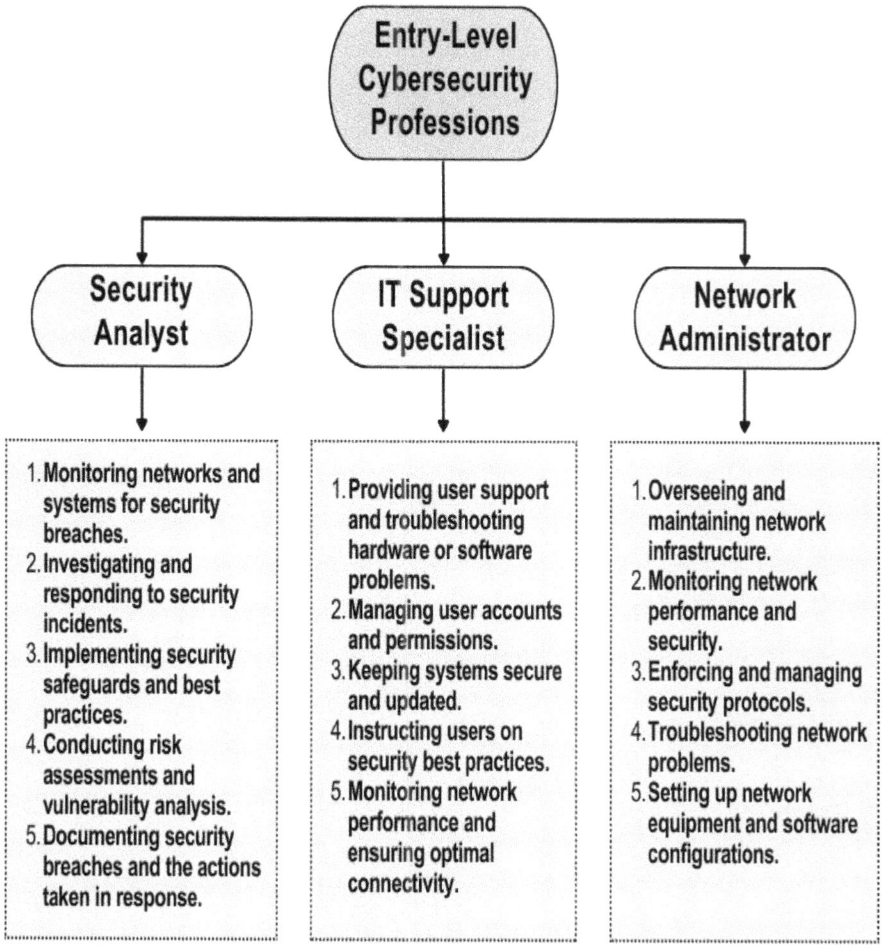

Security Analyst

A Security Analyst, or Information Security Analyst, is vital in defending an organization's digital assets. Their work includes monitoring for security breaches, investigating security events, and initiating preventive measures to prevent future incidents. They often serve as the first line of defense in an organization's cybersecurity strategy.

Skills and Qualifications

To succeed as a Security Analyst, one should have a strong awareness of networking, system administration, and security protocols. Essential skills include analytical thinking, careful attention to detail, and problem-solving capabilities. Typically, a bachelor's degree in cyber security, information technology, or a related discipline is required, though relevant certifications can also enhance one's qualifications.

Job Responsibilities

- Monitoring networks and systems for security breaches.
- Investigating and responding to security incidents.
- Implementing security safeguards and best practices.
- Conducting risk assessments and vulnerability analysis.
- Documenting security breaches and the actions taken in response.

Pathway to Becoming a Security Analyst

Starting with foundational certifications like CompTIA Security+ is a solid entry point. Practical experience through internships or entry-level IT roles can also be invaluable.

IT Support Specialist

An IT Support Specialist handles technical support within an organization. While this role encompasses broader IT duties, it provides a strong foundation in technical skills and security awareness. IT Support Specialists typically address system issues, manage user permissions, and ensure that systems are secure and current.

Skills and Qualifications

Essential qualities include comprehensive technical knowledge, excellent communication abilities, and a customer-focused approach. A degree in information technology or a similar field is advantageous, with certifications such as CompTIA A+ serving as proof of technical expertise.

Job Responsibilities

- Providing user support and troubleshooting hardware or software problems.
- Managing user accounts and permissions.
- Keeping systems secure and updated.
- Instructing users on security best practices.
- Monitoring network performance and ensuring optimal connectivity.

Pathway to Becoming an IT Support Specialist

Earning a CompTIA A+ certification and gathering experience in technical support are effective steps toward progressing into more specialized cybersecurity roles.

Network Administrator

A Network Administrator oversees an organization's network infrastructure, ensuring security, efficiency, and reliability. This role is crucial for implementing and maintaining protective measures to safeguard the network from unauthorized access and cyber threats.

Skills and Qualifications

A deep understanding of networking protocols, along with hardware and software knowledge, is crucial. Attention to detail and strong problem-solving abilities are also vital. A degree in cyber security or a related area is typical, supplemented by certifications like CompTIA Network+ or Cisco's CCNA.

Job Responsibilities

- Overseeing and maintaining network infrastructure.
- Monitoring network performance and security.
- Enforcing and managing security protocols.
- Troubleshooting network problems.
- Setting up network equipment and software configurations.

Pathway to Becoming a Network Administrator

Acquiring certifications such as CompTIA Network+ or Cisco CCNA and gaining hands-on experience through internships or entry-level roles can set the stage for a career as a Network Administrator.

Example of the Wilson Family

For the Wilsons, these entry-level positions offer a definite pathway into the cybersecurity field. David could look into hiring a Security Analyst to secure his architectural firm's sensitive data. Sarah might introduce her students to these roles by incorporating basic cybersecurity principles into her lessons. Emma and Jack could start their journey with certifications like CompTIA Security+ or CompTIA A+, establishing a robust foundation for their future in cybersecurity.

Entry-level roles in cybersecurity serve as gateways to impactful and fulfilling careers. Starting as a Security Analyst, IT Support Specialist, or Network Administrator allows you to acquire the fundamental skills and experience necessary for career advancement. With the appropriate credentials and a commitment to lifelong learning, you can develop a successful career dedicated to safeguarding our digital realms against cyber threats.

8.3 Intermediate Cybersecurity Professions

As your career in cybersecurity grows from the foundational levels, the next step involves intermediate roles, where specialized knowledge and a deeper awareness of cybersecurity concepts become essential. This section will cover typical mid-level cybersecurity positions, emphasizing the necessary skills, typical responsibilities, and the ways to enter these roles.

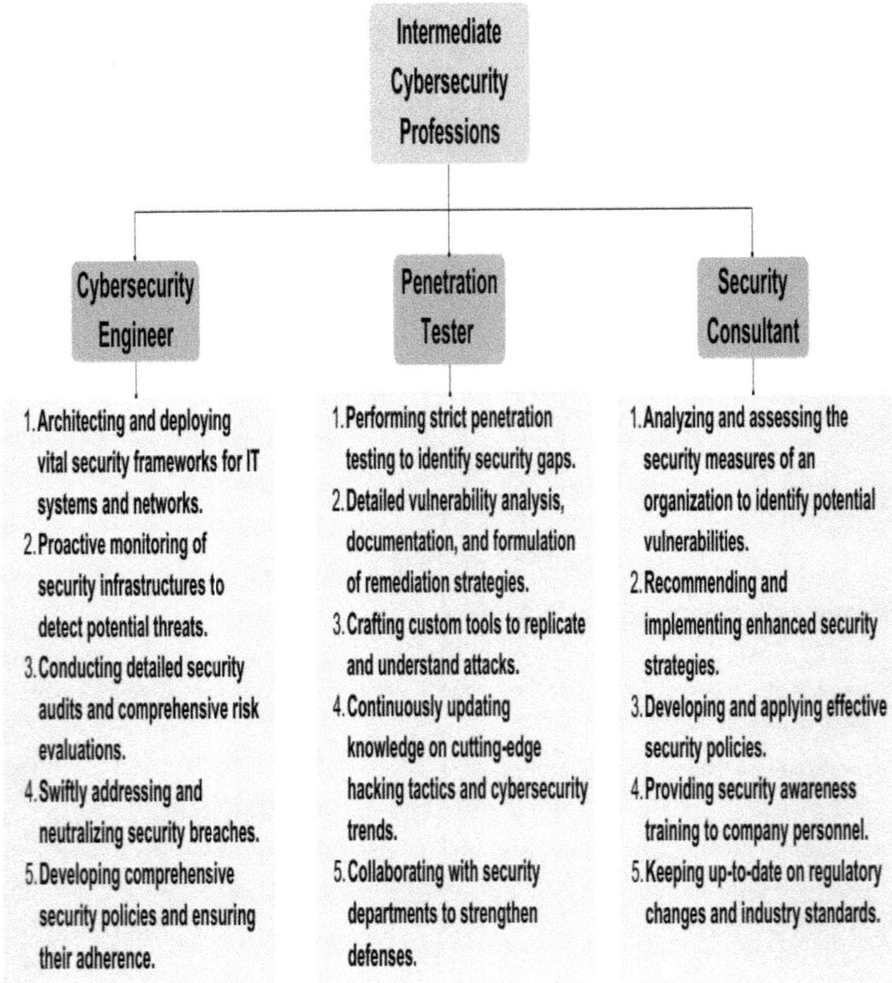

Cybersecurity Engineer

Tasked with the design, implementation, and management of security defenses, Cybersecurity Engineers ensure the effective protection of organizational networks and systems. This role demands a deep understanding of traditional security practices and modern technological solutions, coupled with a strategic response capability to complex security issues.

Skills and Qualifications

Candidates for this role typically possess a solid IT background with a keen understanding of cybersecurity techniques, including expertise in firewalls, VPNs, IDS/IPS systems, and encryption techniques. Beyond technical skills, analytical thinking and proficient problem-solving are crucial. A bachelor's degree in fields like cyber security or information technology is usually expected, enhanced by certifications such as the Certified Information Systems Security Professional (CISSP) or Certified Ethical Hacker (CEH).

Job Responsibilities

- Architecting and deploying vital security frameworks for IT systems and networks.
- Proactive monitoring of security infrastructures to detect potential threats.
- Conducting detailed security audits and comprehensive risk evaluations.
- Swiftly addressing and neutralizing security breaches.
- Developing comprehensive security policies and ensuring their adherence.

Pathway to Becoming a Cybersecurity Engineer

Progressing from foundational roles, pursuing relevant professional certifications, and continually updating oneself on emerging security technologies and threats are essential for advancing into this role.

Penetration Tester (Ethical Hacker)

Ethical Hackers, or Penetration Testers, undertake simulated cyber-attacks against systems, networks, and applications to identify and fix security weaknesses. This position demands a sophisticated understanding of offensive security tactics and cyber attackers' mindsets.

Skills and Qualifications

Technical skills in networking, command over operating systems, and scripting (in languages like Python or Bash) are essential. A deep familiarity with common exploitation techniques and vulnerability assessments is expected. Professional certifications such as the Certified Ethical Hacker (CEH) or Offensive Security Certified Professional (OSCP) are valuable assets.

Job Responsibilities

- Performing strict penetration testing to identify security gaps.
- Detailed vulnerability analysis, documentation, and formulation of remediation strategies.
- Crafting custom tools to replicate and understand attacks.
- Continuously updating knowledge on cutting-edge hacking tactics and cybersecurity trends.
- Collaborating with security departments to strengthen defenses.

Pathway to Becoming a Penetration Tester

Initiating with a solid foundation in IT or cybersecurity, building experience in security roles, and achieving specialized certifications like CEH or OSCP are essential steps.

Security Consultant

Security Consultants offer strategic advice and develop solutions to strengthen organizational security postures. This role involves a thorough evaluation of current security protocols, identifying vulnerabilities, and suggesting vital improvements.

Skills and Qualifications

An extensive understanding of cybersecurity fundamentals, risk analysis, and protective frameworks is necessary. Effective communication and strong analytical capabilities are also required. Credentials like a bachelor's degree in a related field and certifications such as CISSP or Certified Information Security Manager (CISM) are advantageous.

Job Responsibilities

- Analyzing and assessing the security measures of an organization to identify potential vulnerabilities.
- Recommending and implementing enhanced security strategies.
- Developing and applying effective security policies.
- Providing security awareness training to company personnel.
- Keeping up-to-date on regulatory changes and industry standards.

Pathway to Becoming a Security Consultant

A pathway through various cybersecurity roles, gaining relevant certifications, and developing effective consulting skills are vital for success in this capacity.

Example of the Wilson Family

For the Wilsons, moving into these intermediate roles offers a chance to deepen their engagement with the cybersecurity field. David could consider bringing on a Cybersecurity Engineer to advance his firm's security capabilities. Sarah might inspire her students towards careers in ethical hacking by introducing them to basic concepts and practices. For Emma and Jack, pursuing further certifications such as CEH or CISSP could be a natural progression, enriching their potential in the industry.

Intermediate cybersecurity roles offer opportunities to specialize and handle complex challenges within the industry. Roles like Cybersecurity Engineer, Penetration Tester, and Security Consultant require advanced skills and provide rewarding career paths. Through continued experience, acquiring relevant certifications, and a dedication to lifelong learning, you can ascend in your career and significantly impact the cybersecurity landscape.

8.4 Advanced Cybersecurity Professions

As cybersecurity professionals earn extensive experience and refine their expertise, they often progress to more specialized and senior-level roles. These advanced positions demand a deep understanding of complex security concepts, substantial hands-on experience, and typically leadership abilities. This section investigates some of the notable advanced cybersecurity professions, detailing the requisite skills, job responsibilities, and pathways to ascend to these roles.

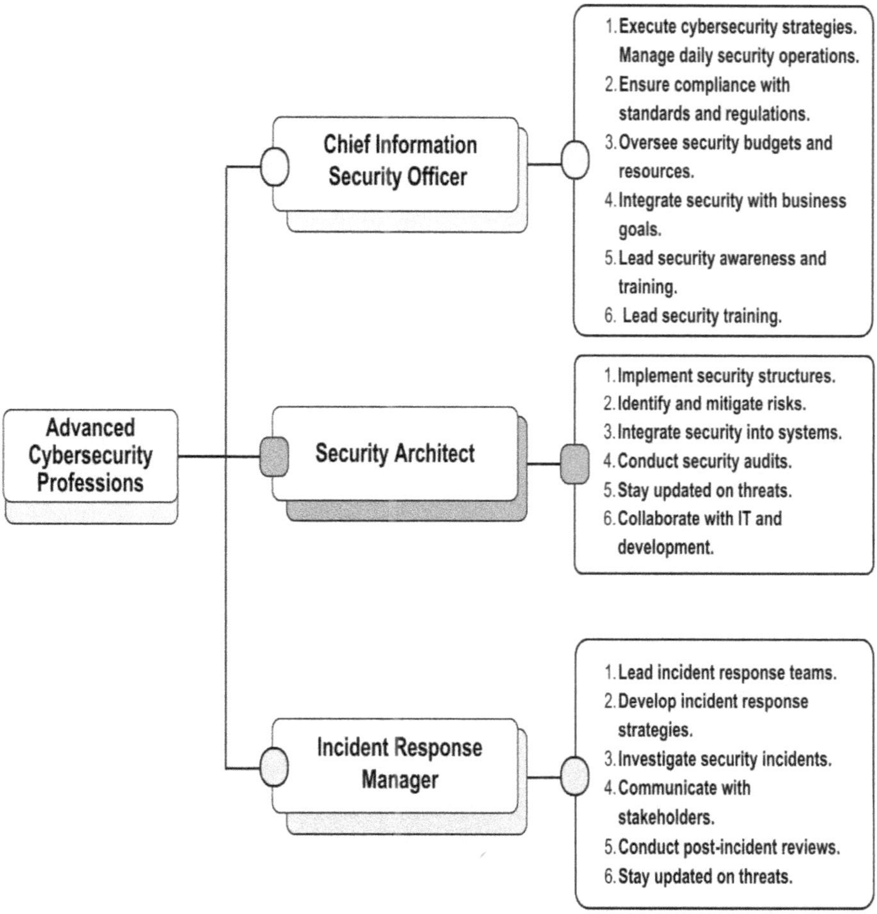

Chief Information Security Officer (CISO)

The Chief Information Security Officer (CISO) is a prominent senior executive who directs an organization's entire cybersecurity strategy and its execution. This role is essential in managing security policies, directing security operations, and maintaining compliance with regulatory frameworks. Additionally, the CISO is integral to incident response and risk management strategies.

Skills and Qualifications

A forthcoming CISO must have a significant background in cybersecurity management and risk assessment, paired with professional strategic planning capabilities. Exceptional leadership and communication skills are necessary, as the role involves extensive collaboration with other executives and departments. Preferred qualifications include a master's degree in cybersecurity, information technology, or a related discipline. Professional certifications such as Certified

Information Systems Security Professional (CISSP) and Certified Information Security Manager (CISM) are also valuable.

Job Responsibilities

- Formulating and executing the organization's cybersecurity strategies.
- Managing daily security operations and incident management.
- Ensuring adherence to industry standards and regulatory mandates.
- Managing security budgets and resource allocation.
- Collaborating with executive leadership to integrate security with overall business objectives.
- Leading initiatives for security awareness and staff training.

Pathway to Becoming a CISO

A career pathway starting from security management positions, enriched with extensive field experience, advanced degrees, and professional certifications, is crucial. Developing vital leadership and strategic planning skills is also vital.

Security Architect

The Security Architect is tasked with designing and executing comprehensive security systems to safeguard an organization's IT infrastructure. This role entails evaluating security risks, crafting security frameworks, and ensuring the integration of security measures within all technological aspects of the organization.

Skills and Qualifications

Security Architects require an in-depth understanding of security protocols, network architecture, and software development processes. Analytical skills and the ability to solve complex problems are essential. Educational qualifications typically include a bachelor's or master's degree in computer science or a related field, with certifications like CISSP, Certified Information Systems Auditor (CISA), and Certified Information Security Manager (CISM) providing additional benefits.

Job Responsibilities

- Architecting and implementing security structures and frameworks.
- Identifying and mitigating security risks.
- Integrating security measures into system development and operational procedures.
- Conducting comprehensive security audits and assessments.
- Keeping up-to-date with the latest security technologies and threats.
- Collaborating with IT and development teams to strengthen security measures.

Pathway to Becoming a Security Architect

Experience in network security, system administration, and security analysis, coupled with relevant certifications, make the way into a Security Architect role. Advanced academic qualifications and a commitment to continual learning are also beneficial.

Incident Response Manager

An Incident Response Manager works to detect, respond to, and recover from cybersecurity incidents. This role involves directing the incident response teams, developing response strategies, and ensuring efficient and effective incident management.

Skills and Qualifications

Necessary skills for an Incident Response Manager include strong analytical capabilities and organizational prowess, alongside extensive experience in incident detection and response. An in-depth knowledge of network and system security is crucial. Typically, a bachelor's degree in cybersecurity, information technology, or a related field is required, with certifications such as CISSP or Certified Incident Handler (GCIH) enhancing credentials.

Job Responsibilities

- Leading and coordinating the incident response teams.
- Developing and implementing comprehensive incident response strategies.
- Investigating and analyzing security incidents.
- Communicating with stakeholders during and following incidents.
- Conducting reviews post-incident to refine response strategies.
- Staying informed about emerging threats and response practices.

Pathway to Becoming an Incident Response Manager

Foundational experience in security analysis and incident response, along with relevant certifications and developed leadership and communication skills, are essential for advancing into this role.

Example of the Wilson Family

For the Wilsons, these advanced roles provide a glimpse into the benefits of cybersecurity career paths. David might envision himself in the strategic role of a CISO, ensuring his architectural firm's security is tightly aligned with its business goals. Sarah could motivate her students to consider a career as a Security Architect, emphasizing the significance of secure design in technology applications. Emma and Jack, who are deepening their interests in cybersecurity, might see the role of an Incident Response Manager as both dynamic and challenging.

Advanced cybersecurity roles signify the standard of professional development in the field, requiring years of experience, specialized education, and dedication. Positions like CISO, Security Architect, and Incident Response Manager necessitate advanced skills and offer substantial opportunities for leadership and impact within the cybersecurity domain. By continually enhancing their knowledge, acquiring pertinent certifications, and shining strategic and leadership skills, cybersecurity professionals can attain these respectable roles and contribute significantly to the security and resilience of their organizations.

8.5 Essential Certifications for Beginners

Starting a career in cybersecurity can be challenging, but earning the right certifications can provide a solid foundation and guide you towards success. For newcomers, these certifications require essential knowledge and skills that employers highly value. This section highlights some of the most crucial certifications for those embarking on a cybersecurity career.

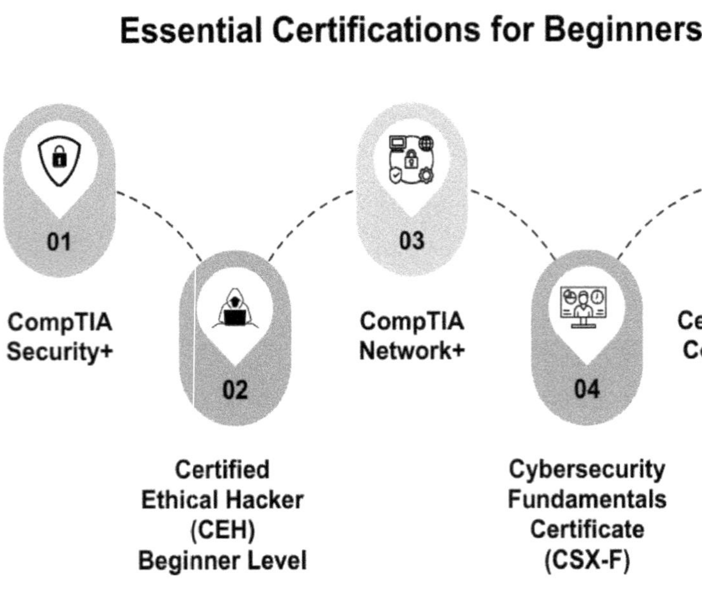

CompTIA Security+

CompTIA Security+ is often considered an entry-level certification that encompasses the core principles of network security and risk management. It serves as an excellent starting point for individuals new to cybersecurity.

Skills and Knowledge

- Knowing fundamental security concepts and best practices.
- Familiarity with network security, cryptography, and risk management.
- Capability to identify and mitigate security threats.

Benefits

- Widely recognized by employers as a foundational certification.
- Prepares individuals for more advanced cybersecurity roles and certifications.
- Offers a broad overview of cybersecurity, providing a thorough introduction.

Example of the Wilson Family

Emma and Jack could begin their cybersecurity journey with CompTIA Security+, acquiring a solid understanding of essential security concepts that will form the basis for their future studies and careers.

Certified Ethical Hacker (CEH) – Beginner Level

The Certified Ethical Hacker (CEH) certification is designed for those interested in learning to think like a hacker to better secure systems. It covers fundamental hacking techniques and tools, making it suitable for beginners.

Skills and Knowledge:

- Basic understanding of hacking tools and procedures.
- Understanding of penetration testing and vulnerability assessment.
- Ability to recognize and exploit common security vulnerabilities.

Benefits

- Provides practical experience with hacking tools.
- Enhances understanding of cyber-attack methods.
- Prepares individuals for roles in ethical hacking and penetration testing.

Example of the Wilson Family

Jack, who is fascinated by the technical aspects of cybersecurity, might find the CEH certification engaging and rewarding, learning to secure systems by understanding how they are attacked.

CompTIA Network+

CompTIA Network+ is another foundational certification focusing on networking concepts and practices. It is ideal for beginners aiming to build a strong understanding of network infrastructure and operations.

Skills and Knowledge

- Understanding of network protocols and configurations.
- Knowledge of network security and troubleshooting.
- Ability to manage and maintain network infrastructure.

Benefits

- Provides a solid foundation in networking, crucial for many cybersecurity roles.
- Prepares individuals for more specialized certifications in network security.
- Recognized by employers across IT and cybersecurity sectors.

Example of the Wilson Family

David, who operates an architectural firm, might consider CompTIA Network+ to enhance his knowledge of network security and ensure his firm's network is secure.

Cybersecurity Fundamentals Certificate (CSX-F)

The CSX-F certification is designed for individuals starting their journey in cybersecurity. It provides foundational knowledge and understanding of essential security concepts and practices.

Skills and Knowledge

- Basic understanding of cybersecurity principles and frameworks.
- Knowledge of cybersecurity architecture, concepts, and techniques.
- Ability to apply fundamental cybersecurity skills in various scenarios.

Benefits

- Provides a solid foundation for further cybersecurity certifications and career advancement.
- Enhances comprehension of core cybersecurity practices.
- Recognized globally by employers and industry professionals as a valuable entry-level certification.

Example of the Wilson Family

Sarah, with her educational background, could pursue the CSX-F certification to integrate cybersecurity topics into her curriculum and prepare her students for future cybersecurity careers.

Certified Secure Computer User (CSCU)

The CSCU certification is tailored for individuals who want to understand the basics of computer and network security, making it ideal for non-technical users who need to secure their personal and professional digital environments.

Skills and Knowledge

- Basic understanding of computer security threats and best practices.
- Knowledge of secure browsing, email security, and data protection techniques.

- Ability to implement fundamental security measures to protect personal and organizational data.

Benefits

- Provides practical knowledge for secure computing in everyday use.
- Enhances awareness and ability to protect against common cyber threats.
- Recognized by employers as a valuable certification for all employees, regardless of technical background.

Example of the Wilson Family

Emma, who favors a hands-on learning approach, could benefit from CSCU by acquiring practical experience in securing her computer and online activities and effectively protecting her personal information.

Essential certifications for beginners offer the foundational knowledge and skills necessary for a successful career in cybersecurity. Certifications such as CompTIA Security+, CEH, CompTIA Network+, CSX-F, and CSCU provide valuable insights and practical experience, preparing individuals for various roles in the cybersecurity field. For the Wilson family and others, these certifications can open doors to exciting career opportunities and lay a strong foundation for continuous learning and advancement in cybersecurity.

8.6 Intermediate Certifications

When advancing in your cybersecurity career, intermediate certifications are important factors in deepening your expertise and preparing for higher-level roles. These certifications expand upon basic knowledge, focusing on specialized areas of cybersecurity to prepare you with the skills needed to address complex security challenges. This section discusses some essential intermediate certifications for cybersecurity professionals.

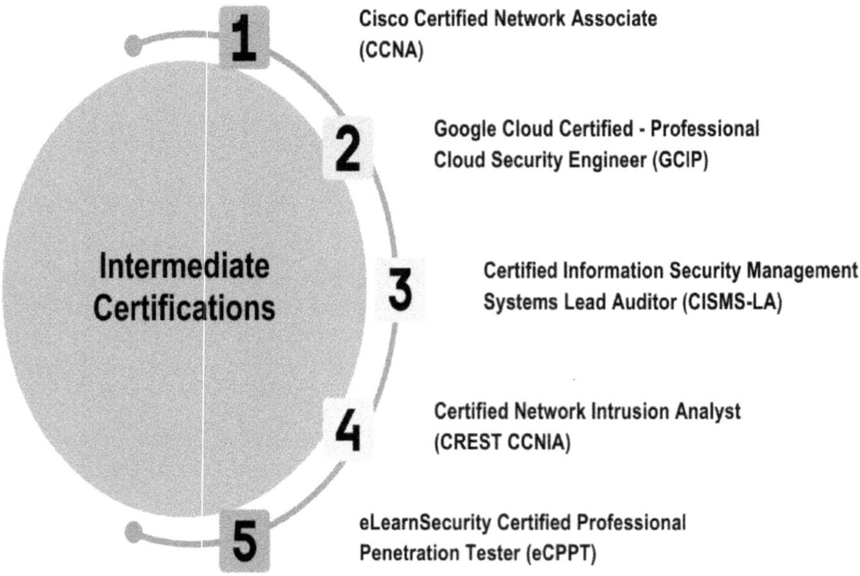

Cisco Certified Network Associate (CCNA)

The CCNA certification provides foundational networking knowledge and skills, making it valuable for cybersecurity professionals who focus on network security.

Skills and Knowledge

- Broad understanding of networking principles and protocols.
- Proficiency in configuring, managing, and troubleshooting network devices.
- Capability to implement and maintain network security measures.

Benefits

- Globally acknowledged and respected among employers.
- Facilitates advancement to specialized cybersecurity and networking positions.
- Signals a high degree of expertise and dedication to network security.

Example of the Wilson Family

David, aiming to boost cybersecurity within his architectural practice, could benefit from the CCNA to gain a more in-depth understanding of vital network security practices, thus enhancing his firm's protective measures.

Google Cloud Certified - Professional Cloud Security Engineer (GCIP)

The GCIP is designed for professionals responsible for designing and managing secure cloud infrastructure on the Google Cloud Platform.

Skills and Knowledge

Insight into cloud security architecture, best practices, and compliance.

Skills to design, develop, and manage secure cloud solutions.

Understanding of regulatory compliance and security policies for cloud environments.

Benefits

- Internationally recognized, strengthening your professional reputation.
- Confirms your capability to secure and manage cloud infrastructure.
- Prepares you for advanced roles in cloud security.

Example of the Wilson Family

Sarah, who wants to incorporate cloud security into her teaching, could adopt GCIP to deepen her understanding of cloud security management and administration.

Certified Information Security Management Systems Lead Auditor (CISMS-LA)

The CISMS-LA certification is targeted at professionals responsible for auditing and managing information security management systems (ISMS) within an organization.

Skills and Knowledge

- Comprehensive knowledge of ISMS audit processes and principles.
- Understanding of ISO/IEC 27001 standards and compliance requirements.
- Ability to lead ISMS audit teams and evaluate security controls.

Benefits

- A leading credential globally recognized for ISMS auditors.
- Enhances qualifications for roles in IT auditing, compliance, and risk management.
- Demonstrates proficiency in managing and assessing ISMS effectively.

Example of the Wilson Family

David committed to ensuring his firm meets industry standards and regulations, could explore CISMS-LA to acquire the necessary skills for effective ISMS auditing and risk management.

Certified Network Intrusion Analyst (CREST CCNIA)

The CREST CCNIA certification focuses on advanced network intrusion analysis, making it ideal for professionals specializing in identifying and responding to network security incidents.

Skills and Knowledge

- Practical skills in network intrusion detection and analysis.
- Ability to identify and respond to network security incidents effectively.
- Knowledge of advanced intrusion detection tools and techniques.

Benefits

- Valued by employers for roles requiring advanced network security analysis capabilities.
- Provides practical experience with sophisticated intrusion detection methods.
- Prepares for specialized positions in network security and incident response.

Example of the Wilson Family

Jack who is passionate about network security, might find advancing to the CREST CCNIA certification enriches his technical skills and opens up specialized career opportunities.

eLearnSecurity Certified Professional Penetration Tester (eCPPT)

The eCPPT certification is respected for its focus on practical, hands-on penetration testing skills, perfect for professionals aiming to excel in offensive security and ethical hacking.

Skills and Knowledge

- Practical skills in penetration testing tools and techniques.
- Ability to identify and exploit vulnerabilities to conduct thorough security evaluations.
- Knowledge of scripting and programming for automated security testing.

Benefits

- Acknowledged as a rigorous and significant certification in the industry.
- Provides extensive, hands-on experience in penetration testing.
- Prepares for advanced roles in offensive security and ethical hacking.

Example of the Wilson Family

Jack, willing to deepen his penetration testing expertise, could pursue eCPPT to enhance his practical skills and qualify for advanced positions in ethical hacking.

Intermediate certifications are crucial for advancing in the cybersecurity field. Certifications like CCNA, GCIP, CISMS-LA, CREST CCNIA, and eCPPT provide essential insights and hands-on experience, preparing you for more sophisticated security roles and challenges. For the Wilson family and others, these certifications can significantly enhance their expertise and open up new career opportunities in cybersecurity.

8.7 Advanced Certifications

For cybersecurity professionals aiming for advancement in their careers, advanced certifications deliver the specialized knowledge and capabilities required for leadership and expert roles. These certificates are developed for those with considerable experience in the field who are looking to deepen their expertise and demonstrate their commitment to the highest professional standards. This section outlines some of the most advanced certifications available.

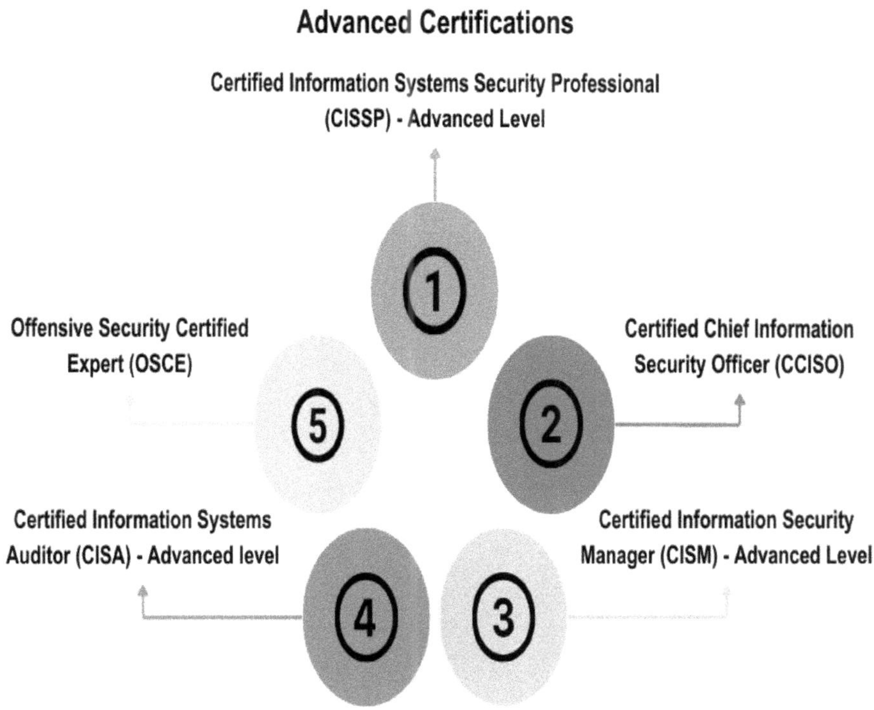

Certified Information Systems Security Professional (CISSP) – Advance Level

The CISSP is globally acclaimed as one of the top certifications in the cybersecurity domain. It confirms a professional's competence in creating, implementing, and managing top-level cybersecurity programs.

Skills and Knowledge

- Extensive knowledge of cybersecurity architecture, management, and operations.
- Expertise in areas like security and risk management, asset protection, security engineering, and network security.
- Capacity to manage and direct comprehensive security programs and initiatives.

Benefits

- Highly respected by both employers and industry peers.
- Opens pathways to high-level positions, such as Chief Information Security Officer (CISO) and Security Director.
- Signifies a dedication to ongoing professional development and adherence to rigid cybersecurity standards.

Example of the Wilson Family

David, having refined his cybersecurity skills, might pursue the CISSP to validate his expertise and advance into leadership roles within the industry.

Certified Chief Information Security Officer (CCISO)

Designed for senior-level information security executives, the CCISO certification focuses on governance, risk management, and the strategic management of information security at the executive level.

Skills and Knowledge

- In-depth knowledge of information security governance and risk management.
- Skills in strategic planning, financial management, and vendor relations.
- Competence in leading and managing an organization's information security at the executive level.

Benefits

- Recognized worldwide as an exclusive certification for information security leaders.
- Bolsters qualifications for top executive roles like CISO, CIO, and Security Executive.

- Validates the capability to align security strategies with business objectives and oversee complex security frameworks.

Example of the Wilson Family

David, desiring to ascend to an executive position, could benefit from the CCISO to enhance his strategic and leadership skills, positioning him for relevant roles.

Certified Information Security Manager (CISM) – Advance Level

The CISM certification is aimed at those who manage and govern an enterprise's information security, making it ideal for professionals who manage security programs.

Skills and Knowledge

- Comprehensive understanding of information security governance, risk management, and incident response.
- Proficiency in developing and administering information security strategies.
- Ability to accompany information security plans with business objectives.

Benefits

- Widely recognized among employers and industry colleagues.
- Prepares candidates for senior management roles in information security.
- Demonstrates deep expertise in managing and governing an information security program.

Example of the Wilson Family

Sarah, looking to merge cybersecurity management into her career, could find the CISM certification beneficial in developing her capabilities to manage security programs effectively.

Certified Information Systems Auditor (CISA) – Advance Level

The CISA is invaluable for those specializing in IT auditing and compliance. It is targeted at professionals charged with auditing, controlling, and overseeing an organization's IT and business systems.

Skills and Knowledge

- Deep understanding of IT audit processes, governance, and management.
- Expertise in evaluating and managing IT risks and controls.
- Skill in ensuring adherence to industry standards and regulatory demands.

Benefits

- Recognized globally as a leading certification for IT auditors.
- Enhances credentials for senior roles in IT auditing, compliance, and risk management.

- Confirms the ability to assess and oversee IT and business systems effectively.

Example of the Wilson Family

David, who is focused on ensuring his firm meets industry regulations, might consider the CISA to increase his capabilities in auditing and risk management.

Offensive Security Certified Expert (OSCE)

The OSCE is renowned for its rigid approach to penetration testing and offensive security, making it one of the most challenging and respected certifications in these fields.

Skills and Knowledge

- Advanced expertise in penetration testing tools and strategies.
- Proficiency in identifying vulnerabilities and executing comprehensive security evaluations.
- Capability to develop custom exploits and perform sophisticated attack simulations.

Benefits

- Respected by employers as a strict and vital certification.
- Offers extensive practical experience in advanced penetration testing.
- Equips candidates for expert roles in offensive security and ethical hacking.

Example of the Wilson Family

Jack, willing to master advanced penetration testing, might pursue the OSCE to further his skills and qualify for expert-level roles in offensive security.

Advanced certifications provide the specialized knowledge and skills essential for excelling in leadership and expert positions within cybersecurity. Credentials such as CISSP, CCISO, CISM, CISA, and OSCE provide valuable insights and hands-on experience, equipping professionals for the most demanding and rewarding roles in the industry. For the Wilson family and others, these certifications can significantly elevate their careers and enhance their ability to impact their organizations' security strategies.

8.8 Specialized Certifications

In the rapidly evolving field of cybersecurity, having specialized certifications and skills is crucial for those aiming to focus on particular areas within this sector. Such certifications offer precise knowledge and capabilities, equipping individuals to excel in specialized roles and address distinct security challenges. This section discusses some of the vital specialized certifications and skills critical in cybersecurity.

Specialized Certifications

1. Certified Cloud Security Professional (CCSP)
2. ISA/IEC 62443 Cybersecurity Expert (IC33E)
3. GIAC Certified Forensic Analyst (GCFA)
4. Offensive Security Wireless Professional (OSWP)

Certified Cloud Security Professional (CCSP)

As cloud services become more prominent, possessing a Certified Cloud Security Professional (CCSP) certification is vital for those in charge of cloud security. This credential verifies expertise in the domains of cloud security design, operations, and management.

Skills and Knowledge

- Comprehensive understanding of cloud technology and associated security challenges.
- Skilled in safeguarding cloud infrastructures, data, and applications.
- Capable of managing cloud security practices and maintaining regulatory compliance.

Benefits

- Widely acknowledged as a leading cloud security certification.
- Equips professionals for roles in cloud security planning and oversight.
- Demonstrates your proficiency in managing sophisticated cloud environments.

Example of the Wilson Family

David, who manages cloud solutions for his architectural firm, might find CCSP invaluable for increasing his ability to secure cloud setups and safeguard data.

ISA/IEC 62443 Cybersecurity Expert (IC33E)

The IC33E certification focuses on the cybersecurity of industrial automation and control systems (IACS), essential for professionals working in sectors such as energy, manufacturing, and critical infrastructure.

Skills and Knowledge

- Thorough understanding of ISA/IEC 62443 standards and their application.
- Expertise in designing and implementing security measures for industrial control systems.
- Skilled in assessing and mitigating cyber risks in critical infrastructure environments.

Benefits

- Acknowledged as a significant certification in industrial cybersecurity.
- Prepares individuals for roles in critical infrastructure and industrial control system security.
- Confirms your expertise in securing IACS and adhering to international standards.

Example of the Wilson Family

David, who is involved in projects that include industrial control systems, would benefit from IC33E in ensuring the security of these systems from cyber threats.

GIAC Certified Forensic Analyst (GCFA)

The GCFA certification, which concentrates on digital forensics and incident response, is suited for professionals who investigate and manage security incidents.

Skills and Knowledge

- Advanced knowledge of digital forensics and incident handling techniques.
- Proficient in analyzing digital evidence and pinpointing security breaches.
- Capable of conducting detailed forensic investigations and assisting legal processes.

Benefits

- Renowned globally as an exclusive certification for digital forensics.
- Prepares you for roles in forensic analysis and incident management.
- Confirms your ability to handle and respond to security incidents.

Example of the Wilson Family

Jack, ready for digital forensics, would find GCFA beneficial for acquiring skills in investigating cyber incidents and assisting in legal matters.

Offensive Security Wireless Professional (OSWP)

The OSWP certification, which specializes in wireless network security and penetration testing, is ideal for professionals who want to secure wireless infrastructures.

Skills and Knowledge

- In-depth knowledge of wireless network protocols and security challenges.
- Proficient in executing wireless penetration tests and detecting vulnerabilities.
- Skilled in designing and implementing security strategies for wireless networks.

Benefits

- Valued as an essential certification for wireless security experts.
- Prepares individuals for roles in wireless security testing and assessments.
- Demonstrates your ability to protect wireless setups.

Example of the Wilson Family

Emma, fascinated by the unique challenges of wireless security, might consider OSWP to specialize in safeguarding wireless networks.

Specialized certifications and skills are indispensable for professionals aspiring to excel in specific areas of cybersecurity. Credentials like CCSP, IC33E, GCFA, and OSWP deliver targeted knowledge and expertise, making you ready for specialized roles and distinct security challenges. For the Wilson family and others, these certifications can enhance their career opportunities and enable them to contribute significantly to their organization's security strategies.

8.9 Career Pathways and Progression

Building a successful career in cybersecurity requires knowledge of the various paths and advancement opportunities within this dynamic industry. This field offers a broad range of roles, each characterized by unique responsibilities, necessary skills, and potential for growth. This section highlights typical career pathways in cybersecurity and ways for professionals to guide through their career stages.

Entry-Level Positions

Beginning at the entry-level offers a solid grounding in cybersecurity fundamentals and strategies. These positions suit newcomers to the field and provide chances to acquire practical experience and develop critical competencies.

Typical Entry-Level Roles

- **Security Analyst:** Engages in monitoring and analyzing security events, detecting potential threats, and enforcing security protocols.
- **IT Support Specialist:** Assists in technical support while ensuring the security of IT systems and networks.

- **Penetration Tester (Junior):** Performs basic penetration tests to discover and fix security vulnerabilities.

Example of the Wilson Family

Jack, who is willing to learn cybersecurity, could start as a Security Analyst, learning to oversee network traffic and handle security incidents.

Intermediate Positions

After gaining experience and earning further certifications, professionals can progress to intermediate roles. These positions carry more responsibility and involve more specialized activities, often concentrating on distinct cybersecurity areas.

Typical Intermediate Roles

- **Security Engineer:** Crafts and deploys security solutions like firewalls, intrusion detection systems, and encryption technologies.
- **Incident Responder:** Handles and reacts to security incidents, carries out investigations, and formulates recovery plans.
- **Forensic Analyst:** Examines digital evidence to investigate security breaches and assist legal processes.

Example of the Wilson Family

David, now seasoned and certified in CISSP, might advance to a Security Engineer position, creating sophisticated security systems for his company.

Advanced Positions

These roles are generally reserved for highly experienced professionals with deep specialized knowledge. Such positions entail strategic planning, leadership, and management of extensive security programs.

Typical Advanced Roles

- **Chief Information Security Officer (CISO):** This person directs the organization's security strategy and manages all security operations and policies.
- **Security Architect:** Develops and implements comprehensive security architectures to safeguard the organization's IT infrastructure.
- **Cybersecurity Consultant:** Offers expert advice and solutions to firms, enhancing their security frameworks.

Example of the Wilson Family

Sarah, with a strong background in security management, might target a CISO role, directing security strategies for a school or company.

Specialized Career Pathways

Cybersecurity also offers specialized paths that focus on specialized areas like cloud security, IoT security, and ethical hacking. These paths demand particular skills and knowledge, which are often verified through specialized certifications.

Typical Specialized Roles

- **Cloud Security Specialist:** Concentrates on securing cloud platforms and ensuring adherence to cloud security standards.
- **IoT Security Expert:** This position protects Internet of Things (IoT) devices and networks, handling the distinct vulnerabilities of connected devices.
- **Ethical Hacker:** Performs penetration tests and vulnerability assessments to find and mitigate security risks.

Example of the Wilson Family

Emma, fascinated by the unexplored field of IoT security, might seek specialized certifications and roles in securing smart devices and networks.

Continuous Learning and Professional Growth

Advancing in cybersecurity necessitates ongoing education and professional growth. As cyber threats evolve, it is crucial to keep up with the newest technologies, tools, and best practices.

Strategies for Continuous Learning

- **Advanced Certifications:** Acquire certifications like CISSP, CISM, and CEH for more profound knowledge and skills.
- **Professional Organizations:** Join groups such as $(ISC)^2$, ISACA, and the SANS Institute for resources, networking, and professional growth.
- **Industry Conferences:** Participate in cybersecurity conferences and workshops to stay updated on the latest trends and innovations.

Example of the Wilson Family

Jack, committed to his career growth, might regularly attend industry events and seek advanced certifications to remain at the forefront of the sector.

Understanding the career pathways and advancement opportunities in cybersecurity helps professionals in planning and achieving their career objectives. From entry-level to advanced roles and specialized tracks, the sector offers diverse prospects for growth and impact. For the Wilson family and others, exploring these paths can lead to rewarding and influential careers in cybersecurity. By dedicating themselves to continuous learning and professional development, they can maintain their relevance and value in this ever-changing field.

8.10 Continuous Learning and Professional Development

In the fast-paced world of cybersecurity, consistently upgrading one's knowledge and skills is not just advantageous—it is necessary. The landscape of cyber threats and technologies shifts rapidly, and keeping up-to-date on these changes is critical to upholding strong security measures. This Section highlights the value of continuous learning and outlines various strategies for professional growth, helping you maintain a competitive edge in your cybersecurity career.

The Necessity of Constant Learning

Constant learning ensures that cybersecurity professionals stay informed about the latest threats, tools, and best practices. It empowers them to handle new challenges effectively and expands their capability to safeguard digital environments. For individuals like the Wilson family, staying updated on cybersecurity trends can greatly enhance their digital security and professional prospects.

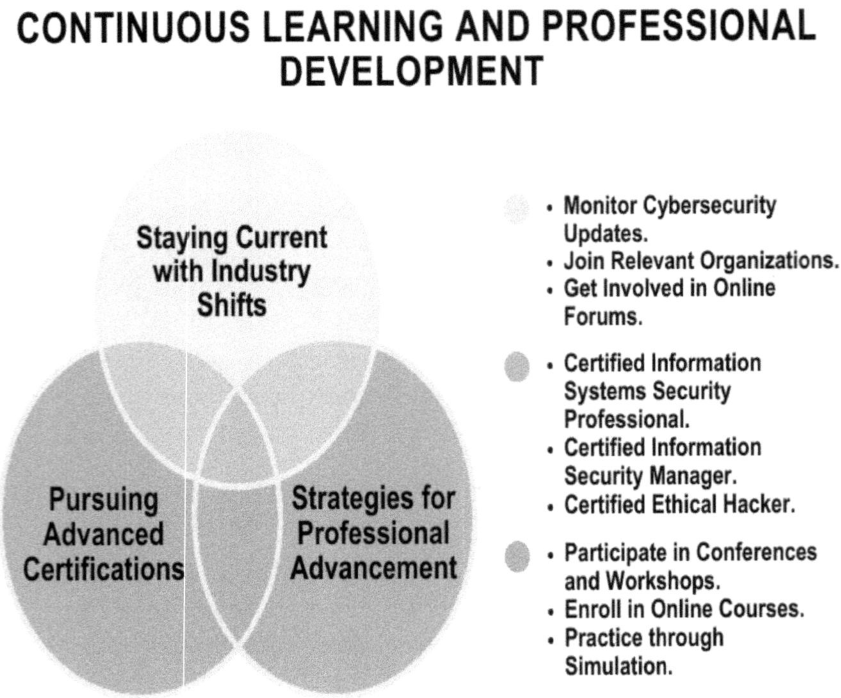

Staying Current with Industry Shifts

Cybersecurity is a rapidly evolving domain characterized by frequent innovations and new threats. To remain informed, professionals should:

- **Monitor Cybersecurity Updates:** Regularly engage with industry publications, blogs, and news outlets to keep track of emerging trends and threats.
- **Join Relevant Organizations:** Joining groups like (ISC)², ISACA, and the SANS Institute grants access to essential resources like research papers, webinars, and discussion forums.
- **Get Involved in Online Forums:** Participate in online forums and communities where cybersecurity experts exchange the latest insights, support each other, and discuss recent developments.

Pursuing Advanced Certifications

Acquiring advanced certifications is crucial for career progression in cybersecurity. These credentials affirm one's expertise and pave the way for more senior roles. Notable certifications include:

- **Certified Information Systems Security Professional (CISSP):** This globally recognized certification underscores a deep understanding of comprehensive security practices.
- **Certified Information Security Manager (CISM):** This certification focuses on the oversight and management of enterprise information security.
- **Certified Ethical Hacker (CEH):** Specializes in ethical hacking techniques and penetration testing.

Example of the Wilson Family

David, with intermediate certifications, might consider pursuing the CISSP to upgrade his qualifications and progress to higher-level security positions.

Strategies for Professional Advancement

Cybersecurity professionals should employ various tactics to refine their skills continually:

- **Participate in Conferences and Workshops:** Events such as the RSA Conference, Black Hat, and DEF CON are excellent for learning from leading experts, discovering new tools, and networking.
- **Enroll in Online Courses:** Platforms like Coursera, edX, and Cybrary offer a plethora of cybersecurity courses, allowing for self-paced learning.
- **Practice through Simulation:** Engage in online labs and simulations to build skills in a risk-free setting. Sites like Hack the Box and TryHackMe offer hands-on cybersecurity practice.

Example of the Wilson Family

Jack, who is inclined to ethical hacking, could benefit from platforms like Hack the Box to sharpen his skills in spotting vulnerabilities.

Advancing Through Higher Education

Attaining an advanced degree in cybersecurity or a related area can significantly strengthen one's expertise and career opportunities. Degrees like a Master's in Cybersecurity or Information Assurance offer thorough education and research opportunities.

Example of the Wilson Family

Sarah, who aims to incorporate cybersecurity into her academic career, pursuing a Master's degree in cybersecurity could provide deep insights into the field and enhance her teaching methods.

Networking and Finding Mentors

Establishing a solid professional network and seeking mentors are essential for career development. Connecting with colleagues, attending sector events, and finding mentors can offer valuable guidance and open doors to new opportunities.

Example of the Wilson Family

Emma, who is new to the field, might find it beneficial to join local cybersecurity groups and seek a mentor to help guide her career path.

Maintaining Certification

Keeping certifications active requires earning continuous professional education (CPE) credits. By participating in educational activities such as webinars, writing articles, and attending trainings, professionals can keep their certifications valid and stay updated.

Example of the Wilson Family

David, who holds several certifications, needs to regularly engage in CPE activities to maintain his qualifications and keep up with sector developments.

Ongoing learning and professional development are crucial for success in the dynamic field of cybersecurity. By keeping up with industry trends, earning advanced certifications, and engaging in continuous education, professionals can enhance their abilities and advance their careers. For individuals like the Wilson family, a commitment to lifelong learning ensures they are well-prepared to protect their digital environments and adapt to the ever-evolving cybersecurity landscape. Embracing these strategies is essential for achieving long-term success and making meaningful contributions to the field.

This chapter has outlined a wide range of career paths and specific certifications within the cybersecurity sector, charting a course from beginner positions to advanced expert roles. This chapter explained various certifications, from basic to highly specialized, assisting individuals in planning their career courses with precision. Initially, it introduces fundamental certifications that set the foundation for a cybersecurity career, progresses to intermediate certifications enhancing both experience and expertise and tops with advanced certifications that denote high-level proficiency and open routes to leadership positions. It further stresses the significance of continuous professional growth and skill enhancement, acknowledging that the dynamic field of cybersecurity demands ongoing dedication to education and mastery. For families like the Wilsons, this chapter acts as a navigational tool for securing long-term achievement and influence within the cybersecurity domain. Whether embarking on a new career journey or advancing to higher positions, the outlined strategies and certifications can direct individuals towards a fulfilling and vibrant professional life. By pursuing appropriate certifications, engaging in continual learning, and developing specialized skills, one can ensure their expertise remains current and invaluable, thereby positioning oneself as a fundamental protector in our digital era. The chapter has underlined that engaging in cybersecurity exceeds a mere career choice—it is a critical element in safeguarding our interconnected digital landscape, with its practitioners playing an essential role in defending our digital future.

Chapter 9: Cybersecurity for Emerging Technologies

9.1 Introduction to Emerging Technologies

Today's digital era is rapidly transformed by cutting-edge technologies that redefine our day-to-day activities, professional operations, and worldwide connections. Influential innovations such as artificial intelligence (AI), the Internet of Things (IoT), blockchain, and quantum computing not only unlock remarkable opportunities but also give rise to cybersecurity risks. It is vital to manage these effectively to safeguard their secure implementation.

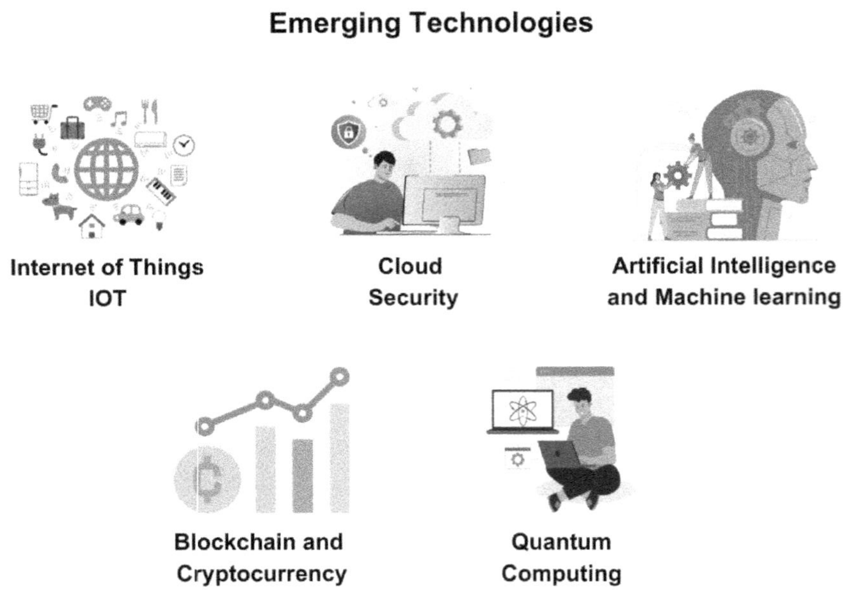

These advanced technologies are revolutionizing various industries by encouraging innovation and enabling unexplored business frameworks. AI is changing our approach to data analysis and decision-making, while IoT is integrating billions of devices into a unified network. Blockchain ensures secure, transparent dealings and quantum computing is set to handle complex challenges that traditional computing cannot handle. As these technologies evolve, they significantly enhance efficiency, productivity, and convenience in our lives.

For instance, the Wilsons—a typical family—could greatly benefit from these technologies. David might integrate AI to refine workflows in his architectural works, while Sarah could use IoT solutions to enhance their home's connectivity. Their children, Emma and Jack, will probably engage with these technologies in both their schooling and daily routines. Thus, understanding the distinction between these technologies is essential for families like theirs to protect their personal and digital data.

The Critical Role of Cybersecurity in the Modern World

As we incorporate these advanced technologies into our everyday lives, they expose us to new security risks. AI, while powerful, is vulnerable to attacks if not sufficiently secured. IoT devices, designed for ease of use, often lack in-depth security measures, making them prime targets for cyber threats. While blockchain is mostly secure, it is not immune to all attacks. Moreover, quantum computing could soon outpace current encryption methods, posing a direct challenge to existing cybersecurity measures.

It is crucial to have vital cybersecurity strategies in place to protect these technologies. These strategies must ensure the confidentiality, integrity, and availability of data and systems. As the technological landscape evolves, so must our cybersecurity approaches to handle new and emerging threats.

Adapting to Technological Evolution

Staying updated with the latest technology and cybersecurity best practices is crucial for both individuals and organizations to safeguard emerging technologies efficiently. Continuous education and skill development are essential for cybersecurity professionals to keep up with the rapid pace of technology. Similarly, families should be proactive about implementing recommended security measures to minimize potential risks.

Emerging technologies promise to transform our world, offering extensive benefits and opportunities. However, they also bring new cybersecurity challenges that must be encountered to guarantee their safe utilization. By comprehending these technologies and the associated risks, families like the Wilsons can actively secure their digital interactions. The upcoming sections will explore specific cybersecurity considerations for these technologies in greater detail, providing essential advice and insights to ensure you navigate this evolving landscape securely.

9.2 Internet of Things (IoT) Security

The Internet of Things (IoT) is a vast network of interconnected devices that interact and share data over the Internet. These devices include smart thermostats and security cameras for the home, as well as industrial gear and medical devices. For the Wilsons and many other families, Internet of Things (IoT) devices provide convenience, efficiency, and greater usefulness. However, they raise serious cybersecurity concerns that must be addressed in order to maintain the safety and privacy of their digital environment.

Understanding IoT Security Challenges

IoT devices are frequently designed with usefulness and convenience of use as main concerns, sometimes at the sacrifice of solid security measures. This makes them appealing targets for hackers who use their weaknesses to obtain illegal access, steal data, and disrupt operations. Some of the leading security problems related to IoT devices are:

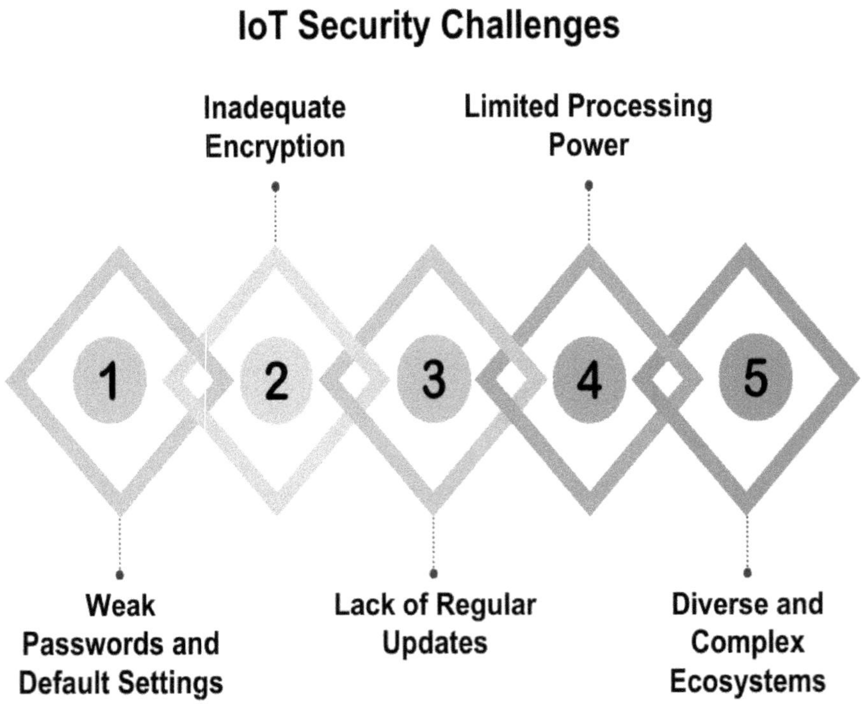

- **Weak Passwords and Default Settings:** Many IoT devices include default passwords and settings that users frequently fail to alter, making them ideal targets for attackers.
- **Inadequate Encryption:** Data sent between IoT devices and networks is not always encrypted, making it subject to intercepting and modification.
- **Lack of Regular Updates:** IoT devices usually lack automated update systems, leaving security vulnerabilities unpatched and vulnerable.
- **Limited Processing Power:** Many IoT devices have limited computing power, making it challenging to integrate solid security measures without sacrificing efficiency.
- **Diverse and Complex Ecosystems:** The IoT ecosystem's diverse range of devices, manufacturers, and communication protocols makes it challenging to apply standardized security requirements.

Secure IoT Devices: Practical Steps

To safeguard their IoT devices and provide a secure digital environment, the Wilson family and others may adopt a few recommended practices:

Change the Default Settings

Changing the default usernames and passwords on all IoT devices is one of the most straightforward but efficient security solutions. Using strong, unique passwords for each device can help to decrease the danger of illegal access.

Enable Encryption

Assure that the data transmitted by IoT devices is encrypted. This may be accomplished by activating encryption capabilities on the devices and utilizing secure communication protocols. For example, when David installs a new smart security camera in his house, he should make sure it uses an encrypted connection to prevent the video stream from being intercepted.

Regular Software Updates

Regularly upgrading IoT devices with the most recent firmware version helps defend against known vulnerabilities. If automated updates are available, enable them to ensure that devices receive security fixes as soon as possible. Sarah, for example, should check for and apply updates to her smart home hub on a regular basis to ensure its security.

Secure Network Configuration

IoT devices should be connected to a secure Wi-Fi network that uses a strong password and WPA3 encryption. Setting up a separate network for IoT devices improves security by separating them from other sensitive data on the leading network. For example, the Wilsons can set up a guest network just for their devices that are smart.

Use a Firewall

Implementing a firewall protects the home network from external threats. Firewalls may monitor incoming and outgoing communications and prevent suspicious activity. This is especially critical for David, who conducts his architectural practice from home and must secure vital business information.

Disable Unnecessary Features

Many IoT devices provide functionalities that may not be required for their intended usage. Turning off unneeded features and services decreases the attack surface and lowers the chance of exploitation. For example, if the Wilsons do not utilize their smart TV's built-in camera and microphone, they should disable these functions.

Monitor Device Activity

Regularly monitoring the activities of IoT devices helps detect unexpected behavior that might signal a security compromise. Most devices keep logs or activity reports, which users may inspect. If Sarah sees strange behavior on her smart thermostat, it may indicate that the device has been hacked.

The Internet of Things has several benefits, but it also poses considerable cybersecurity problems. By recognizing these problems and applying proper security measures, the Wilson family, like any other family, can safeguard their IoT devices from cyber-attacks. Securing IoT devices is critical for protecting the privacy and integrity of their digital environment, allowing them to reap the benefits of intelligent technology without endangering their safety.

9.3 Cloud Security

Cloud computing has transformed how we store, access, and manage data. It provides exceptional simplicity, scalability, and cost-effectiveness, making it a necessary component of both personal and business digital worlds. The Wilson family, like any other family, now relies on cloud services for everything from photo storage to business document management. However, the move to the cloud presents substantial security problems that must be addressed in order to secure sensitive information.

Understanding Cloud Security

Cloud security refers to a collection of rules, methods, and controls used to safeguard data, applications, and related infrastructure in cloud settings. The shared responsibility model is a basic idea in cloud security, in which both the cloud service provider and the user share responsibility for data protection. While the provider assures the infrastructure's security, consumers must manage their data safely in the cloud.

A cloud services provider, such as Google or Amazon, is responsible for safeguarding the infrastructure, which includes physical data centers, servers, and networks. However, the Wilson family is responsible for safeguarding their own data and apps inside this infrastructure, which includes creating secure passwords, activating encryption, and controlling access limits.

Key Cloud Security Challenges

Using cloud services presents many security risks that consumers must be aware of:

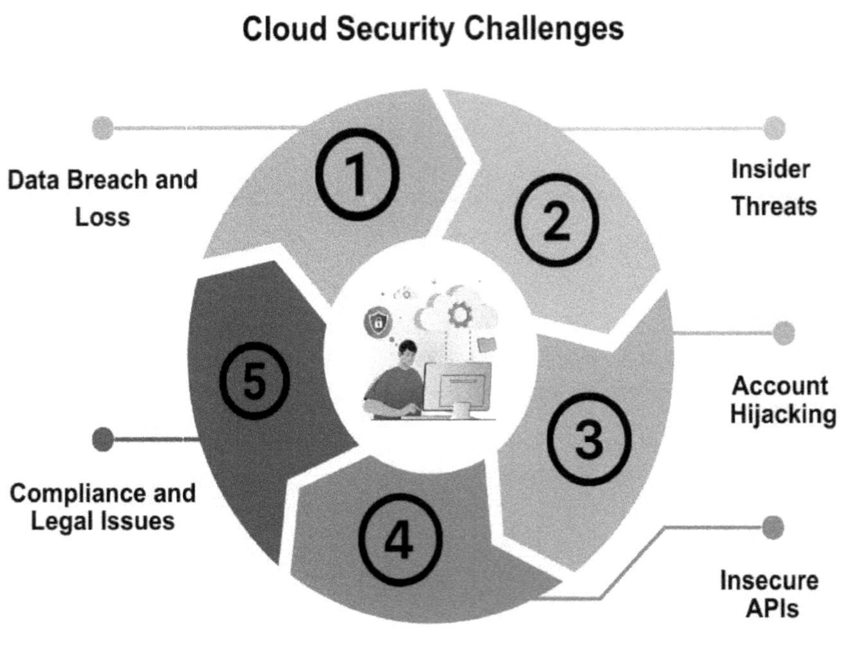

Data Breach and Loss

Storing sensitive data in the cloud exposes it to security risks and loss. Cybercriminals target cloud services to get access to valuable information, and misconfigurations can result in unintentional data disclosure. For example, a poorly set cloud storage pool may be publicly accessible, allowing anybody to see or download the stored data. This was the case in numerous high-profile breaches in which sensitive data, such as personal information and financial records, were exposed as a result of setup errors.

Insider Threats

Employees and users with malicious intent, as well as those who mistakenly mishandle data, can represent considerable hazards. Insider attacks are challenging to identify and can lead to significant data breaches. For example, an employee who has access to sensitive client data may purposefully or mistakenly communicate this information outside of the firm. Implementing strict access restrictions and routinely analyzing access records can assist in reducing this danger.

Account Hijacking

Weak passwords and a lack of multi-factor authentication (MFA) can result in account hijacking, in which attackers gain unauthorized access to cloud accounts and potentially compromise all stored data. Once an attacker has access to an account, they can steal data, install malware, or use the account to launch more harm. For the Wilson family, protecting their cloud accounts with strong, unique passwords and MFA is critical to preventing account hijacking.

Insecure APIs

Application Programming Interfaces (APIs) are critical to cloud operation, but they can be abused if not adequately protected, resulting in data breaches and other security concerns. APIs enable diverse software components to communicate and interact, but if not adequately protected, they can provide entry points for attackers. Ensuring that APIs are appropriately authenticated and permitted is critical to ensuring cloud security.

Compliance and Legal Issues

Data storage on the cloud frequently necessitates compliance with a variety of rules, including the General Data Protection Regulation (GDPR) and the California Consumer Privacy Act. Failure to comply may result in legal action and penalties. Organizations and individuals must understand the regulatory obligations that apply to their data and verify that cloud service providers follow these standards.

Best Practices in Cloud Security

To guarantee their cloud settings are safe, the Wilson family, like any other family, should embrace a few best practices:

Use Strong Authentication

Using robust authentication techniques is crucial. This includes employing multi-factor authentication (MFA), which needs a second form of verification in addition to a password. To prevent unwanted access, David should setup MFA on his cloud storage accounts. MFA provides an extra layer of security by requiring both what the user knows (password) and what the user has (a code texted to their phone).

Encrypt Data

Data at rest and in transit should be encrypted to prevent unwanted access. Cloud service providers frequently provide encryption services; however, customers must ensure that they are activated. Sarah, for example, should encrypt her cloud-stored medical documents to protect their privacy. Encryption scrambles data so that it can only be read by someone who has the correct decryption key, ensuring that it is not intercepted or accessed without authority.

Regularly Monitor and Audit Accounts

Regular monitoring and auditing of cloud accounts assists in the early detection of suspicious actions. Most cloud service providers give tools for monitoring account behavior, which can notify customers of possible security risks. Emma and Jack should verify their cloud-based educational account activity logs on a regular basis to confirm that there has been no unwanted access. Regular audits can help detect and address security weaknesses before they are exploited.

Secure APIs

Make sure all Application Programming Interface (APIs) are safe by implementing correct authentication and permission protocols. David should collaborate with developers to protect the APIs used by his architectural firm's cloud apps. This includes utilizing safe coding techniques, checking for vulnerabilities on a regular basis, and putting rate limits in place to avoid misuse.

Data Backup and Recovery

Regularly backing up cloud data to a secure place guarantees that it may be restored in the event of an accidental deletion or a ransomware attack. The Wilsons should set up automatic backups of their key papers and images saved on the cloud. Backups should be encrypted and kept in many locations so that data may be restored even if one backup is compromised.

Understand the Compliance Requirements

Understanding and adhering to appropriate rules is critical. If Sarah keeps medical records on the cloud, she should be aware of healthcare data protection requirements. This includes verifying that the cloud service provider follows all applicable legislation and installing extra measures as needed to secure sensitive data.

Choose Reputable Cloud Providers

It is critical to choose reputed and reliable cloud service providers who have strong safety precautions in place and compliance certifications. David should analyze companies based on their security solutions and adherence to industry norms.

Reputable suppliers often use strong security measures such as physical security controls, frequent security audits, and compliance with industry rules.

Practical Tips for the Wilson Family

For the Wilsons, safeguarding their cloud environment requires performing practical actions that fit into their regular routines. David can verify that his cloud-stored business records are encrypted and protected from unauthorized access. Sarah may teach Emma and Jack about the value of secure passwords and multi-factor authentication for their cloud accounts. Regularly evaluating and upgrading security settings across all cloud services may help them maintain a strong security posture.

Cloud computing has several benefits, but it also poses unique security difficulties. Understanding these problems and establishing appropriate security measures allows the Wilson family and any other family to secure their data while taking use of cloud services.

9.4 Artificial Intelligence and Machine Learning in Cybersecurity

Artificial Intelligence (AI) and Machine Learning (ML) are revolutionizing a variety of industries, including cybersecurity. These technologies provide unmatched capabilities for detecting, preventing, and responding to cyber-attacks. Understanding the function of AI and ML in cybersecurity can give insights into how these technologies improve protection in an increasingly digital environment.

Understanding Artificial Intelligence and Machine Learning in Cybersecurity

AI refers to the emulation of human intellectual processes by computers, specifically computer systems. These processes include learning (acquiring knowledge and rules for utilizing it), reasoning (using rules to arrive at approximate or definite conclusions), and self-correction. A subset of AI, machine learning (ML), focuses on the development of algorithms that allow computers to learn from and make predictions or judgments based on data.

In the context of cybersecurity, AI and machine learning may be used to rapidly evaluate large volumes of data, discover trends, and detect abnormalities that may signal a cyber-threat. These technologies improve the capacity to respond to security problems quickly and efficiently, decreasing the severity of prospective attacks.

Applications of Artificial Intelligence and Machine Learning in Cybersecurity

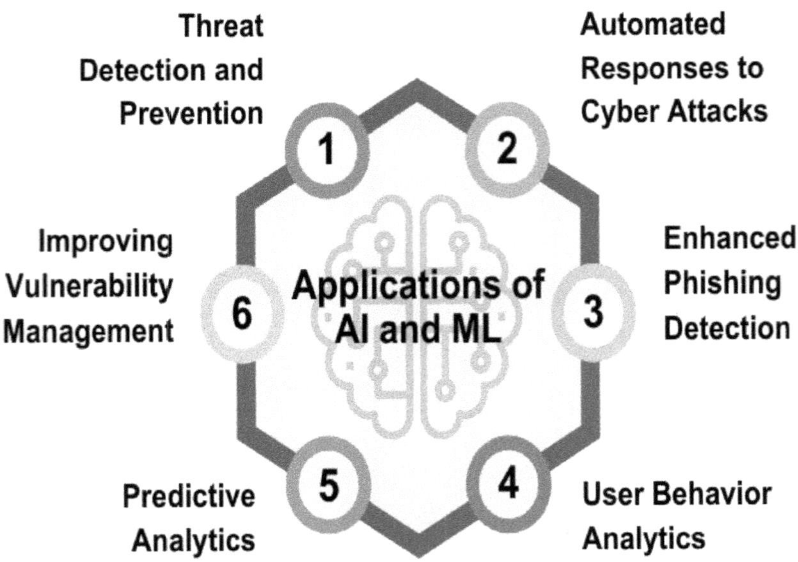

Threat Detection and Prevention

Artificial intelligence and machine learning algorithms can monitor network data in real-time to detect and prevent attacks. They can recognize strange patterns of activity that might indicate a cyber-attack. For example, suppose an AI system detects an unusually high number of login attempts from a single IP address. In that case, it may identify a potential brute-force assault and take preventative steps, such as banning the IP address.

Automated Responses

AI can automate responses to certain sorts of cyber-attacks. For example, if a system detects malware, AI may start automatic quarantine and eradication processes. This quick response helps to limit the harm and spread of the infection.

Enhanced Phishing Detection

Phishing attacks frequently utilize sophisticated social engineering approaches to trick people into disclosing critical information. AI can evaluate email content and metadata to detect phishing attempts, including suspicious links, sender information, and linguistic trends. AI can help consumers avoid phishing attempts by spotting potentially dangerous emails.

User Behavior Analytics

ML models may learn and comprehend typical user behavior over time. Any departure from this behavior may result in an alert. For example, suppose David regularly enters his cloud storage account from home in the evening and tries to log in from a different place during the day. In that case, the system will detect the anomaly and require extra verification.

Predictive Analytics

AI can forecast possible security risks by evaluating patterns and past data. Predictive analysis enables businesses to predict and prepare for future threats, increasing their overall security posture. For example, if Sarah's medical data storage system exhibits characteristics indicative of ransomware incidents, AI may notify her to take precautionary measures.

Improving Vulnerability Management

AI can help find and prioritize vulnerabilities in software and systems. By constantly scanning for flaws and estimating the risk associated with each one, AI helps guarantee that the most serious vulnerabilities are fixed as soon as possible. This proactive approach is critical to maintaining safe settings.

Practical Examples for the Wilson Family

For the Wilson family, AI and machine learning could substantially enhance their cybersecurity measures:

Smart Home Security: AI-powered home security systems can identify odd behavior in the home and notify the family. For example, if the security camera detects activity when the home is vacant, it might send an alarm to David's phone.

Email Security: AI-powered email filters can help Sarah prevent phishing emails by detecting questionable communications before they get into her inbox.

Parental Controls: Artificial intelligence can help Emma and Jack set up and manage parental controls on their devices, keeping them safe from improper information and online risks.

Financial Security: AI may monitor financial transactions and notify the family of any strange activity, therefore preventing fraud and identity theft.

Challenges and Considerations

While Artificial Intelligence and Machine Learning provide substantial advantages, they also pose challenges:

- **Data Privacy:** AI systems must have access to vast volumes of data to work properly. Ensuring that this data is gathered, kept, and utilized in accordance with privacy standards is crucial.
- **Bias and Fairness:** AI models can carry biases from the data on which they are trained, resulting in unfair or discriminating outputs. It is critical to incorporate mechanisms to detect and reduce bias in AI systems.
- **False Positives:** Artificial intelligence systems may occasionally yield false positives, identifying acceptable actions as dangers. Sensitivity must be balanced with accuracy to minimize interruption.

Artificial intelligence and machine learning are transforming cybersecurity by delivering sophisticated capabilities for detecting, preventing, and responding to attacks. Integrating these tools into the Wilson family's cybersecurity plan, as well as any other family, can dramatically improve their security. By knowing the potential and uses of artificial intelligence and machine learning, individuals can better protect their digital lives.

9.5 Blockchain and Cryptocurrency Security

Blockchain technology and cryptocurrencies have emerged as critical developments in the world of technology. While they provide various advantages, such as increased security, transparency, and efficiency, they also create new security issues. Understanding blockchain and cryptocurrency security is critical for the Wilson family and any other family seeking to secure their money and manage this ever-changing world responsibly.

Understanding Blockchain and Cryptocurrencies

Blockchain Technology

A blockchain is a decentralized and distributed ledger that records transactions across several computers in such a way that the registered transactions cannot be changed later. Each block in the chain comprises a list of transactions, and when a block is finished, it is added to the chain in a sequential sequence. This structure protects the integrity and security of data by making it nearly hard to change or tamper with.

Cryptocurrencies

Cryptocurrencies are digital or virtual currencies that employ cryptography to ensure security. They rely on blockchain technology, which offers a decentralized means of recording transactions. Bitcoin, Ethereum, and Litecoin are among the most well-known cryptocurrencies. These digital assets may be used for a variety of reasons, including making online purchases, investing, and moving funds across borders.

Key Security Challenges

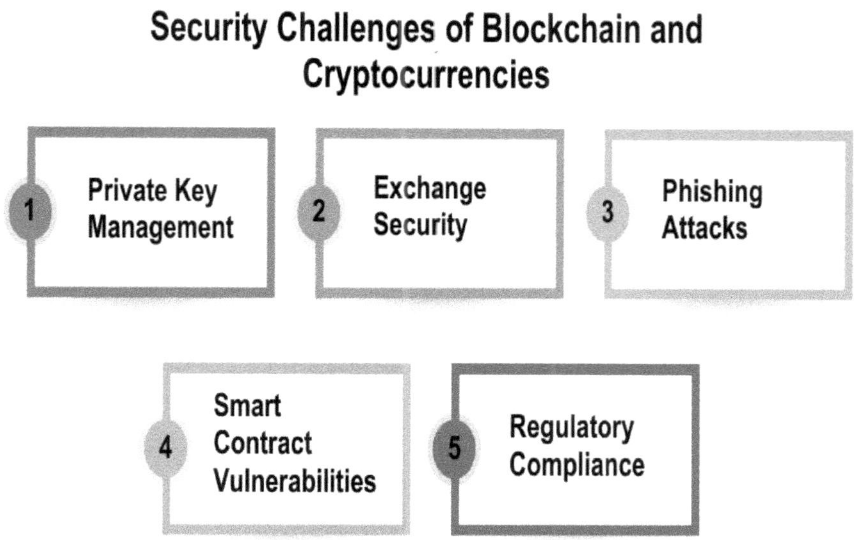

Private Key Management

In the context of cryptocurrencies, private keys function similarly to passwords, granting access to your cash. If someone acquires access to your private keys, they can take control of your Bitcoin. Managing these keys safely is critical. To avoid illegal access, David must ensure that his private keys are maintained securely, such as through hardware wallets or encrypted digital wallets.

Exchange Security

Cryptocurrency exchanges are platforms that allow users to purchase, sell, and trade cryptocurrency. However, hackers frequently target these transactions. It is critical that an exchange implements strong security measures like as two-factor authentication (2FA), cold storage for cash, and frequent security audits. Sarah should undertake extensive research before deciding on an exchange to trade cryptocurrency.

Phishing Attacks

Phishing incidents are widespread in the Bitcoin community. Cybercriminals may set up counterfeit websites or send false emails to fool people into disclosing their private keys or login credentials. Emma and Jack should exercise caution when receiving unsolicited emails about cryptocurrency and should always verify the legitimacy of websites before providing personal information.

Smart Contract Vulnerabilities

Smart contracts are self-executing contracts in which the terms of the agreement are encoded directly into code. They operate on blockchain networks like Ethereum. However, weaknesses in intelligent contract programming might be exploited by attackers, resulting in significant financial losses. Prior to implementation, intelligent contracts must be thoroughly inspected and tested.

Regulatory Compliance

Cryptocurrencies operate in a fast-changing regulatory framework. Different nations have different laws governing the usage, trading, and taxation of cryptocurrencies. Staying educated about legal requirements and maintaining compliance is critical for avoiding legal problems and potential penalties.

Best Practices in Blockchain and Cryptocurrency Security

Use Hardware Wallets

Hardware wallets are physical devices used to store private keys offline securely. They are regarded as one of the safest ways to keep cryptocurrency. For example, David can keep his Bitcoin in a hardware wallet, guaranteeing that his private keys are not vulnerable to internet attacks.

Enable Two Factor Authentication (2FA)

Enabling 2FA on Bitcoin exchanges and wallets provides an additional degree of security. This necessitates a secondary method of verification, such as a code delivered to your phone in addition to your password. Sarah should set up 2FA on all of her Bitcoin accounts to prevent unwanted access.

Regularly Update Software

Keeping software up to date is critical for protecting against known vulnerabilities. This covers wallet software, exchange systems, and other programs for Bitcoin administration. Regular updates guarantee that the most recent security fixes are deployed, which reduces the chance of exploitation.

Be wary of Phishing Scams

Phishing schemes are typical in the Bitcoin community. Emma and Jack should be cautious about the emails they receive and avoid clicking on any questionable links. They should also verify that the websites they visit are authentic by checking the URL and looking for security certifications.

Backup Private Keys

Private keys should be backed up on a regular basis and stored in secure locations. Backups should be stored in several locations, including safe physical locations and encrypted digital forms. This guarantees that if one backup is lost or corrupted, others are accessible to restore access.

Conduct Security Audits

Regular security audits are critical for anybody building or utilizing intelligent contracts. These audits assist in identifying and fixing code vulnerabilities, hence averting possible attacks. David, who could utilize intelligent contracts in his architectural business, should have them reviewed by credible security firms.

Stay Informed About Regulations

Maintaining awareness of the regulatory environment is critical for compliance and security. Distinct jurisdictions have distinct rules governing Bitcoin use and trade. The Wilson family should check for regulatory changes on a regular basis to guarantee compliance.

Practical Tips for the Wilson Family

Implementing these recommended practices can dramatically improve the Wilson family's blockchain and cryptocurrency security.

- David may employ hardware wallets to protect his Bitcoin investments and ensure that his private keys are safely stored.
- Sarah may set up two-factor authentication on all of her Bitcoin accounts and ensure that her wallet software is constantly updated.
- Emma and Jack may keep aware of phishing schemes and avoid clicking on strange links or inputting personal information on untrustworthy websites.

Blockchain and cryptocurrencies provide intriguing potential, but they also present unique security issues. Understanding these problems and employing appropriate security measures allows the Wilson family and any other family to preserve their wealth and navigate the Bitcoin market safely. This chapter emphasizes the value of private key management, exchange security, phishing prevention, smart contract audits, and regulatory compliance. By following these instructions, users can guarantee that their blockchain and cryptocurrency operations are safe and resistant to cyber-attacks.

9.6 Quantum Computing and Cybersecurity

Quantum computing, which uses quantum physics concepts, has the potential to transform the world of computers. This developing technology has the ability to address complicated problems far faster than traditional computers. However, it provides both substantial obstacles and potential for cybersecurity. Understanding the influence of quantum computing on cybersecurity is critical for the Wilson family, as well as any other family, in order to future-proof their digital security measures.

Understanding Quantum Computing

Quantum computing makes use of quantum bits, or qubits, which may exist in several states at the same time due to superposition and entanglement principles. Qubits, unlike traditional bits, may represent both 0 and 1. This capacity enables quantum computers to process massive volumes of data at unprecedented rates, therefore addressing issues that are now intractable for traditional computers. Quantum computing, for example, can handle sophisticated simulations, optimization issues, and cryptography activities that need massive processing resources more effectively.

Impact on Cybersecurity

While quantum computing has immense potential, it also poses considerable risks to existing cybersecurity methods. Due to quantum computers' computing capacity, traditional encryption methods, which rely on the difficulty of solving mathematical problems, may become outdated.

Key Threats and Challenges

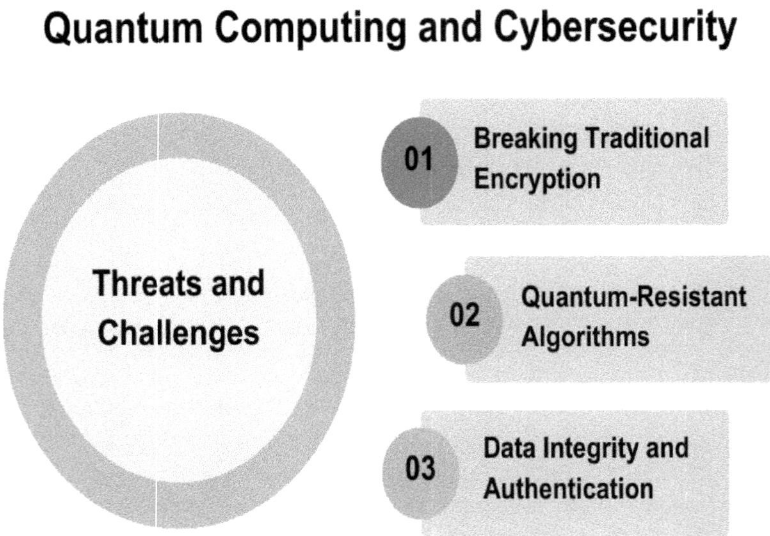

Breaking Traditional Encryption

Most current encryption techniques, such as RSA and ECC, rely on the difficulty of factoring huge numbers or solving discrete logarithm issues. Quantum computers could address these issues much quicker than classical computers, possibly decrypting sensitive information in seconds that traditional computers would take decades to break. For example, if a quantum computer acquires access to David's encrypted architectural designs, it may rapidly decipher and reveal them, creating a serious security concern.

Quantum computing employs methods such as Shor's algorithm to effectively factor big numbers, which has a direct influence on the security of RSA encryption. This capacity implies that commonly used encryption standards are vulnerable to compromise, endangering the security of financial transactions, communications, and stored data.

Quantum-Resistant Algorithms

To counteract the threat posed by quantum computing, academics are working on quantum-resistant algorithms, often known as post-quantum cryptography. These algorithms are intended to be safe against both classical and quantum attacks. Implementing these algorithms in current systems will be critical to ensuring security as quantum computing improves. The transition to post-quantum cryptography entails upgrading existing cryptographic standards and protocols to guarantee they can resist the processing capability of quantum computers.

Quantum-resistant algorithms include multivariate polynomial cryptography, hash-based cryptography, and lattice-based encryption. Organizations like the National Institute of Standards and Technology (NIST) are standardizing these algorithms in preparation for the quantum future.

Data Integrity and Authentication

Quantum computing might have an influence on data integrity and authentication operations. Current digital signature and hashing techniques may become susceptible, necessitating the development of new ways to ensure data authenticity and integrity. For example, Sarah's medical records on the cloud must be safeguarded with quantum-resistant authentication mechanisms to maintain their integrity and validity.

Quantum-resistant digital signatures are critical for preserving confidence in digital communications and transactions. Without safe authentication mechanisms, it would be difficult to authenticate the authenticity of documents, emails, and other digital assets.

Opportunities in Quantum Computing

Quantum Cryptography

Quantum computing also provides new options to improve cybersecurity. Quantum cryptography, specifically Quantum Key Distribution (QKD), secures data transmission by applying quantum mechanics principles. QKD allows two parties to communicate encryption keys with complete security since any effort to eavesdrop on the key exchange alters the quantum states and is observable.

Quantum cryptography uses quantum entanglement and superposition to generate encryption keys that cannot be intercepted without notice. This technique has the potential to revolutionize secure communications, making eavesdropping almost impossible.

Enhanced Security Protocols

Quantum computing can improve existing security protocols by giving new methods for generating truly random numbers, which are an essential component of encryption techniques. This capacity can increase the strength and unpredictability of cryptographic keys.

Actual random number creation is critical for producing safe encryption keys. Quantum random number generators (QRNGs) employ quantum processes to generate really random numbers, as opposed to conventional random number generators, which rely on algorithms and are predictable.

Practical Steps for the Wilson Family

While the entire impact of quantum computing may not be realized for years, the Wilson family may take many practical actions to prepare for the future:

Stay Informed

It is critical to stay up to date on developments in quantum computing and post-quantum cryptography. David, Sarah, Emma, and Jack should stay up to speed on cybersecurity news and changes to understand how they may influence their digital security. Understanding the evolution of quantum computing breakthroughs and the creation of quantum-resistant algorithms allows for more educated cybersecurity judgments.

Use Strong Encryption

Until quantum-resistant algorithms become mainstream, the Wilson family should continue to use the most powerful encryption methods available for their sensitive data. This involves employing AES-256 for data encryption and implementing strong protocols to safeguard communication routes. AES-256 is currently deemed quantum-resistant because of its long bit length, making it a safe choice in the meantime.

Plan for Change

As quantum-resistant algorithms become available, the Wilson family should prepare to upgrade their data and communication infrastructure to meet these new requirements. This might include upgrading software, re-encrypting sensitive data, and assuring compatibility with quantum-resistant protocols. Early adoption of post-quantum cryptography standards allows a smooth transition and long-term security as quantum computing capabilities advance.

Advocate for Security Awareness

Educating oneself and others about the possible implications of quantum computing on cybersecurity can contribute to a better-informed and prepared community. The Wilsons can communicate knowledge about quantum dangers and remedies with their colleagues and networks. Raising awareness of quantum computing's implications promotes societal readiness and preventive steps.

Quantum computing is a sword with two sharp edges in cybersecurity. While it provides tremendous processing capacity, which can improve security measures, it also has the potential to break present encryption systems. Understanding these problems and opportunities allows the Wilson family and any other family to take proactive actions in preparing for the quantum age. Staying educated, utilizing strong encryption, preparing for the transition to quantum-resistant algorithms, and raising security awareness are all critical methods for navigating the future of cybersecurity in the age of quantum computing. Quantum computing's transformational potential necessitates a proactive and educated strategy to ensure ongoing security and resilience against emerging cyber threats.

As we approach a time of advancements that are set to transform our digital world, it is more crucial than ever to understand and tackle the cybersecurity challenges that come with these new technologies. This section has delved into the range of cybersecurity obstacles and possibilities brought about by the Internet of Things (IoT), cloud computing, artificial intelligence (AI), Mac, machine learning (ML), blockchain and cryptocurrencies, as well as quantum computing. Each of these innovations comes with its advantages and vulnerabilities, emphasizing the need for security measures that can adapt to changing circumstances. For families like the Wilsons, as with any other family navigating the online realm, implementing strong cybersecurity practices is vital to safeguard personal information, uphold privacy and defend against increasingly sophisticated online threats. By keeping up to date with information, utilizing security resources, and promoting a culture of education and awareness, both individuals and businesses can fortify their resilience against evolving cyber dangers. The journey through technologies highlights a core truth: cybersecurity is not stagnant. An ever-evolving and essential aspect of our daily existence. As we welcome these advancements, let us also pledge to protect the confidentiality, integrity and accessibility of our possessions for a prosperous future for everyone.

Chapter 10: Global Cybersecurity Landscape

10.1 Introduction to Global Cybersecurity

In today's globally connected environment, cybersecurity extends beyond local or national concerns to become a worldwide imperative. As technology eliminates geographical boundaries, cyber threats similarly spread across borders, impacting individuals, businesses, and governments globally. Learning the worldwide cybersecurity scenario is vital for understanding the extent and complexity of challenges before us and the united actions needed to handle them.

Global Cybersecurity Significance

Cybersecurity on an international scale involves a broad range of measures to protect the integrity, confidentiality, and availability of information that crosses international lines. These measures are crucial for defending critical infrastructure, securing financial transactions, safeguarding personal privacy, and upholding national security. The connection of digital networks means a violation in one region can trigger devastating impacts worldwide. For families like the Wilsons, this means the security of their personal information relies on the robustness of global cybersecurity protocols and methods.

Cyber Threats without Borders

The variety of cyber threats is vast and continuously evolving, including ransomware, data violations, cyber spying, and government-backed cyber activities. These threats do not adhere to geopolitical boundaries; hence, international collaboration is essential. An attack on one nation's financial sector could destabilize financial markets globally, just as a compromise in a global corporation's data can affect consumers around the world.

Global Cybersecurity Efforts

Numerous global entities and associations focus on elevating worldwide cybersecurity. Key initiatives like the EU's General Data Protection Regulation (GDPR), the US's Cybersecurity and Infrastructure Security Agency (CISA), and international alliances such as the United Nations' International Telecommunication Union (ITU) are critical in shaping cybersecurity strategies and standards. These bodies aim to establish common protocols, help in information exchange, and coordinate collective responses to cyber threats.

Governmental Involvement in Cybersecurity

Governments worldwide acknowledge the critical nature of cybersecurity, passing laws and regulations and creating agencies dedicated to protecting their constituents and infrastructures. National approaches typically include cybersecurity defense actions, public education initiatives, and partnerships with the private sector. For example, the GDPR in the EU mandates strict data security norms that influence global practices, ensuring that personal data is managed with utmost security.

Public and Private Sector Collaboration

Achieving strong cybersecurity necessitates cooperation between governmental bodies and private enterprises. Private sectors often bring advanced technological prowess and innovation, whereas governments provide the necessary regulatory frameworks and enforcement mechanisms. Collaborations between these sectors strengthen cyber defenses by combining resources, expertise, and critical data. For families like the Wilsons, such partnerships ensure that the technological products and services they rely on are built and operated with solid cybersecurity measures in place.

Navigating the global cybersecurity landscape requires continual alertness and collaborative effort. By recognizing the international dimensions of cyber threats and the joint actions required to mitigate them, individuals and organizations can better understand the significance of global cybersecurity initiatives. For families like the Wilsons, appreciating the global interconnectedness of digital security emphasizes the importance of staying informed and employing best practices to safeguard their online activities.

10.2 International Cyber Threats

In today's digital era, cyber threats have grown into a significant global issue. These threats, unrestricted by geographical boundaries, can originate from any corner of the globe, targeting people, businesses, and government entities across various nations. Gaining an in-depth understanding of international cyber threats is essential for crafting effective cybersecurity strategies and enhancing worldwide collaboration.

Diverse International Cyber Threats

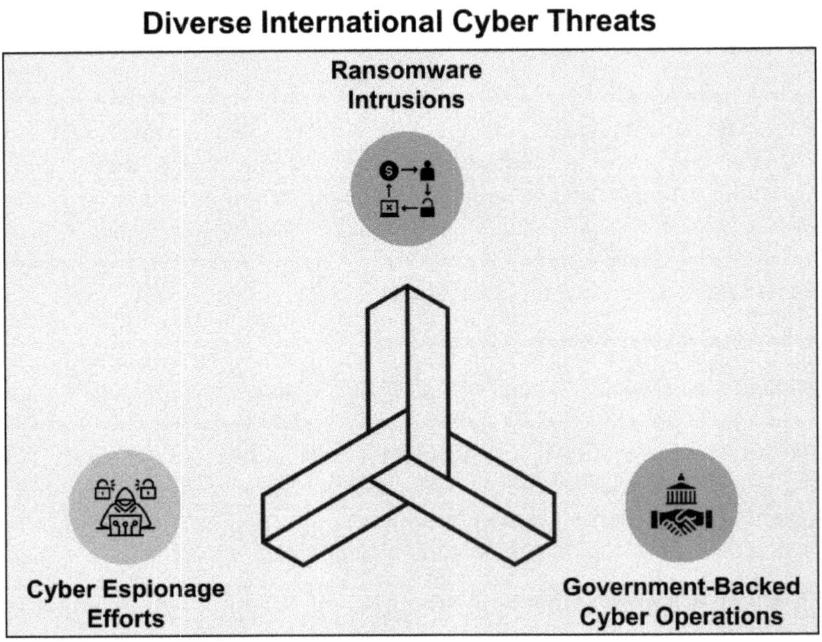

Ransomware Intrusions

Ransomware, a malicious software variant, encrypts the victim's data, demanding a ransom for the decryption key. Such intrusions can disrupt businesses, healthcare facilities, and vital infrastructure globally. Significant incidents like the WannaCry and NotPetya attacks have led to extensive damage across continents, affecting countless systems.

Government-Backed Cyber Operations

These cyber operations are executed by entities sponsored by national governments aiming to gather intelligence, disrupt foreign affairs, or inflict damage on other countries. These operations are typically sophisticated and well-resourced. Examples include the purported Russian involvement in the 2016 U.S. elections and North Korea's attack on Sony Pictures, highlighting the geopolitical stakes.

Cyber Espionage Efforts

This involves illegal access and theft of critical data by state-aligned or independent actors. Such espionage targets governmental bodies, defense establishments, and multinational corporations to secure strategic edges. A case in point is Operation Cloud Hopper by the Chinese APT10 group, which compromised global IT service providers to obtain intellectual property and sensitive data.

Phishing and Social Engineering Schemes

Utilizing misleading communications, phishing schemes trick recipients into revealing sensitive information or installing harmful software. These schemes often employ social engineering techniques to exploit human vulnerabilities, targeting a global audience.

Distributed Denial-of-Service (DDoS) Disruptions

DDoS attacks flood a system's online services with excessive traffic to restrict them. These attacks are employed against critical online services like financial platforms and government portals. The 2016 attack on Dyn, a primary DNS provider, disrupted access to major platforms, including Twitter, Reddit, and Spotify, impacting users worldwide.

Consequences of Global Cyber Threats

Economic Fallout

International cyber incidents can lead to substantial economic downturns. Companies may suffer from expenses linked to data restoration, legal consequences, and damaged reputations. For instance, the NotPetya attack led to multi-billion-dollar losses for global giants like Maersk and FedEx.

Risks to National Security

Cyber operations backed by national entities can compromise critical national infrastructure, military communications, and governmental networks, posing significant threats to a country's security framework.

Privacy Breaches

Invasions like cyber espionage and data leaks threaten personal and organizational privacy, leading to risks like identity theft, financial scams, and loss of competitive standing.

Global Countermeasures against Cyber Threats

Cross-Border Collaborations

Considering global cyber threats necessitates partnerships across countries. Entities such as the United Nations, NATO, and the European Union facilitate strategic alliances, sharing of crucial information, and collective tactical responses. The Budapest Convention on Cybercrime exemplifies an international treaty designed to unify cybercrime legislation and promote cooperation.

Public-Private Sector Alliances

Vital cybersecurity frameworks demand cooperation between government agencies and private enterprises. These alliances maximize the strengths and resources of both sectors to devise effective cybersecurity measures and responses.

Adherence to Cybersecurity Norms and Protocols

International standards and guidelines like ISO/IEC 27001 and the NIST Cybersecurity Framework outline strategies for cyber risk management and mitigation.

Implementing these standards empowers organizations to adopt industry best practices and enhance their security measures.

The risk of international cyber threats, ever-present and evolving, calls for a unified and attentive global response. By understanding the nature of these threats and their potential repercussions, individuals, organizations, and governments can better safeguard themselves. For every family, including the Wilsons, being well-informed about these threats is crucial for maintaining strong cybersecurity practices and supporting global efforts aimed at strengthening collective digital resilience.

10.3 Cross-Border Cybercrime

In our increasingly connected world, cybercrime has developed into a sophisticated and widespread threat that ignores national borders. This type of crime, known as cross-border cybercrime, involves unlawful activities conducted through digital channels that affect people, organizations, and governments worldwide. Getting the importance of cross-border cybercrime, its consequences, and the joint efforts needed for its mitigation is critical to maintaining global cybersecurity.

Exploring the Dynamics of Cross-Border Cybercrime

Cross-border cybercrime involves a range of harmful activities that leverage the extensive reach of the internet. These acts are particularly harmful as they impact victims across multiple nations, thus complicating traditional law enforcement approaches. Notable forms of cross-border cybercrime include:

System Infiltrations and Data Compromises

Cyber attackers infiltrate global networks, systems, and databases, stealing critical information such as personal identities, financial details, and intellectual assets. Major incidents like the Equifax breach have underscored the far-reaching consequences of these breaches, affecting millions globally.

Online Deception and Identity Theft

Cyber fraudsters deploy methods like phishing, social engineering, and harmful software to conduct fraud and steal identities, imposing financial and emotional harm globally. For instance, a single phishing expedition originating from one country can trick individuals in another into submitting their banking details.

Ransomware Disruptions

These attacks involve encrypting a victim's data and demanding a ransom for its release, targeting global entities from individuals to critical infrastructure. The widespread impact of the WannaCry ransomware attack, which hit over 150 countries, illustrates the global scale of such threats.

Banned Digital Marketplaces

The dark web hosts marketplaces that facilitate the trade of illegal goods such as narcotics, weaponry, and stolen data, connecting sellers and buyers worldwide and making it challenging to shut these networks down.

Exploitation and Trafficking

The internet is also exploited for unfortunate crimes like child exploitation and human trafficking, often involving actors and victims from various nations, which demands a concerted international response to counter effectively.

Impacts and Challenges of Cross-Border Cybercrime

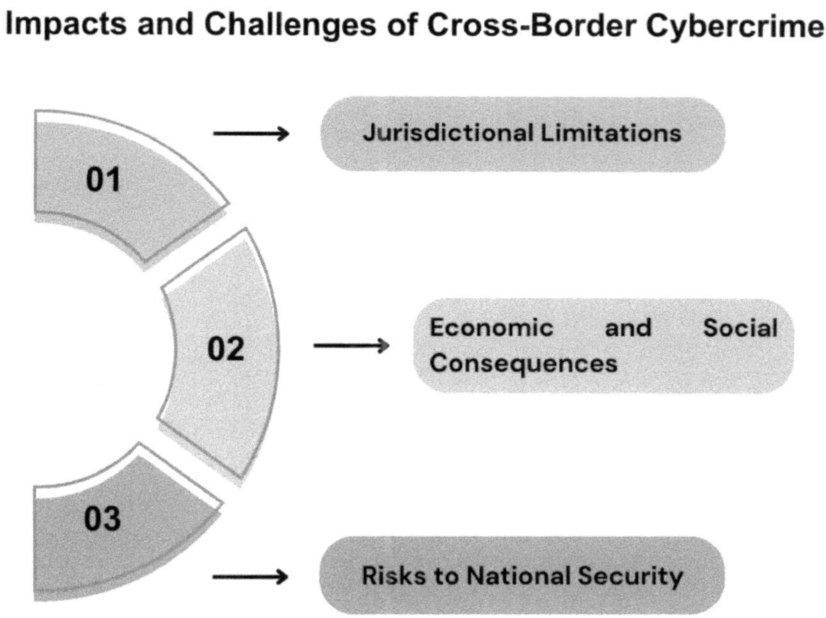

Jurisdictional Limitations

These crimes present substantial jurisdictional issues as attackers often operate from regions with weak cybersecurity measures or inadequate enforcement capabilities, complicating the pursuit and prosecution efforts. Variations in legal systems and enforcement priorities add layers of complexity to international cybercrime management.

Economic and Social Consequences

Cross-border cybercrime leads to significant economic damages for businesses and individuals, including financial losses, reputational harm, and operational interruptions. The social consequences are also severe, impacting victims' emotional well-being and sense of security.

Risks to National Security

Cross-border cybercrimes pose severe threats to national security by targeting vital infrastructure and governmental systems. State-sponsored attacks and espionage present critical challenges to global stability and safety.

Global Counteractions to Cross-Border Cybercrime

Strengthening International Ties

Addressing these cyber threats necessitates solid international collaborations. Agencies like Interpol, Europol, and the United Nations play pivotal roles in promoting communication, synchronizing investigative efforts, and crafting unified strategies to combat cybercrime. For instance, Europol's European Cybercrime Centre (EC3) aids European law enforcement in handling cyber threats through shared intelligence and operational support.

Unifying Cybercrime Legislation

Aligning cybercrime laws across nations is critical for seamless international cooperation. The Budapest Convention on Cybercrime exemplifies a crucial international agreement that aims to standardize laws and enhance collaborative efforts among its signatories.

Enhancing Enforcement Capabilities

Improving the skills and resources of law enforcement and judicial entities to handle cybercrime effectively is vital. Initiatives that focus on training, technical support, and sharing resources are essential for preparing these agencies to face advanced cyber threats.

Encouraging Public-Private Alliances

Effective cybersecurity strategies often rely on partnerships between the public and private sectors. These collaborations enrich the collective capacity to identify, prevent, and tackle cyber threats through shared knowledge, advanced threat intelligence, and innovative security solutions.

The challenge of cross-border cybercrime demands a unified and sharp global response. By deepening our understanding of these threats and enhancing international cooperation, we can better defend against and mitigate these pervasive dangers. For all families, including the Wilsons, being informed about the risks of cross-border cybercrime is crucial for maintaining strong cybersecurity measures and supporting global efforts aimed at strengthening collective digital strength.

10.4 International Cooperation and Treaties

In the world of digital security, international alliances and formal agreements are critical for presenting a united front against cybercrime. As cyber threats often effortlessly cross international boundaries, cooperative efforts are essential for protecting citizens, enterprises, and governments globally. Learning the crucial role of global collaborations and the significant treaties that support these efforts is critical to developing a strong worldwide cybersecurity infrastructure.

Urgency for Worldwide Collaboration

Cyber threats have an inherently international character, affecting several countries at once, often originating from remote locations. This reality demands a cooperative approach among nations for effective cybercrime management. Individual nations need more capacity to tackle these threats single-handedly, as cybercriminals utilize gaps in international law to their advantage. Collective action enables nations to exchange vital intelligence, unify their strategies, and design comprehensive approaches to counteract cyber threats effectively.

Prominent Global Treaties and Agreements

Convention on Cybercrime (Budapest Convention)

This landmark treaty, initiated by the Council of Europe in 2001, is held to fight cybercrime. It seeks to align domestic laws, promote international collaboration, and streamline procedures for tracking and charging cybercrimes, addressing offences ranging from computer-related fraud to severe network violations. It also enhances cooperation on extradition and mutual legal support, growing global law enforcement harmony.

General Data Protection Regulation (GDPR) of the European Union

Implemented in 2018, the GDPR is a critical declaration within the EU that enforces strict data protection protocols. Primarily focused on privacy, its broader cybersecurity implications are significant, enforcing strict security protocols, mandatory breach reporting, and responsibility for data handlers. This regulation has set a benchmark worldwide, prompting nations outside the EU to uplift their data protection statutes.

International Telecommunication Union (ITU) of the United Nations

The ITU operates under the UN to handle global issues related to information and communication technologies. It initiates the Global Cybersecurity Agenda (GCA), which aims to strengthen international collaboration, formulate cybersecurity strategies, and enhance the preparedness of member states to handle cyber threats. The ITU is critical in promoting global best practices and standardizing cybersecurity measures.

NATO's Cooperative Cyber Defence Centre of Excellence (CCDCOE)

Established in Estonia in 2008, the CCDCOE is a key NATO-affiliated hub focusing on cyber defense, offering research and training to NATO members and allies. It organizes significant initiatives like the Locked Shields exercise, which critically evaluates the cyber defense capabilities of its participants.

Shanghai Cooperation Organization (SCO) Cybersecurity Agreement

The SCO enables security collaborations among member states like China, Russia, and India, focusing on cybersecurity challenges. Its agreements are aimed at addressing cyber terrorism, cybercrime, and digital warfare by promoting cooperative exercises, information exchange, and policy development across member states.

ASEAN's Strategy for Cybersecurity Cooperation

This strategy addresses the rising cyber threats within Southeast Asia, emphasizing skill development, information dissemination, and establishing regional cybersecurity standards. ASEAN's collaborative efforts include coordinated cyber exercises and incident management, strengthening the cybersecurity posture of the member states.

Significance of Public-Private Partnerships

Collaborations between the public and private sectors are invaluable for strengthening global cybersecurity. Entities from technology, cybersecurity, and finance contribute critical expertise and resources that strengthen national and international cyber defenses. These partnerships are vital for enhancing information exchange, improving threat detection capabilities, and driving the creation of cutting-edge cybersecurity innovations.

International solid cooperation and structured legal frameworks are the foundations for handling the complex and dynamic challenges posed by cyber threats. By standardizing laws, promoting collaborative initiatives, and aligning defensive tactics, the global community can create a robust cybersecurity framework that provides vital protection across all levels of society. For families like the Wilsons, awareness of these international efforts is crucial to ensuring a secure digital existence.

10.5 Cybersecurity in Different Regions

The techniques and constraints encountered in the digital age of defense might vary substantially across various places due to varied economic, political, and technical settings. Understanding these regional variances is critical for gaining a broad picture of the global cybersecurity landscape and comprehending each country's comprehensive tactics to fight cyber threats. This section examines cybersecurity practices throughout North America, Europe, Asia, Africa, and Latin America, emphasizing their distinct methods and common concerns.

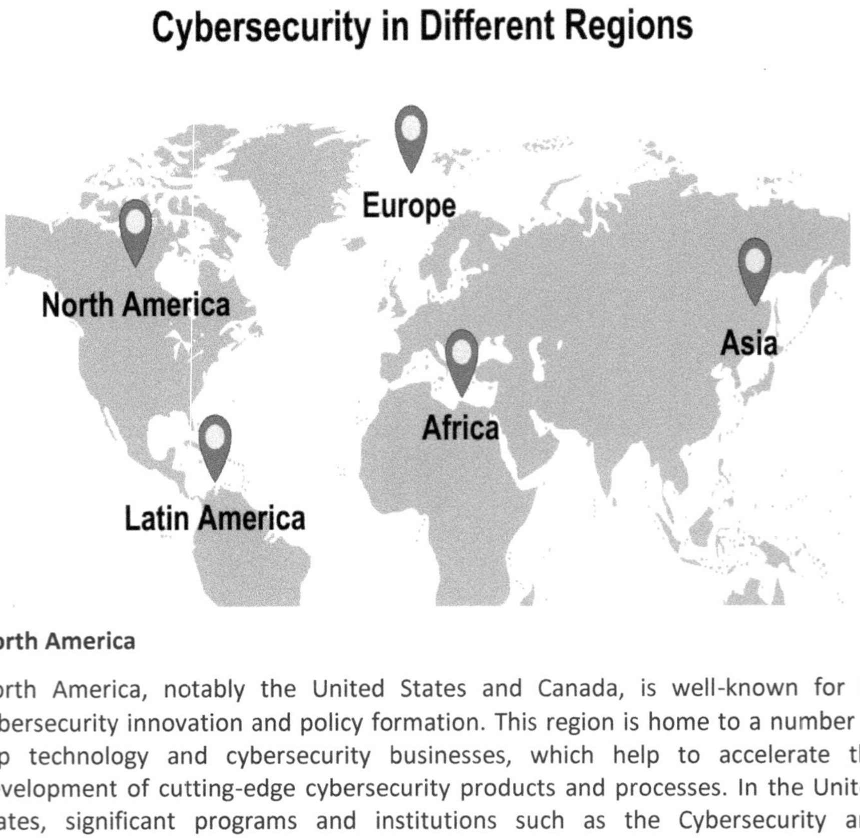

North America

North America, notably the United States and Canada, is well-known for its cybersecurity innovation and policy formation. This region is home to a number of top technology and cybersecurity businesses, which help to accelerate the development of cutting-edge cybersecurity products and processes. In the United States, significant programs and institutions such as the Cybersecurity and Infrastructure Security Agency (CISA) and the National Institute of Standards and Technology (NIST) Cybersecurity Framework strengthen national cyber defenses. Canada has a similar emphasis on digital security, primarily through its National Cyber Security Strategy, which aims to secure government networks, key infrastructure, and citizens' data. Despite these achievements, North America faces complicated concerns, such as sophisticated ransomware attacks and the need for greater collaboration between the public and commercial sectors.

Europe

Europe differentiates itself through strong data protection laws and a significant emphasis on privacy. The General Data Protection Regulation (GDPR) is a key component of Europe's data protection policy, establishing a high standard that impacts global practices. European states collaborate through organizations such as the European Union Agency for Cybersecurity (ENISA) to develop uniform cybersecurity policies and actions. Other measures, including the Network and Information Systems (NIS) Directive, seek to strengthen the security of critical infrastructure and digital services among EU member states. The NATO Cooperative Cyber Defence Centre of Excellence (CCDCOE) in Estonia is likewise located in Europe and plays an important role in cyber defense research and training. Nonetheless, Europe has challenges in managing various legislative frameworks and disparities in cybersecurity maturity among its members.

Asia

Asia's cybersecurity ecosystem is solid and diverse, with nations such as China, Japan, and South Korea at the forefront of cybersecurity progress and investment. China has built strong cybersecurity regulations and is well-known for its state-sponsored cyber efforts. Japan and South Korea prioritize critical infrastructure protection and public-private collaborations. Meanwhile, the Association of Southeast Asian Nations (ASEAN) promotes regional collaboration through programs such as the ASEAN Cybersecurity Cooperation Strategy. Challenges for Asia include:

- Geopolitical concerns.
- Different levels of cybersecurity preparation.
- The need for more regional coordination.

Africa

Africa is evolving its digital security, with an increased recognition of the importance of cybersecurity. Many African governments are developing national cybersecurity policies to tackle the rising threat of cybercrime. The African Union (AU) has adopted the Malabo Convention on Cyber Security and Personal Data Protection to promote cybersecurity and data protection across the continent. However, Africa has significant challenges, including insufficient resources, low cybersecurity knowledge, and weak regulatory frameworks. International assistance, skill building, and regional collaboration are critical to strengthening Africa's cybersecurity capabilities.

Latin America

Latin America is increasing its attention on cybersecurity to protect its digital infrastructure and commercial interests. Nations such as Brazil, Mexico, and Argentina have developed national cybersecurity policies and are strengthening their cyber defense measures. The Organization of American States (OAS) supports regional cybersecurity initiatives through venues such as the Inter-American Committee against Terrorism (CICTE) and the Cybersecurity Program. Collaboration on threat intelligence sharing and capacity building is critical for Latin America. Nonetheless, the area must address issues such as economic disparities, varying degrees of cybersecurity maturity, and the creation of comprehensive regulatory frameworks.

The global cybersecurity environment is defined by its diverse regional practices and problems. North America's technical leadership, Europe's regulatory stringency, Asia's inventive dynamism, Africa's evolving tactics, and Latin America's collaborative breakthroughs all contribute to the intricate fabric of global cybersecurity. Understanding these variances is critical for any family, including the Wilsons, and emphasizes the significance of a united cybersecurity strategy. Recognizing each region's unique capabilities and problems promotes greater international collaboration and leads to more successful global cyber security plans.

Conclusion: Safeguarding the Digital Fortress

As we conclude 'Cybersecurity: The Ultimate Beginner's Roadmap,' it is essential to take a moment to reflect on the journey we have undertaken through the domain of cybersecurity. This guide has been designed to simplify the complexities of cybersecurity, making it both approachable and engaging for individuals and families. By learning and implementing the principles presented in this book, individuals and families can boost their digital safety, secure their data, and move through the digital domain with increased assurance.

We started by highlighting the vital role of cybersecurity in everyday life, showcasing its importance in safeguarding financial details, personal identities, and sensitive data. The foundation was set by explaining the CIA Triad—confidentiality, Integrity, and Availability—as the essential objectives of cybersecurity.

Progressing to the basics, we understood the different states of data—resting, in transit, and use—and the strategies to secure them. We examined various hacking methods and emphasized the need for solid defenses, while also stressing the significance of adhering to legal and ethical norms, which support the broader societal impacts of cybersecurity.

The book then introduced practical steps for everyday digital protection, empowering readers to defend against prevalent cyber threats. Techniques such as secure internet use, fortifying social media profiles, recognizing scams, and crafting strong passwords were discussed as essential habits for protecting digital activities.

An overview of vital cybersecurity tools and technologies, including antivirus programs, encryption methods, firewalls, VPNs, and multi-factor authentication, was also provided. These tools play a critical role in risk mitigation and increasing digital safety.

Recognizing that technology is not the only solution, the human element of cybersecurity was emphasized. Education, training, and cultivating security-focused habits are crucial in preventing social engineering attacks and internal threats. Promoting proactive cybersecurity practices within families encourages a culture of alertness and accountability.

We explored the pivotal aspect of privacy, discussing data protection regulations like the GDPR and CCPA and strategies for establishing strong privacy practices. Techniques for data minimization and anonymization, as well as handling privacy breaches, are fundamental in protecting personal information.

For those considering a cybersecurity career, the book offered insights into necessary skills, qualifications, and certifications. Various career paths and the expanding roles within the field were outlined, showcasing the escalating demand for cybersecurity experts and the opportunities in this evolving industry.

Expanding on career options, we discussed specific cybersecurity roles from entry to advanced levels, detailing the certifications and specialized skills required for each position and providing a roadmap for aspiring professionals.

We also considered the cybersecurity implications of emerging technologies such as IoT, cloud services, AI, blockchain, and quantum computing. Understanding these innovations and their security aspects equips individuals and organizations for future cybersecurity challenges.

Lastly, we discussed the universal aspect of cybersecurity threats and the critical nature of international collaboration. By recognizing the diverse cybersecurity practices globally, we understand the importance of a collective effort in fighting cybercrime.

This guide serves as a comprehensive resource for understanding and applying cybersecurity in daily life. It addresses both the technical and human elements and aims to provide readers with the necessary knowledge and tools to secure their digital domains.

For any family like the Wilsons, this book provides valuable advice and practical steps for enhancing digital security. By adhering to the recommendations outlined, readers can establish a vital defense against cyber threats and ensure a secure digital environment.

'Cybersecurity: The Ultimate Beginner's Roadmap' is not merely a handbook—it is a call to remain attentive. In an era where cyber threats persist and evolve, staying informed and proactive is crucial. By adopting the principles and practices detailed in this book, we can collectively enable a safer digital landscape for ourselves and future generations. Remain watchful, secure, and dedicated to defending your digital fortress.

Glossary

- **Advanced Persistent Threat (APT):** A long-term cyber-attack, often state-sponsored, designed to steal sensitive data or disrupt operations over time.
- **Authentication:** The process of verifying the identity of a user or device, ensuring that only authorized individuals can access a system.
- **Authorization:** The process of granting or denying access to resources based on the user's identity and their permissions.
- **Artificial Intelligence (AI):** The ability of machines to simulate human intelligence and perform tasks like problem-solving, learning, and decision-making.
- **Attack Surface:** The total set of points where an unauthorized user could potentially access a system, such as software, hardware, or network vulnerabilities.
- **Blockchain:** A decentralized, digital ledger that records transactions across multiple computers to ensure transparency and security.
- **Botnet:** A network of infected computers or devices that are controlled by cybercriminals to carry out malicious tasks, like sending spam emails or launching DDoS attacks.
- **Cyber Espionage:** The act of spying on governments, organizations, or individuals to steal sensitive information or intellectual property for political or economic gain.
- **Cybercrime:** Criminal activities conducted using computers or the internet, such as fraud, hacking, and identity theft.
- **Cybersecurity:** Measures taken to protect digital systems, networks, and data from attacks, theft, or damage.
- **Data Encryption:** The process of converting information into a code to prevent unauthorized access during transmission or storage.
- **Data Privacy:** Protecting personal or sensitive data from unauthorized access, use, or disclosure, ensuring individuals' control over their own information.
- **Denial-of-Service (DoS) Attack:** A type of cyber-attack where a system or network is overwhelmed with excessive traffic, causing it to crash or become unavailable.

- **Distributed Denial-of-Service (DDoS) Attack:** A DoS attack carried out using multiple systems, making it harder to defend against due to the scale of the attack.
- **Firewall:** A security system that monitors and controls incoming and outgoing network traffic to protect against unauthorized access.
- **Hacker:** A person who gains unauthorized access to systems or networks, often for malicious purposes, though some may hack for ethical reasons (e.g., ethical hackers).
- **Intrusion Detection System (IDS):** A system that monitors network traffic for suspicious activity or potential security breaches.
- **Malware:** Malicious software designed to damage, disrupt, or gain unauthorized access to systems or data. Examples include viruses, worms, and ransomware.
- **Phishing:** A deceptive method of obtaining sensitive information, like passwords or financial details, by pretending to be a trustworthy entity, usually via email.
- **Ransomware:** A type of malware that locks or encrypts a victim's data and demands a ransom payment to restore access.
- **Risk Assessment:** The process of identifying, evaluating, and prioritizing risks to an organization's assets or operations, followed by applying appropriate security measures.
- **Social Engineering:** Manipulative tactics used to deceive people into revealing confidential information, often exploiting human psychology rather than technical vulnerabilities.
- **Spyware:** A type of malware that secretly gathers information from a user's device without their consent, often for malicious purposes like identity theft.
- **Threat Intelligence:** Information about potential or current threats that can help organizations understand, detect, and defend against cyber-attacks.
- **Two-Factor Authentication (2FA):** A security process where users must provide two types of identification (like a password and a fingerprint) before gaining access.
- **Vulnerability:** A weakness in a system or network that can be exploited by attackers to gain unauthorized access or cause harm.

- **Zero-Day Exploit:** A cyber-attack that takes advantage of a previously unknown vulnerability in a system, leaving no time for security patches or defenses to be implemented.
- **Cloud Security:** Protection of data, applications, and services stored or operated in cloud environments from cyber threats and unauthorized access.
- **Data Breach:** An incident where unauthorized individuals gain access to sensitive or confidential data, often with the intent of stealing or using it maliciously.
- **Distributed Ledger Technology (DLT):** A system for storing data across multiple locations to ensure transparency, security, and tamper-proof records, commonly used in blockchain.
- **Compliance:** Adhering to laws, regulations, and guidelines related to cybersecurity and data protection to ensure organizations meet required standards.
- **ISO/IEC 27001:** An international standard for information security management, focusing on protecting sensitive data through a systematic approach.
- **Incident Response:** The steps taken by an organization to detect, respond to, and recover from a cybersecurity incident, such as a data breach or cyber-attack.
- **Penetration Testing (Pen Testing):** A simulated attack on a system to identify security weaknesses before malicious actors can exploit them.
- **Red Team/Blue Team:** A simulation of real-world cyber threats where the Red Team attacks a system and the Blue Team defends it. This exercise helps identify vulnerabilities and improve security posture.
- **Network Security:** Measures taken to protect the integrity, confidentiality, and accessibility of computer networks from attacks, damage, or unauthorized access.
- **Regulatory Compliance:** The act of conforming to rules, laws, and guidelines set by authorities to ensure cybersecurity practices align with legal standards.
- **Encryption Key:** A piece of information used to encrypt and decrypt data, ensuring that only authorized users can access it.

- **Identity Theft:** The fraudulent acquisition and use of someone's personal information, typically for financial gain.
- **Cyber Hygiene:** Best practices and habits aimed at maintaining a secure and safe digital environment, such as regularly updating software and using strong passwords.
- **Digital Forensics:** The process of investigating and analyzing digital devices and data to uncover evidence related to cybercrime or security breaches.
- **Security Operations Center (SOC):** A centralized unit that monitors, detects, and responds to cybersecurity threats in real-time, ensuring quick and effective responses.
- **Data Integrity:** Ensuring that data remains accurate, consistent, and trustworthy throughout its lifecycle, from creation to storage and use.
- **Bot:** A software application that performs automated tasks, which can be used for both beneficial (e.g., search engine indexing) and malicious (e.g., launching DDoS attacks) purposes.
- **Cybersecurity Framework:** A structured approach to managing cybersecurity risks, such as the NIST Cybersecurity Framework, which outlines best practices for protecting systems and data.

www.ingramcontent.com/pod-product-compliance
Lightning Source LLC
LaVergne TN
LVHW050930210926
848482LV00013B/593

* 9 7 8 1 9 1 6 8 6 5 4 1 9 *